$ 2/00

140
10/85
Academy

לשרים,

כפורים עלם

וכן לם?

לידי אקטרלים

D1435202

**Evangelicals
and Jews
in Conversation
on Scripture, Theology,
and History**

Evangelicals and Jews in Conversation on Scripture, Theology, and History

Edited by
Marc H. Tanenbaum
Marvin R. Wilson
A. James Rudin

BAKER BOOK HOUSE
Grand Rapids, Michigan

PHOTOLITHOPRINTED BY CUSHING - MALLOY, INC.
ANN ARBOR, MICHIGAN, UNITED STATES OF AMERICA
1978

Contents

Introduction

"All real living is meeting," the late Martin Buber wrote in his *Life of Dialogue*. In that sense, the majority of evangelical Christians and Jews in America have been existing, not actually living together in vital relation with one another. Whereas the theological and cultural differences are clear and substantial, the common spiritual affirmations and ideals should be no less so. In light of this, it is all the more poignant that bridges of understanding and friendship between both faith communities have been so limited until this time.

Today's images of both evangelicals and Jews have to some degree been falsely depicted. This has largely resulted from a majority culture and literature that for decades have in various ways emptied both faith communities of their true humanity, background, and distinctiveness. All too often the rich faith traditions of each group have been projected as little more than cardboard constructions, which did not have to be taken seriously. Can anyone honestly believe that the popular images such as "rednecks," "crackers," "wild-eyed religious fanatics," "narrow-minded bigots," "Bible thumpers," and "street preachers" do justice to the present-day reality of Southerners and of evangelical Christians? Can anyone honestly believe that the epithets of "Christ-killers," "Pharisees," "Shylock," "Elders of Zion" have any basis in the empirical fact of Jewish history, religion, or contemporary society?

Ironically, these distorted views of evangelicals and Jews

have not been due simply to a faulty portrayal by others. Far too frequently they themselves have interiorized these external biases. These misconceptions were then magnified through the dark lenses of various stereotypes, caricatures, and cartoonlike images. The geographical concentration of evangelicals in the South and Southwest, and of Jews in the North, Midwest, and West only deepened the mutual isolation. This resulted in large vacuums that came to be filled by mythic half-truths and sordid preconceptions. Only recently have we begun to see these views corrected through expanding interreligious dialogue and personal encounter.

The unfairness, immorality, and social havoc that such stereotyping has wrought came to the surface dramatically during President Jimmy Carter's election campaign. Carter was the first evangelical Baptist from the Deep South to be elected President of the United States in more than a century. Those who shared his religious commitments were sometimes made to suffer a special burden of suspicion and misunderstanding. This state of affairs largely derived from nearly two hundred years of lack of knowledge and experience on the part of "the rest of America" regarding who evangelical Southerners really are, what they actually believe, and what might result if an evangelical Christian were entrusted with the leadership of America and the destiny of its two hundred million people.

In large measure, as reflected in the voting pattern, this free-floating expression of national ambivalence toward (even distrust of) an evangelical Christian was but the end product of widely-held cultural images. These commonplace ideas unfortunately portrayed evangelicals as a "fringe group," largely steeped in ignorance and superstition, and given to exaggerated emotionalism in their religious behavior. Many nonevangelicals, in fact, articulated the view that all evangelicals stand only for aggressive proselytism that holds no respect or sensitivity for the religious commitments of Catholics, Jews, and others. It was readily concluded, therefore, that evangelicals cannot be trusted with the precious legacy of democratic pluralism, the keystone of American society and of world order.

Beyond that, there prevailed the image in large sectors of sophisticated urban America that evangelical Christians care only about being "born again," that is, personal salvation. By implication, therefore, it was assumed that evangelicals are weary of this world and thus indifferent to social justice, economic betterment for the under-privileged, eradication of prejudice, international peace, and reconciliation in the real world. Unfortunately, this caricature has failed to see evangelicalism as a movement historically concerned with maintaining a vital emphasis on both personal and societal redemption.

During the same election period, Jews were subjected to similar verbal violence and stereotyping. The Chairman of the Joint Chiefs of Staff, General George Brown, and the former Vice-President of the United States, Spiro Agnew—who was forced to resign from his office in disgrace—both abused the honor and dignity of the Jewish people. These men made the same infamous charges that were hurled against Jewry nearly a century before in Czarist Russia—namely, that the Jews (collective guilt, once again) are a conspiracy who secretly connive to dominate the financial and media centers of America. (A study of the religious identification of the chief executive officers of the "Fortune 500 Corporations"—who are the real power of America—shows that there are very few Jews employed in the upper management levels of "the executive suites" of our nation's banks, public utilities, insurance companies, and heavy industry. But those who profit from making the Jewish people scapegoats refuse to yield their mythologies to factual truth.)

This shared vulnerability as objects of prejudice, misun-derstanding, and hatred in the American past was but one factor that prompted the exchange of viewpoints found in this book. These perspectives were first shared on De-cember 8-10, 1975, in New York City at a national confer-ence of evangelical and Jewish scholars and religious lead-ers. The gathering was co-sponsored by the Interreligious

Affairs Department of the American Jewish Committee and the Institute for Holy Land Studies (an evangelical school of higher education based in Jerusalem). In more than twenty hours of formal dialogue, representatives of both faith communities had opportunity to present and discuss their respective positions on many of the substantive issues of Scripture, theology, and history.

There were other reasons for this "dialogue," equally compelling and far more positive. The bicentennial observance commemorating our nation's two hundredth birthday brought millions of American citizens to reflect on the origins of American democracy, on the sources of the values and ideals that have forged the distinctive qualities of this "experiment in democracy." In the course of this reflection, it became clear as seldom before, especially to evangelicals and Jews, how deeply indebted this republic is to the biblical world view and to the inspiration of the prophets of Israel.

The founding fathers repeatedly referred to the Bible as "the arsenal of democracy," and the early colonists of Massachusetts Bay Colony launched their career in the New Zion of America by entering into a Mosaic covenant. Exodus, Sinai, and Calvary were the pivotal commitments on which they staked their existence and the future destiny of their nation. The fundamental values were as engraved on their consciousness as they have been carved into the tablets of the Decalogue—love of God experienced in love of neighbor, the sacred dignity of every human personality created in the image of the Holy One, the covenanted people, the priesthood of all believers, the Divine Presence experienced in the liberation of slaves from oppression, the biblical commonwealth and its jubilee year requiring human liberation, freedom from economic oppression, ecological renewal, and education for a spiritual strength and revitalization.

Evangelicals and Jews have been the unique carriers of these central biblical ideals on the American landscape. Many evangelical Christians, as they sought to penetrate beneath the clichés and to relate to the living reality of the

Jewish presence in America and to Israel reborn, began to develop a new appreciation of the continuity of the Jewish witness in the world across thirty civilizations down to our own. They also perceived anew that Jewish life not only survived the Nazi holocaust some thirty years ago, but prevailed and, by the grace of God, created the state of Israel out of the ashes of the ovens of Europe, and built a flourishing spiritual, cultural, and intellectual life in this blessed land. That turmoil and triumph became signs of the times worthy of theological reflection by evangelicals as well as Jews.

Jews learned a new appreciation and gratitude for the evangelical reality in America as well. As they sorted out their readings of American history, it became evident as seldom before how deeply indebted the Jewish community, as all Americans, must be to the Baptist revivalists for their contributions to the distinctive traditions of American democracy. Baptists Roger Williams and Anne Hutchinson risked their lives to bring about the separation of church and state. In his lovely parable of the ship at sea, Williams upheld freedom of conscience for "Jews, Papists, and Turks" as central to his Christian faith. There would be no democratic pluralism without their vision and sacrifice.

Jews also began to know the much less celebrated facts that the evangelical Christians were central in establishing the institutions of higher learning in America, making them democratic institutions available to the poor and disinherited rather than aristocratic havens as they had been in the old country. The movements to abolish slavery would have collapsed without the major involvement of Baptist and Methodist pastors and lay people. The entire network of social welfare and social service institutions, based on voluntarism, is also inexplicable without their leadership. And during the frontier period when violence, drunkenness, lynchings, and law by six-shooters made human life precarious, the revivalist churches became the moral courts of this fragile nation.

These were the concerns that brought this national conference of evangelical Christians and Jews into assembly. The objectives for this conference were, quite frankly, ambitious—how to start a process of unlearning the bad teaching about each other; how to mobilize the best resources of scholarship in both communities to share systematically what we have in common and what binds us together in our religious beliefs, in our history, and in our present-day society. This volume contains the texts of the papers presented at the conference; the reader can assess for himself the degree to which the stated goals were realized.

Two final things need saying. As important as the study of the past and the present was throughout these deliberations, it was a concern for the future that imparted a sense of urgency to our discussions. We sharpened our perceptions of the spiraling threat to the human condition—the proliferation of nuclear installations, the insane arms race, the rise in crime, violence, terrorism, the epidemic violation of human rights, the rampant hunger and starvation in the human family, the poverty at home and abroad, the public immoralities and corruptions on every level of society, the widespread religious illiteracy and, at the same time, the unparalleled hunger for the life of the spirit.

As People of the Book, we knew that the obligation the Holy One laid upon us through his prophet Isaiah was inescapable:

> Wash you, make yourselves clean.
> Put away the evil of your doings from
> before Mine eyes,
> Cease to do evil, learn to do right,
> Seek justice, relieve the oppressed,
> Judge the fatherless, plead for the widow.
> (1:16, 17)

For

> The Lord of hosts is exalted through
> justice,
> God, the Holy One, is sanctified
> through righteousness. (5:16)

Evangelicals and Jews joined in conversation not as a matter of social tolerance, nor nice manners, nor to conform to the custom of the American way of life. Rather, their deepest spiritual and moral commitments in the face of a confused and needy world made their meeting, their living in harmony, the highest necessity.

Finally, whatever wisdom and insight these pages contain, they cannot communicate the most precious thing of all that happened when evangelicals and Jews were in true conversation—they ceased to be abstractions and became friends; there was expression of love, mutual respect, and deep caring for one another.

And these were some of the signs that God was present and blessed the work of our hands.

The editors wish to express their thanks and deepest appreciation to several who have rendered special assistance along the way: Nancy Anderson, Florence Mordhorst and Rita Reznik for their secretarial skills; and Nan Johnson for preparing the indices at the end of this volume. Likewise the editors wish to acknowledge the kind help and counsel of Dan Van't Kerkhoff of Baker Book House in seeing this project through to completion.

Marc H. Tanenbaum
Marvin R. Wilson
A. James Rudin

Contributors

Marvin R. Wilson Professor and Chairman of the Department of Biblical and Theological Studies, Gordon College, Wenham, Massachusetts.

Michael Wyschogrod Professor of Philosophy, Baruch College, City University of New York.

Ellis Rivkin Adolph S. Ochs Professor of Jewish History, Hebrew Union College—Jewish Institute of Religion, Cincinnati, Ohio.

William Sanford LaSor Professor of Old Testament, Fuller Theological Seminary, Pasadena, California.

Seymour Siegel Professor of Theology, Jewish Theological Seminary of America, New York.

Carl Edwin Armerding Associate Professor of Old Testament, Regent College, Vancouver, British Columbia.

Asher Finkel Professor of Graduate Jewish-Christian Studies, Seton Hall University, South Orange, New Jersey.

Edwin M. Yamauchi Professor of History, Miami University, Oxford, Ohio.

Roger Nicole Professor of Theology, Gordon-Conwell Theological Seminary, South Hamilton, Massachusetts.

Bernard Martin Abba Hillel Silver Professor of Jewish Studies, Case Western Reserve University, Cleveland, Ohio.

Marc H. Tanenbaum National Interreligious Affairs Director, American Jewish Committee, New York.

Paul E. Toms Pastor of Park Street Church, Boston, Massachusetts; Immediate Past President of the National Association of Evangelicals.

Vernon C. Grounds President, Conservative Baptist Theological Seminary, Denver, Colorado.

Emanuel Rackman President, Bar-Ilan University, Ramat-Gan, Israel.

G. Douglas Young President, Institute of Holy Land Studies, Jerusalem.

Albert Vorspan Vice-President, Union of American Hebrew Congregations, New York.

Leighton Ford Associate Evangelist, Billy Graham Evangelistic Association, Charlotte, North Carolina.

A. James Rudin Assistant National Interreligious Affairs Director, American Jewish Committee, New York.

PART 1

**Evangelical Christians and Jews
Share Perspectives**

1

MARVIN R. WILSON

An Evangelical Perspective on Judaism

Modern religious history painfully indicates that evangelical Protestants and American Jews have largely remained aloof from one another. Especially since the twenties, American religious life has been characterized by a noticeable lack of communication and dialogue between evangelicals and nonevangelical groups. To be sure, until most recently, the mere suggestion that meaningful inter-religious discussion could be pursued between American Jews and evangelical Christians would have been "rejected out of hand."[1]

But today, we stand at the threshold of a new era. It is my conviction that we must heed the words of evangelical writer, Paul Carlson, who states in his book, *O Christian! O Jew!*, that both communities must now enter into a "deeper understanding of their *Akeida*—or binding—to one another. For the survival of the one is eternally linked to the survival of the other."[2]

Over the years I have learned much from my varied contacts within the Jewish community. I have grown to appreciate especially the significant contribution this has made to my understanding of the background of the Christian faith.[3] For me, therefore, to try to present a concise evangelical perspective on Judaism is indeed a difficult task. In so doing, however, it must be emphasized that I do not speak for all evangelicals, for we—like Jews—are, in certain ways, a diverse people. Rather, I speak as only one evangelical within a vast and growing movement. Nonetheless, in this paper, I trust that I speak as much—if not more—to my own evangelical community as I do to the Jewish community.

The approach I have followed is not that of a definitive discussion of one single issue. Rather, by way of introduction to this conference, I have deemed it to be more appropriate to present an overview of several important preliminary matters of concern relating to the broad areas of Scripture, faith, and history. It is my belief that this approach will be especially useful in pointing the need for further clarification of self-definition within each community.[4] Accordingly, it is my personal hope that through a candid look at the past, both evangelical and Jew may look forward to the opening up of future opportunities for interfaith discussion along some of the major areas broached in this paper.

I.   What is Evangelicalism?

Evangelicalism today is perceived in a variety of ways. Harold Lindsell, editor of *Christianity Today*, has stated that "Christian history at its best is the lengthened shadow of evangelical Christianity."[5] Yale professor Paul Holmer, however, says of evangelicals that "they look marginal if you are very churchly; they appear intolerant if you are ecumenical; they seem anti-intellectual just when everything looks systematic and about to be settled."[6] Rabbi Balfour Brickner, director of the Commission of Interfaith Activities of the Union of American Hebrew Congregations, provides yet another perspective:

> "Key 73" died for many reasons. I think it died because Americans came to understand that the great social problems facing the nation were not going to be resolved by the simplistic slogan, "Believe and be saved!" Neither were these

> problems—racism, ethnic enmity, the urban blight, poor public education, corruption in high places—going to be solved by an evangelical Christianity that spoke of salvation in terms of the "other world" and asked people to rely on some Messiah-like "Big Daddy."
>
> The Billy Grahams and Oral Roberts types of evangelizers will always "pack 'em in" because they are wonderful entertainers and tell people what they *wish* was true.[7]

With such a spectrum of representative viewpoints, it is of first priority that we begin to clarify this question by placing the distinctive tenets of evangelicalism in historical perspective.

Evangelicalism has been called one of the "unanticipated trends of the modern age" which may soon be—if it is not already—"the dominant religious orientation in Protestant America."[8] It is estimated that there are about forty million evangelical Protestants (including self-termed "conservatives" and "fundamentalists") in this country.[9] As a result, church historian Sydney Ahlstrom has called evangelicalism the "third force" in American Christianity.[10]

The term *evangelical* comes from the New Testament word *euangelion*[11] meaning "good news," "gospel," or "evangel." Its theological definition is rooted in such kerygmatic texts as I Corinthians 15: 3, 4, which stress the joyous announcement of the death and resurrection of Jesus in the sinner's behalf. Thus, "to be evangelical," states theologian Donald Bloesch, "means to believe that we are justified only by grace through faith in Him who suffered and died for our sins."[12] As a consequence of this life-changing belief, an evangelical is one who is interested in bearing witness of this gospel message to all men. In short, an evangelical is a Christian who believes, lives, and desires to share the gospel.

The emphasis in evangelicalism upon the doctrine of salvation by faith in Christ alone has been tied for centuries to the priority of preaching, rather than ritual, as a means of saving grace.[13] Hence, "evangelical" is sometimes used to indicate the spirit of zeal and earnestness in which this preaching is carried on.[14]

In historical perspective, evangelicalism sees itself as a movement of rediscovery. At the time of the Reformation, the element of gospel, which had been so clearly a part of apostolic Christianity, remained submerged and largely forgotten. The Reformers were termed "evangelicals" to set them apart from "Catholics" because they redirected their followers to a rediscovery of the biblical concept of gospel, rooted in the authority of Scripture alone.[15]

The century following the Reformation saw the "evangel" once again become obscure—if not lost—in the institutionalized lifelessness of the church. The eighteenth century, however, saw its recovery through what is now called the "Evangelical Awakening." This renewal involved a series of movements which included Methodism in England, Pietism in Germany, and the Great Awakening in America.[16] The emphasis this time, however, was less doctrinally orientated and more experiential; it stressed the life of holiness and made the Christian life more practically centered by its accent on the "doing" of theology.[17] In sum, the evangelical heritage is rooted in a vital Christian experience which has sought for balance vertically through a growing personal relationship of love and commitment to God through Jesus Christ, and horizontally through practical outreach to one's fellow men.[18]

The rise of modern evangelicalism must be understood against the background of the fundamentalist-modernist controversy of the first half of this century. At that time, evangelicals became known as "fundamentalists," holding to the so-called five fundamentals of the faith:[19] (1) the infallibility of Scripture; (2) the virgin birth of Jesus; (3) his substitutionary atonement; (4) his bodily resurrection; (5) his personal second coming.[20] It was not so much the theology of fundamentalism, however, but the negativism which emerged from the subsequent battle against liberalism, that began to shape the movement. Fundamentalists began to separate themselves from mainline denominations and also began to pull back from relating the "evangel" to societal needs. A gradual preoccupation with peripheral areas of theology and culture created a shift which resulted in a more anti-intellectual and cultic stance. Hence, fundamentalists[21] have often been pejoratively labeled "obscurantist, heretical, sectarian, schismatic, and atavistic."[22]

A growing awareness of their misplaced emphases began to prick the conscience of the leadership of fundamentalism during the forties.[23] With the founding of such organizations as the National Association of Evangelicals under the presidency of Harold Ockenga (1942),[24] Fuller Theological Seminary (1947), and the Evangelical Theological Society (1949), a "New Evangelicalism"[25] began slowly to emerge. This began to bring a needed corrective to some of the lopsided peripheral emphases of earlier fundamentalism. A resurgence of interest in mainline denominationalism, in social and political concerns, and a renewed focus on the central themes of the faith[26] were to become gradually apparent during the fifties and sixties.

Evangelicalism, like Judaism, is still experiencing growing pains. Today, on the cutting edge of this movement, there is increased concern for such matters as a more concentrated social witness, the indigenization of theology, and ecumenical dialogue.[27] Accordingly, Martin Marty speaks of an "increasing cultural openness" among evangelicals.[28] Contemporary evangelicalism,[29] however, is by no means united on where one should draw the line on these and other issues.

Despite such diversity of opinion, most evangelicals would likely agree that there is one doctrinal issue which may be called the "formal principle" for separating evangelicalism from other Protestant movements. That singular issue is biblical authority.[30] In general, evangelicals would seem to concur with apologist Francis Schaeffer, who argues that "holding to a strong view of Scripture or not holding to it is the watershed of the Evangelical world."[31] For many evangelicals, this implies the concept of biblical infallibility, that is, whatever the Bible intends to teach, is true. No evangelical scholars, however—despite widespread rumors to the contrary—hold to a mechanical "dictation" view of Scripture; rather they have generally held to the concept of "verbal" inspiration.

At present, many theologians—evangelicals included—are struggling to redefine more precisely the concepts of inspiration and biblical authority.[32] It would seem, however, that despite periodic rumblings, within contemporary evangelicalism there remains an over-all consensus of belief in the complete reliability and trustworthiness of Scripture and a corresponding conviction that Scripture stands as the final authority in matters of faith and practice.[33] The understanding and implications of this point are of utmost significance for the Jewish community when involved in theological dialogue with evangelicals. For any attempt to grasp correctly the evangelical attitude toward the Bible, and its role in the formulating of theological statements, begins here.

II. The Dilemma of Dialogue

Is genuine dialogue between evangelicals and Jews really possible? What about the barriers to dialogue and the spirit in which we face it? And what can we hope to accomplish? In this regard, Marc Tanenbaum has stated: "It is inherent in the Christian situation that the Jew will never be entirely understood to the satisfaction of Christians."[34] If this is so for the Jew, then the reverse is also true for the Christian. Accordingly, Martin Buber was correct in saying that "we are not capable of judging . . . [the] meaning [of the faith which someone else confesses] because we do not know it from within as we know ourselves from within."[35] An understanding of another's faith based solely on external knowledge is always deficient; it has never been fleshed-out and tested in the crucible of the experience of daily life. Acknowledging this lack of total existential commitment to the life and principles of each other's communities, we must begin dialogue on a different level. Together we have chosen to participate in this historic gathering with the realization that we come to understand a faith better, as Eugene Borowitz reminds us, by "knowing its believers, than by reading its theoreticians!"[36]

There is the potential—if not the reality—that any dialogue between Jews and evangelicals begins with both communities being worlds apart—not speaking *with* each other, but *past* each other. Such may be symbolized by the difference between the terms *Anno Mundi* and *Anno Domini*.[37] That each community bases its beliefs on a different set of presuppositions is to be candidly understood. Effective dialogue does not require that either of us underplays or dilutes our differences. Indeed, as Israel Mowshowitz has correctly observed: "One of the most welcome by-products of the dialogue may very well be the development of a spirit of acceptance of differences as a desirable good."[38] We must, however, be honest with one another. Judaism and evangelical Christianity have some sensitive areas of tension where theological antitheses of centuries past have resulted in a seemingly perpetual impasse—a sort of ideological cul-de-sac—which may never be fully resolved until the end of this age. But at this point we must conclude together that it would be wrong to insist that if the one facing us in dialogue does not accede to our viewpoint, it was hardly worth talking. Indeed, as evangelical philosopher Arthur Holmes points out, "If all truth is God's truth wherever it be found, why should we not learn though fragmentarily from those of different persuasion?"[39]

In every attempt at interfaith discussion, there is always a risk. There are those in both of our communities who feel dialogue cannot help; rather it has the ultimate effect of undermining one's own religious commitment. But, as Emil Fackenheim has clearly stated, "The heart of dialogue [is to] risk self-exposure. If Jew and Christian are both witnesses, they must speak from where they are."[40] Ofttimes, however, this has not been without the feeling of deep emotion, with past experiences at dialogue being carried on in anything but an irenic and dispassionate spirit.[41] Notwithstanding, as a prelude to dialogue, both

Christian and Jew would do well to hold in highest regard the old Jewish proverb which says: "He who puts his neighbor to shame [lit., "makes his face white"] in public will have no share in the World to Come" (*Baba Metzia* 59a; cf. DSS, 1QS, 6:23—7:5).

Perhaps the greatest potential barrier to effective dialogue between evangelicals and Jews is the attitude in which we choose to view the misunderstandings and scars of the past. It would be presumptuous—downright foolish—to assume that no problems exist. When approaching Jews in the past, Christians have not always been fully sensitive to the admonition that "good theology cannot be built on bad history."[42]

One of the historical barriers affecting evangelicalism has been its lack of aggressive desire to understand accurately the structure and life—religious and otherwise—of contemporary Judaism. The subtitle of Franklin Littell's recent volume, *The Crucifixion of the Jews*, conspicuously calls attention to this barrier, namely, "The Failure of Christians to Understand the Jewish Experience."[43] Unfortunately, too many evangelicals continue to equate modern Judaism with biblical Judaism. They have failed to realize that Judaism is not the religion of the Old Testament, but one which developed from it. The essence of Judaism today will never be correctly grasped by evangelicals until these wise words of Rabbi Joseph Soloveitchik are taken to heart: "They [Christians] have never tried to penetrate the soul of the Jews. They have read the Bible but neglected the oral tradition by which we interpret it. This makes a different Bible altogether."[44] Confessedly, there remains a great need for evangelicalism in general to be introduced not only to Talmudic materials,[45] but to other postbiblical rabbinic sources as well. It has been keenly noted that Jews sadly lament the fact that while Christians search for Christ in the Old Testament, they hear next to nothing from their pulpits about Hillel in the New.[46] Unfortunately, Christians are so far removed from the world of postbiblical Judaism that their misunderstandings of Judaism are not only legion, but sometimes both ignorant and painfully naive.[47] Rabbis, for instance, have been asked how Jews baked matzoth from blood, and whether a Sunday school class could visit a synagogue at the time while the animal sacrifices were going on.[48] There is but one solution to this problem: education, and more education.

The deepest historical wound, however—one which has cut world Jewry to its very bone—is that of anti-Semitism. Though seldom a factor to motivate the Christian to seek dialogue with the Jew, this painful sore of the Jew remains unhealed, and he seems willing—even desirous at times— to talk about it. Though Arthur Hertzberg's view may not be shared by every Jew, he admits that the discussion of anti-Semitism is carried on for "purely theoretical purposes." Yet he insists, "We must keep retesting the temperature of the waters in which we must swim and the indices of our own strength to survive, because these are everyday matters of the most profound personal concern."[49] We need not wonder why Hertzberg writes this way, for past relationships between the church and synagogue have been gnarled and twisted because of coercive and devious efforts employed to convert Jews. When this has been the case, the "evangel" hardly came across as "good news." To the contrary, it was "bad news." It is clear that most evangelicals would disavow any direct connection of anti-Semitic persecutions with those who are "true-to-their-faith" Christians, as opposed to those who are of a "different kind."[50] Nevertheless, the pain remains; and accordingly, it is needful that the evangelical community not pass over lightly Franklin Littell's sobering comment: "It is not the Jewish people that has become incredible; it is Christianity and those who call themselves 'Christians.' "[51] Irrespective of the exact sources responsible for all the horrors of anti-Semitism perpetrated throughout the centuries, we as evangelicals must become more painfully aware of how difficult it must be for today's Jew to rise above the burden of historical memories and admit to the importance for Jews to give serious ear to the Christian "evangel."[52]

The dilemmas of dialogue are many; we have mentioned only a few. Yet one major consideration remains: interfaith discussion can achieve very little unless each participant is willing to accept with a spirit of true repentance the misdeeds in his group. To our disadvantage, we, as humans, are all proud people. Humility of spirit has never come easily to anyone—especially to that one who may feel that not only his hands, but also those of his ancestors, are totally clean of innocent blood. Nevertheless, we who are of the American evangelical community would do well to appropriate for ourselves as a prelude to dialogue the repentant attitude of the noted British evangelical scholar, H. L. Ellison, who said: "When I come to know a Jew, I must be prepared to say to him as occasion serves, My people has sinned, My Church has sinned, and, it may well be, I have sinned, where the Jew is concerned."[53] Anything short of this, may serve only to further fortify that barrier which has divided us for nearly two thousand years.

III. Our Common Heritage

One of the greatest threats now facing both synagogue and church is the increasing trend toward the secularization of modern man. The drift to conformity is an ever present evil in American culture. There always exists the temptation for man to turn his back on his sacred heritage and to forget what he represents. A recent cover story in *Time* magazine clearly pinpointed the challenge we now face: "How do you preserve faith in the Bible in a world that seems increasingly faithless?"[54] The moral and ethical values upon which our nation was founded now find themselves in a continuous state of flux. Could this bicentennial year be the hour for evangelical and Jew to seek a level of rapprochement by affirming together the eternal validity of those broadly based biblical ideals needed to bring renewed stability to the societal foundations we see crumbling around us? Appropriately, the Talmud mentions that not one of us lives in total isolation from the other—"We're *all* in the same boat."[55]

The New Testament teaches that the destinies of Judaism and Christianity are inextricably bound together. Like mother and child, Judaism has given birth to and nourished Christianity. With this in mind, the apostle Paul in Romans 11 cautioned the Gentile believers of his day not to "boast" (v. 18) or become "proud" (v. 20), for they were but wild branches grafted in (v. 24), allowed by God's grace to "share the richness of the olive tree [Israel]" (v. 17). Paul instructed these early Christians: "It is not you that support the root [Israel], but the root that supports you" (v. 18).[56] In a number of areas—spiritual and otherwise—Christianity is debtor to biblical Judaism for the sharing of her heritage. Though Judaism as a whole has never sensed its need of the Christian gospel from the time of the "parting of the way" until now, the Jewish scholar, Eugene Borowitz, says that today Judaism does need Christianity. It needs Christianity, however, Borowitz specifies, "as its ally against the paganization of our civilization."[57] Despite the fact that conservative biblical Christianity does not believe that an alliance against paganization is the best it has to offer Judaism, it would seem that this is one significant area where evangelical and Jew can in some way stand together in calling America back to the values of its ancient biblical heritage which are vital to the strengthening of today's society.

The impact of Jewish thought and life upon American society has been great.[58] Lecky's famous saying, "Hebraic mortar cemented the foundations of American democracy," has become a truism. Typical of this are the words inscribed on the Liberty Bell, taken from Leviticus 25:10, "Proclaim liberty throughout all the land to all the inhabitants thereof." Often characterized as a "religion of optimism,"[59] Judaism has passed down to evangelicalism from the Old Testament the concept that history is not going in circles, but moving forward toward a definite goal and a glorious climax. Standing upon the shoulders of Judaism, evangelicalism holds that whether one confesses Jesus as the Christ or not, all men and all nations are accountable for social righteousness. And though evangelical Christianity would insist that the historical record of the past indicates man's inability to eliminate societal evil, it does emphasize that God is now working redemptively in history and that he achieves—at least in part—his redemptive purpose within the concrete historical situation of this world.[60] For this reason, evangelicalism continues to cherish those biblically rooted ideals which have historically contributed to the stability and meaning of family and society. These have included such timeless values as the dignity of manual labor,[61] reverence for wisdom,[62] love of justice, desire for peace, and the sacredness of the family.[63]

But in dealing with our common heritage, we must be more specific about how the Old Testament has had such a far-reaching impact on the life of the church. It is abundantly clear, as acknowledged by one Jewish scholar, that innately, Judaism and Christianity have a "large measure of overlap."[64] Indeed, evangelicals cannot fully understand the nature of their lives as Christians until they first understand the nature of Israel.[65] If Jews have been called "the People of the Book,"[66] it is equally true that evangelicals have been called—albeit pejoratively, by those outside their wing of the church—"bibliolaters" or venerators of a "paper pope." The centrality of the Bible in Protestant Christian experience is reflected in the great Reformation emphasis on *sola scriptura*. The Reformers, however, were but building upon the concept of revelation found originally in Judaism which affirmed the "divine character of the Torah as the absolute word . . . [being] a common authoritative basis to which all further thinking could refer."[67]

It is unfortunate that today's church—evangelicals included—has not always recognized the importance of the Old Testament for normal healthy maintenance of its spiritual life. Though outwardly confessing the full authority of both Old and New Testaments,[68] evangelicals have not always been conscientious in living up to their Reformation heritage—especially that part derived from biblical Judaism.[69] This has resulted in the ever-present potential of yielding to the temptation to embrace a subtle kind of Neo-Marcionism, that of relegating the first thirty-nine books of inspired Writ to a type of "second class" canonical status.[70] The heresy of Neo-Marcionism thrives today in those churches where Christians fail to form in themselves a truly biblical way of viewing man and the world. A Christian becomes aware of what it means to be a "spiritual Semite" only by recognizing that the Bible reflects mainly not a cultural continuum from the West, but from the ancient Near East.[71] Accordingly, if today's Christian is serious about understanding the Semitic background of the Old Testament and the Jewish life of Jesus and his early followers, then he must take but one road. He must become a "Hebrewphile,"[72] one who has developed "Hebrew eyes" and "Hebrew attitudes" toward life.[73] As Karl Barth has perceptively stated, "The Bible . . . is a Jewish book. It cannot be read and understood and expounded unless we are prepared to become Jews with the Jews."[74]

A key question is raised by Abraham Heschel in regard to the above. He asks, "What is the pedigree of the Christian gospel?"[75] Was the origin of the Christian message in Hellenic soil or Semitic soil? Due to the process of dejudaization in the church and the eventual negation of Judaism, much confusion has resulted. Appropriately, Heschel points to the fact that too often Christians have forgotten how the New Testament opens: "The book of the genealogy of Jesus Christ, the son of David, the son of Abraham" (Matt. 1:1).[76] Despite the fact that the New Testament view of reality is not essentially Greek but Hebrew,[77] the church has often minimized or neglected this Hebraic background. The Christianity of the early New Testament church was predominantly Jewish. Accordingly, Heschel leaves the church to make an all-important decision: "The Church must decide whether to look for roots in Judaism and consider itself an extension of Judaism or to look for roots in pagan Hellenism and consider itself as an antithesis to Judaism."[78] The church can scarcely uncover its Hebraic heritage until it first settles the direction in which it intends to look.

Today's church can provide a strong corrective to the

inroads of Neo-Marcionism if it recognizes the important place that the Old Testament held in the life of Jesus, the apostles, and the early church. Only one document was normative; they lived their lives "according to the Scripture." They knew no Bible but the Hebrew Scriptures, for the New Testament writings did not begin to appear until several decades after the death of Jesus. The Old Testament was the primary source used for teaching and the settling of arguments with opponents. The Book of Psalms was the "Hymn Book" of the early church (cf. I Cor. 14:26), and later became the basis for many songs found in Christian hymnals today.

The theology of the early church—and thus eventually that reflected in evangelicalism today—was founded on the Old Testament Scriptures. It is here that we first learn of the creation, the fall of man, and the divine grace which brings salvation through a faith-love relationship between God and man. Throughout the Old Testament, man's sinfulness is set in contrast with the holiness and righteousness of God. Here also we begin to trace such great overarching theological themes as election-love, the covenant, and the kingdom of God. It is to the Old Testament that we look for the moral law of the Ten Commandments and the social and ethical teachings of the prophets. It is here that we also turn for our biblical background for understanding the claims of Jesus concerning his messiahship, priesthood, and atonement. Furthermore, the last book of the New Testament, the Apocalypse of John, is incomprehensible to the Christian without an understanding of its hundreds of Old Testament allusions. In sum, the church can hardly afford to minimize its appreciation of the Old Testament, for as one writer has aptly concluded: "The New [Testament] is incomplete without the Old. To use it alone is like taking the roof and towers of a great cathedral in isolation and suggesting that the walls exist only that they may bear the roof."[79]

A rediscovery of Judaism by evangelicals is also bound to result in a fresh appreciation of the life and teachings of Jesus. Martin Buber's point is well taken when he claims that there are certain things about Jesus that Jews can understand better than can Gentiles. He says, "We Jews know Jesus internally in his Jewish motivations and moods; this path remains closed to the nations which believe in him."[80] The history of Jewish-Christian relations indicates that there are many Christians who are quick to acknowledge that the synagogue must learn from Jesus, their Messiah; but unfortunately, there seem to be few Christians who are willing to learn from the synagogue. Certainly the Christian is dependent upon Judaism for an understanding of Jesus' comment that the Pharisees "make their phylacteries broad and their fringes long" (Matt. 23:5).[81] The Lord's Prayer (Matt. 6:9-13) is thoroughly Jewish, reflected in such ancient Jewish prayers as the *Kaddish* and the "Eighteen Benedictions" (*Shmoneh Esrai*). In addition, Jesus observed such Jewish holidays as Succoth (John 7:1-39), Hanukkah (John 10:22), and Passover (Mark 14:12-25).

The lives of Hillel, the great rabbi of classical Judaism, and Jesus, overlapped.[82] When Hillel was once asked by a Gentile to teach him the whole of Judaism while standing on one foot, he replied, "What is hateful to yourself do not do to your fellow-man. That is the whole Torah. All the rest is commentary. Now go and study" (*Shabbat*, 31a). Lest one think that Rabbi Hillel and Rabbi Jesus[83] are poles apart, it should be observed that this definition of Judaism is at the heart of Jesus' definition of what it means to have eternal life. Both Hillel and Jesus appeal to Leviticus 19:18, "You shall love your neighbor as yourself." Jesus taught several significant things about this commandment, and another like it, "You shall love the Lord your God with all your heart, and with all your soul, and with all your might" (Deut. 6:5). Jesus said that "on these two commandments depend all the law and the prophets" (Matt. 22:40), and that "there is no other commandment greater than these" (Mark 12:31). Furthermore, Jesus, pointing to obedience of these commandments as the evidence of true and living faith, told a lawyer, "Do this, and you will live" (Luke 10:28).

The debt of Christianity to the synagogue and its teachings is clearer now than ever before. Methods of biblical interpretation, the idea of a canon, the form and order of church worship, the church altar, the titles of church offices ("elder," "teacher," etc.), the public reading and expounding of Scripture[84] and the "family altar"[85] around the table in one's home, have all been taken over and adapted from Judaism. Likewise, in Romans, one of the earliest doctrinal church letters, Paul with his Pharisaic background describes his struggle between the old man (sinful nature) and the new man (spiritual nature). This may well reflect the teaching of Judaism concerning man's drive or inclination toward evil (*Yetzer Ha-Ra*), and his drive or inclination toward good (*Yetzer Ha-Tov*).

The Old Testament, contrary to the teaching of Greek dualism, states that the material world is not evil but that as God's creation, in itself it is good. Though evil is present in the world because of sin—not because of the presence of material things—the Hebrews rejected the Greek notion that an antithesis must be drawn between one's physical and spiritual life. Rather, the Hebrew viewed life in its wholeness. Living simply meant to experience the full enjoyment of all of God's gifts (Ps. 103:1-5) in fellowship with him the Giver.[86] Unfortunately, however, within conservative Christianity, a segment remains which has taken a rather sour or ascetic view toward God's world and the legitimate pleasures he has provided for man's enjoyment. Conscious of the unbiblical foundation of this position, Paul reflects his Old Testament and rabbinical training by cautioning Timothy about those "who forbid marriage, and enjoin abstinence from goods which God created to be received with thanksgiving by those who believe and know the truth." Paul continues, "For everything created by God is good, and nothing is to be rejected if it is received with thanksgiving; for then it is consecrated by the word of God and prayer" (I Tim. 4:3-5).

Since Jewish thinking historically has been orientated mainly to this life and this world, Jews have long known that to enjoy God's good gifts in this life,[87] and to sanctify time,[88] are not incompatible. Indeed, the Preacher admonished, "There is nothing better for a man than that he should eat and drink; and find enjoyment in his toil. This also I saw, that it is from the hand of God" (Eccles. 2:24; cf. 3:12, 13; 5:19). Building on this biblical perspective, the Talmud states, "At judgment day every man will have to give an account for every good thing which he might have enjoyed and did not" (*Jerusalem Kiddushin* 66d). Could this be a factor why statistics suggest that Jews live longer than most other Americans?[89] In any case, though a Jew fulfills a mitzvah when he takes pleasure in material things, he, like the Christian, is warned not to become too attached and forget where his chief duty lies.

There is biblically rooted wisdom here for all evangelicals truly desirous of recovering their full ancient heritage. We are again reminded of the timelessness of scriptural wisdom. Evangelical and Jew can but stand in awe, realizing anew the insight of that modern Jewish sage who wrote, "[The Bible] is a book that cannot die. Oblivion shuns its pages. Its power is not subsiding. . . . If God is alive, then the Bible is His voice."[90]

IV. Facing Our Differences

Within the scope of this paper, it is impossible to discuss the implications of all the areas in which evangelicals and Jews appear to have questions and unresolved differences. Nevertheless, any evangelical perspective on Judaism would be incomplete without at least identifying those areas of confusion and tension where there may be profitable discussion in the future.

First, it must be made clear to the Jewish community that "Christian" and "Gentile" are not interchangeable and synonymous terms. There are many Gentiles who make no Christian profession. As for Jews, the Halakah states that a person may be born a Jew, or formally adopt the Jewish faith through prescribed ritual (conversion). Evangelical Christianity, however, teaches that one is never born a Christian, but rather one may *become* a Christian. Such an experience may be described as a personal faith-love relationship brought about in the believer's heart by the Holy Spirit, whereby he freely decides to commit his life to Jesus Christ as Lord and Savior from sin. If a person claims to love Jesus and hates Jews, it is an outright contradiction of his profession.

A second area in need of clarification concerns the Jewish concept of "chosenness" in relation to claims by both Christians and Jews that their faith is the "true" faith. Many evangelicals would agree that the main emphasis of Scripture is not so much upon the fact that Israel discovered God, but that God, making efficacious his election-love, discovered them. And though there are Jews who approach this issue of chosenness from a different perspective,[91] Abraham Heschel has affirmed, "There is no concept of a chosen God but there is the idea of a chosen people."[92] Evangelicals have sometimes mistaken Jewish chosenness for superiority, rather than responsibility or summons to action. In commenting on the eminence of Jews, Samuel Sandmel sheds further light on the question by stating, "We Jews have no exclusive possession or monopoly of innate gifts."[93] Granting Sandmel's point, one must still face the problem of whether there is *more* truth in Judaism than in other religious faiths.[94] What of Milton Steinberg's claim that someday Judaism, "so long mocked at and scoffed, will be universally recognized as the true faith"?[95] Our problem then is this: if Jews claim "Judaism is the main road and Christianity the turnoff,"[96] and evangelicals claim their New Testament faith has brought Judaism to its spiritual fulfillment through the coming of the Messiah,[97] to what degree has true dialogue been subverted by the fact that each community has antecedently ruled out the claims of the other?[98]

A third area of tension centers around the question of Scripture. Whereas the evangelical claims both Testaments are God's Word and fully authoritative, the Jew recognizes but one covenant to be eternally valid, the so-called Old Testament. Since the answer to the question, "What is Scripture?" differs for both communities, evangelicals must be sensitive as to how Jews view the New Testament.

Jews do not consider the gospels to be sacred. Accordingly, Samuel Sandmel has observed, "When we read them (if we do), we read them as literature, not as Scripture."[99] At the same time, evangelicals would strongly question Sandmel's use of the following analogy: "To the scholar, early Christianity seems like a jigsaw puzzle; more than half of the pieces are missing, and it is possible that pieces from other puzzles have gotten into the box."[100] Though evangelicals have never viewed Christianity as being less than "half there"—not to mention the possibility of its being a kind of "mixed bag"—nonetheless, such an analysis is understandable when made by one standing outside the Christian position, operating with a different set of presuppositions.

One aspect of the gospels that has been burdensome to Jews centers around Jesus' teaching the law on his own authority, and largely by-passing other rabbinic authorities. Another distasteful aspect concerns the purported anti-Semitic slant to the gospels. The implications of this are too extensive to discuss at this point. Nevertheless, most evangelicals would strongly disagree with the viewpoint of one writer who avows, "You cannot teach the present version of the Gospel story, with all its anti-Jewish tendencies, without putting the seed of Jew hatred into the hearts of the readers or listeners, and that is certain."[101] In addition to the problem of anti-Semitism, there are other differences arising from the New Testament such as the faith-works controversy, law and grace, heaven and hell, original sin, and whether or not the title *Jewish Christian* is of necessity a contradiction of terms. For centuries the New Testament has remained a major obstacle to inter-religious discussion. Nevertheless, if it is important that evangelicals become familiar with postbiblical rabbinic literature, it is also needful that Jews become conversant with the last quarter of the Bible—as difficult as that may be.

A fourth and final area of difference concerns the Jewish perception of Jesus. As A. Roy Eckardt has observed, "Jesus of Nazareth, called the Christ, embodies the paradox of uniting Jews with Christians and of separating

Jews from Christians."[102] Rosenstock-Huessy put the issue into clear focus when he wrote, " 'The Word became Flesh'—on that proposition *everything* indeed depends."[103] It is to be recognized that Jews are monotheists, but evangelicals are trinitarian monotheists. The resulting question of God's taking upon himself human flesh is no issue to be quickly brushed aside. For if, as many Jews claim, Jesus is not divine but a gifted man,[104] then such biblically based evangelical doctrines as his mediatorial work (salvation through him), his vicarious atonement (taking the sinner's place), and his second coming (the final establishment of his kingdom) lie in jeopardy.

For nearly two thousand years the question of Jesus has been controversial, for Jesus himself was a controversialist.[105] Indeed, after all the theological dust settles, we are faced with the fact that either he in some way "fulfilled" Judaism, or did not; either his claims to messiahship are true with the spiritual presence of his kingdom now here, or he like Sabbatai Zevi and others was deluded or fraudulent.

In any case, let us be honest. Despite all we have in common, we have our differences. But they mainly center around one person. Jesus remains the key theological barrier which divides us. Yet this is not surprising, as it is nothing new. For whenever Jews and Christians have gathered together from Bible days to the present, the same haunting question about Jesus, arising from the pages of the New Testament, seems to lurk in the mind: Can this be the Son of David (Matt. 12:23) or is this but "the carpenter's son"? (Matt. 13:55).

V. Tomorrow and Beyond

Is the Jew, as the late historian, Arnold Toynbee, once said, merely a dried-up fossil, the vestige of a dead culture? Or, on the other hand, is the very survival of the Jew from biblical times a theological indication of God's faithfulness, a sign that "the gifts and the call of God are irrevocable" (Rom. 11:29)? Indeed, *Am Yisrael Chai* ("The people of Israel lives"). And though there is no Christian consensus—evangelicals included—regarding the relation of the "people" and *Eretz Yisrael*, Franklin Littell has pointed out that American evangelicals are "generally more dependable friends of Israel than liberal Protestants."[106] Littell's observation is likely correct in that many evangelicals see Israel's return to the land as in some way connected with biblical prophecy. In a similar vein— though his case seems overstated—Meir Kahane of the Jewish Defense League has argued that because of the kind of faith in the Bible that evangelical Christians have, they are "the most potent weapon that Israel has within the United States . . . [to] convince others that the United States' true interest is total and unconditional backing for the Jewish State."[107] But, in spite of such positive comments regarding evangelicals and Israel, A. Roy Eckardt looks at the question somewhat differently. He states in a seemingly satirical manner, "What will happen to the evangelicals and their claims as the years pass, and Jesus fails to 'show,' is a portentous question with respect to Christian attitudes toward the State of Israel."[108] Unfortunately, such provocative comments by and large but beg the question, and contribute little to the opening up of the already clogged channels of meaningful dialogue.

That Judaism itself anticipates a brighter tomorrow, few would disagree. In prophetlike style, Abraham Heschel once stated: "Just as Israel is certain of the reality of the Promised Land, so is she certain of the coming of 'the promised day.' "[109] Along similar lines, Arthur Hertzberg concluded a public lecture by saying, "The journey is not yet ended, for the Messiah has not yet come—but, like all of my ancestors, I hear his footsteps."[110] Whether understanding "Messiah" to be one gifted human leader of men, or mankind collectively, Jewish teaching, beginning with the prophets, has pointed to the eventual ushering in of a new society, one founded on universal peace, justice and love.

The idea, held by some within Jewry, that this human drama will find fulfillment on earth through God's direct intervention[111] is not antithetical to New Testament thought. To be sure, Paul sounds an eschatological note by stating, "And so all Israel will be saved; as it is written, 'The Deliverer will come from Zion' " (Rom. 11:26).[112] And though Paul's understanding of this deliverance is tied clearly to Jesus, the one he called the Messiah, the main thrust of Paul's argument in Romans 9-11 is that the destiny of Jew and Gentile is so interlaced that the latter does not come to find God except through the former. Indeed, through Israel, salvation and riches have come to the Gentiles (Rom. 11:11, 12). Paul's metaphorical use of the olive tree suggests a unity between Israel (the tree) and the Gentiles (the branches from the wild olive tree grafted in) (Rom. 11: 17, 24). If I understand Paul correctly, there has been no permanent displacement of God's people. They are still included in the mystery of God's election-love (Rom. 11:1, 2); Israel is yet "beloved for the sake of their forefathers" (Rom. 11:28). And despite unbelief, "Israel in some real sense remains the people of God."[113] Paul's argument is that the Jews still belong to God, and are yet a "holy" people (Rom. 11:16). Unlike Anglican James Parkes, who clearly states that he makes no attempt to reconcile his views with those found in Romans,[114] the great sensitivity on the part of evangelicals to the issue of biblical authority does not permit Paul's teaching concerning the Jews to go unheeded or to be passed over lightly.

But where do we go from here? Religious conviction is a deeply personal matter for both evangelical and Jew. The company of the committed, those whose dedication is sincere, will hardly discard their faith with ease. Accordingly, as one who took his belief seriously, the apostle Paul wrote from Roman imprisonment, in the face of imminent death, "I am already on the point of being sacrificed; the time of my departure has come. I have fought the good fight, I have finished the race, I have kept the faith" (II Tim. 4: 6, 7). Equally persuaded in his commitment was Abraham Heschel, who said, "My being Jewish is so sacred to me that I am ready to die for it. . . . I'd rather go to Auschwitz than to give up my religion."[115] Both of these moving testimonies, filled with unshakable conviction, remind us that Judaism and Christianity are different religions.

But even though evangelicals and Jews continue to stand at variance on certain substantive theological issues, these need not be insuperable barriers for all time to come. God is still Lord of history, and the ultimate Judge of all men. He controls the affairs of his people; he sees as no man can see. As an evangelical, I am deeply indebted to Jews; and I have yet much to learn from them. For as God's divinely established people, the Jews have brought—and will yet bring—riches to me and the rest of the Gentile world (cf. Rom. 11:12). But until each community comes to understand more clearly from Scripture and the events of history its respective relation to the other in the days ahead, evangelicals and Jews—unless God intervenes in a direct way—likely will continue to live in a creative, yet informed, theological tension.

But is there hope that this tension can be eased? Evangelicals recognize that the validity of their claim to ultimate truth rests heavily upon documents of history and upon faith. Here is a problem that should motivate each community to go back and re-examine its historical foundations through the "parting of the ways." For, as one British scholar reminds us, "We are in grave danger of forgetting that the first question about any religion is not whether or not it is useful, but whether or not it is *true*."[116] The evangelical's authority in matters of faith and practice remains the Bible. This position, however, is not foreign to Judaism. Leo Baeck, a heroic leader of German Jewry, has pointed out, "It is a principle in Judaism that truth has to be discovered in, and through, the Bible."[117]

Without debating *which* Bible—Hebrew, or otherwise—there is a mutual need to give high priority to a thorough re-examination of the ancient source materials which reveal the historical roots of both Jewish and Christian faiths. Accordingly, it is my concluding observation that—at least as it concerns evangelicals—any serious adjustment of the focus on the issues must always be examined—and re-examined—in light of the one inspired historical source to which we can confidently appeal, and the one upon which both the knowledge of truth and the hope of our ultimate destiny depend.

NOTES

1. Gerald S. Strober, *American Jews: Community in Crisis* (Garden City, Doubleday & Co., Inc., 1974), pp. 86-87.

2. Paul R. Carlson, *O Christian! O Jew!* (Elgin, IL: David C. Cook Publishing Co., 1974), p. 232.

3. My perspective on Judaism has been largely shaped by three factors: (1) evangelical roots and training; (2) study of ancient and modern Judaism through formal education under Jewish scholars; (3) a strong appreciation of what has been learned, with my students, from personal contact with various segments of the Jewish communities of greater Boston and Rhode Island, and from short stays in Israel.

4. Attention has been called to this through an article by Marc H. Tanenbaum, "What Is a Jew?" *The Star and the Cross*, ed. Katharine T. Hargrove (Milwaukee: The Bruce Publishing Co., 1966), which states: "The most complex challenge the Jew has been faced with since the Emancipation is that of his own self-definition" (p. 18).

5. Harold Lindsell, "Who Are the Evangelicals?" *The Theologian at Work*, ed. A. Roy Eckardt (New York: Harper & Row, 1968), p. 107.

6. Paul L. Holmer, "Contemporary Evangelical Faith: An Assessment and Critique," *The Evangelicals*, ed. David F. Wells and John D. Woodbridge (Nashville: Abingdon Press, 1975), p. 68.

7. Balfour Brickner, "What of the Future?" *Keeping Posted*, XIX (Dec. 1973), 22.

8. Such is the recent assessment of Marquette University sociologist, David O. Moberg, in "Fundamentalists and Evangelicals in Society," *The Evangelicals*, ed. Wells and Woodbridge, pp. 156, 160.

9. See the *New York Times*, June 24, 1974, p. 18. Also note Richard J. Coleman, *Issues of Theological Warfare: Evangelicals and Liberals* (Grand Rapids: Eerdmans, 1972), p. 13. Coleman divides the forty million as follows: (1) thirteen million within the National Council of Churches; (2) nineteen million from major denominations outside the NCC, such as the Southern Baptist Convention; and (3) eight million "outside the conciliar framework."

10. Sydney E. Ahlstrom, *A Religious History of the American People* (New Haven, CT: Yale University Press, 1972), p. 958.

11. Various forms of this root occur over 130 times in the Greek New Testament. It is apparent that the New Testament writers drew heavily on the Old Testament prophetic tradition in developing their own understanding of the "evangel." Cf. Glenn W. Barker, William L. Lane, and J. Ramsey Michaels, *The New Testament Speaks* (New York: Harper & Row, 1969), pp. 248-49.

12. Donald G. Bloesch, *The Evangelical Renaissance* (Grand Rapids: Eerdmans, 1973), p. 48.

13. Bruce L. Shelley, *Evangelicalism in America* (Grand Rapids: Eerdmans, 1967), p. 14.

14. Bloesch, *The Evangelical Renaissance*, p. 48.

15. As a consequence of the Reformation, in Europe today the term *evangelical* is largely used to indicate "Protestant."

16. Note the excellent discussion in Ahlstrom, *Religious History*, pp. 230-329.

17. See Bloesch, *The Evangelical Renaissance*, pp. 101-57, for what he calls "The Legacy of Pietism" in the history of evangelicalism. Other recent works, however, such as Bernard L. Ramm, *The Evangelical Heritage* (Waco, TX: Word Books, 1973), tend to minimize the pietistic heritage of evangelicalism with greater emphasis given to its relation to "Reformation Theology" (pp. 23-40) and "Scholastic Orthodoxy" (pp. 49-63).

18. The evangelical's search for balance between theology and experience, and the question of which is prior to the other, are often highlighted by the place of Pentecostalism and the current charismatic renewal within evangelicalism. See Donald Dayton, "Where Now Young Evangelicals?" *The Other Side*, Vol. 11, No. 2 (March-April, 1975), 32.

19. These were first published in 1910 in twelve pamphlets entitled, *The Fundamentals: A Testimony to the Truth*.

20. It should be observed that these five fundamentals formed the basis of the statement of faith officially adopted at the founding convention of the National Association of Evangelicals. See Shelley, *Evangelicalism in America*, pp. 71-72.

21. Richard Quebedeaux, *The Young Evangelicals* (New York: Harper & Row, 1974), helps to clarify the problem of terminology by stating: "For too long it has been the fault of mainstream Ecumenical Liberalism to lump together with pejorative intent *all* theological conservatives into the worn Fundamentalist category. In general, Evangelicals resent being called Fundamentalists, and Fundamentalists likewise do not usually appreciate the Evangelical designation" (p. 19).

22. Lindsell, "Who Are the Evangelicals?" p. 109.

23. For a case in point, see Carl F. H. Henry, *The Uneasy Conscience of Modern Fundamentalism* (Grand Rapids: Eerdmans, 1947).

24. For a history of the NAE, see Shelley, *Evangelicalism in America*, pp. 69-109.

25. For the origin of this term and a discussion of the new emphases in evangelicalism at this time, see Millard Erickson, *The New Evangelical Theology* (Westwood, NJ: Fleming H. Revell Co., 1968).

26. Bloesch, *The Evangelical Renaissance*, pp. 48-79, sets forth what he considers to be ten "hallmarks of Evangelicalism" which have been given special emphasis throughout the history of this movement. They are: (1) the sovereignty of God; (2) the divine authority of Scripture; (3) total depravity; (4) substitutionary atonement; (5) salvation by grace; (6) faith alone; (7) the primacy of proclamation; (8) scriptural holiness; (9) the church's spiritual mission; (10) the personal return of Christ.

27. See Dayton, "Where Now Young Evangelicals?" pp. 35-37, 55-56.

28. Martin E. Marty, "Tensions Within Contemporary Evangelicalism: A Critical Appraisal," *The Evangelicals*, ed. Wells and Woodbridge, p. 177.

29. Quebedeaux, *The Young Evangelicals*, pp. 18-41, divides the various contemporary expressions of historic biblical orthodoxy in America into four ideological subgroups: (1) separatistic fundamentalism; (2) open fundamentalism; (3) establishment evangelicalism; (4) the new evangelicalism. Quebedeaux states (p. 37) that new evangelicalism today is a movement "wider and deeper" than the original new evangelicalism which began to surface out of postwar fundamentalism. The original new evangelicalism he now calls establishment evangelicalism. One of the features of today's new evangelicalism, says Quebedeaux (p. 39), is the reopening of dialogue with mainstream ecumenical liberalism.

30. Kenneth S. Kantzer, "Unity and Diversity in Evangelical Faith," *The Evangelicals*, ed. Wells and Woodbridge, p. 39.

31. Francis A. Schaeffer, *No Final Conflict* (Downers Grove, IL: InterVarsity Press, 1975), p. 13.

32. For a general discussion of this problem, see "The Bible: The Believers Gain," *Time* (Dec. 30, 1974), pp. 34-41.

33. Cf. John H. Gerstner, "The Theological Boundaries of Evangelical Faith," *The Evangelicals*, ed. Wells and Woodbridge, p. 32; also Quebedeaux, *The Young Evangelicals*, pp. 3-4.

34. Tanenbaum, "What Is a Jew?" pp. 18-19.

35. Quoted in Walter Jacob, *Christianity Through Jewish Eyes* (Cincinnati: Hebrew Union College Press, 1974), p. 173.

36. Eugene B. Borowitz, *How Can a Jew Speak of Faith Today?* (Philadelphia: The Westminster Press, 1969), pp. 219-20.

37. For a further development of this point, see John M. Oesterreicher, *The Rediscovery of Judaism* (South Orange, NJ: The Institute of Judaeo-Christian Studies, Seton Hall University, 1971), p. 9.

38. Israel Mowshowitz, "Why Dialogue," *Face to Face*, ed. Lily Edelman (New York: Crown Publishers, Inc., 1967), p. 10.

39. Arthur F. Holmes, "Evangelical Tensions," *Wheaton Alumni* (Sept. 1968), p. 5.

40. Quoted in Jacob, *Christianity Through Jewish Eyes*, p. 216.

41. A classic example of emotionally charged rhetoric is found in a letter which Franz Rosenzweig (agonizing over Judaism and the thought of converting to Christianity) writes to his Christian friend, Eugen Rosenstock-Huessy: "You won't get rid of us, we are the louse in your fur." See Eugen Rosenstock-Huessy, *Judaism Despite Christianity* (University, AL: University of Alabama Press, 1969), p. 130.

42. This point has been made by James Parkes. See A. Roy Eckardt, *Elder and Younger Brothers* (New York: Schocken Books, 1973), p. 89.

43. Franklin H. Littell, *The Crucifixion of the Jews* (New York: Harper & Row, 1975).

44. Quoted in Carlson, *O Christian! O Jew!*, p. 142.

45. For brief, nontechnical articles which show the influence of Talmudic thought on aspects of the New Testament, see Lee Amber, "Talmud in the New Testament," *Christian Life* (Sept. 1975), pp. 18-19, 36-37; Marvin R. Wilson, "A Question for Rabbis, Pastors, and Teachers," *Christianity Today*, Vol. XIII, No. 10 (Feb. 14, 1969), 5-7.

46. Carlson, *O Christian! O Jew!*, pp. 149-50.

47. It has been bluntly stated by Bernard J. Bamberger (*The Story of Judaism* [New York: Schocken Books, 1970], p. 2) that "few Christians have even a vague notion about Jewish experience and Jewish spiritual creativeness in the last two thousand years."

48. James Yaffe, *The American Jews* (New York: Random House, 1968), p. 55.

49. Arthur Hertzberg, *Anti-Semitism and Jewish Uniqueness: Ancient and Contemporary* (Syracuse, NY: Syracuse University, 1975), p. 17.

50. Though the Minneapolis-based Billy Graham Evangelistic Association has reflected a positive Christian attitude toward Jews and Israel through such films as *His Land* and *The Hiding Place*, it should not go unnoticed that Minneapolis was once known as the "capital of anti-Semitism" (see Yaffe, *The American Jews*, p. 52).

51. Littell, *Crucifixion*, p. 3.

52. Note the discussion of the burden of the Jews' past history by Robert Gordis in *The Root and the Branch* (Chicago: The University of Chicago Press, 1962), pp. 62-65.

53. H. L. Ellison, *The Christian Approach to the Jew* (London: Edinburgh House Press, 1958), p. 52.

54. "The Bible: The Believers Gain," p. 38. See also Samuel Sandmel, *We Jews and You Christians* (Philadelphia: J. B. Lippincott, 1967), p. 84.

55. This moral was drawn by the ancient rabbis from the Talmudic story of three men in a boat. One man began to drill a hole beneath his seat. When his friends aboard pleaded with him to stop, he asked, "What are you worrying about? I'm only drilling under *my* seat." See Morris N. Kertzer, *What Is a Jew?* (New York: Collier Books, 1961), p. 58.

56. Similarly, the Statement on the Jews from Vatican II reads: "Nor can she [the Church] forget that she draws sustenance from the root of that well-cultivated olive tree onto which have been grafted the wild shoots, the Gentiles." Quoted from Augustin Cardinal Bea, *The Church and the Jewish People* (New York: Harper & Row, 1966), p. 151.

57. Borowitz, *How Can a Jew*, p. 211.

58. For an excellent bicentennial summary of the contribution of the Jew to America, see Marcus Konick, "Jewish Influence on American Life and Culture," *The Principal*, Vol. XX, No. 10 (June 1975), 25-32.

59. Cecil Roth, "Our Changing Jewish World," *Jewish Heritage Reader*, ed. Lily Edelman (New York: Taplinger, 1965), p. 376.

60. Carl F. H. Henry, *A Plea for Evangelical Demonstration* (Grand Rapids: Baker, 1971), pp. 53, 67.

61. It is of more than passing interest to note that in modern Hebrew the term *avoda* means both "to work" and "to worship."

62. Marvin R. Wilson, "The Jewish Concept of Learning: A Christian Appreciation," *Christian Scholar's Review*, Vol. V, No. 4 (1976), 350-63.

63. For a discussion of these (and other) ideals, see Abba Hillel Silver, *Where Judaism Differed* (New York: The Macmillan Co., 1956).

64. Samuel Sandmel, *We Jews and Jesus* (New York: Oxford University Press, 1973), p. 150.

65. See the pertinent discussion of this point in Paul and Elizabeth Achtemeier, *The Old Testament Roots of Our Faith* (New York: Abingdon, 1962), pp. 11-16.

66. Mohammed, the founder of Islam, was the first to call Jews by this title. Cf. Kertzer, *What Is a Jew?*, pp. 129-30.

67. Gershom Scholem, "Jewish Theology Today," *The Center Magazine*, Vol. VII, No. 2 (March-April, 1974), 61.

68. Evangelical Christianity has never drawn a formal distinction between the sacred writings produced before Jesus and those after. All sixty-six books have been equally acclaimed to be the Word of God. Such teaching, for example, is clearly set forth in the 1646 Westminster Confession of Faith (article II), which states: "Under the name of holy Scripture . . . are now contained all the Books of the Old and New

Testament . . . all which are given by inspiration of God, to be the rule of faith and life." See *Creeds of the Churches*, ed. John H. Leith (New York: Doubleday & Co., Inc., 1963), pp. 193-95.

69. George A. F. Knight points out in "Building Theological Bridges," *Jews and Christians* (Philadelphia: The Westminster Press, 1965), that the Reformation was called the "rejudaissance" of the Christian faith, the term reflecting in part a rediscovery of the Hebraic biblical categories (p. 109).

70. Marvin R. Wilson, "The Old Testament: Who Needs It?" *Christian Life* (Nov. 1976), pp. 20ff.

71. For a more detailed discussion, see Cyrus H. Gordon, *The Ancient Near East* (New York: W. W. Norton & Co., Inc., 1965).

72. The term *Hebrewphile* is used by John S. Spong in *This Hebrew Lord* (New York: The Seabury Press, Inc., 1974), p. 31.

73. The potential role of the Hebrew Bible in this process should not be underestimated. In 1777, right after the founding of our nation, Ezra Stiles, President of Yale, declared that study of the Hebrew language was "essential to a gentleman's education." In so doing, Stiles was reasoning to himself: "Isn't it the language I am sure to hear first in heaven?" See Konick, "Jewish Influences," p. 25.

74. Karl Barth, *Church Dogmatics*, I. 2 (Edinburgh: T. & T. Clark, 1956), p. 511.

75. Abraham Joshua Heschel, "Protestant Renewal: A Jewish View," *The Insecurity of Freedom* (New York: Schocken Books, 1972), p. 170.

76. Ibid. Here Heschel makes the pertinent observation: "How odd of God not to have placed the cradle of Jesus in Delphi or at least in Athens!"

77. See George E. Ladd, *The Pattern of New Testament Truth* (Grand Rapids: Eerdmans, 1968), pp. 9-40.

78. Heschel, "Protestant Renewal," pp. 169-70.

79. H. L. Ellison, *The Message of the Old Testament* (Grand Rapids: Eerdmans, 1969), p. 11.

80. Quoted in Jacob, *Christianity Through Jewish Eyes*, p. 176.

81. The phylacteries (*tefillin*) are mentioned in Deuteronomy 6:8, and the fringes (*tzitzit*) in Numbers 15:38.

82. Though Hillel still taught after the birth of Jesus, most of his teaching was apparently carried on in the century preceding the Christian era.

83. In the gospels, Jesus is addressed sixteen times by the title *Rabbi*, and forty-one times by the title *teacher* (*didaskalos*). In the *Theological Dictionary of the New Testament*, ed. G. Friedrich (Grand Rapids: Eerdmans, 1968), Lohse points out (Vol. VI, p. 964) that whenever

Jesus is addressed, "Rabbi," by his disciples and others, "this shows that he conducted himself like the Jewish scribes." Like them, he taught in synagogues (Mark 1:21), sat to teach (Matt. 5:1), commented on Scripture (Matt. 5:17-48; Luke 4:16-21) and had disciples.

84. See Frederick C. Grant, *Ancient Judaism and the New Testament* (Edinburgh: Oliver and Boyd, 1960), pp. 153-71. Note also that the terms *Hallelujah* and *Amen* were borrowed from Jewish worship.

85. Judaism has long taught that the table is to be considered an "altar" to sanctify the common daily act of eating, and to provide a place for mealtime prayer and significant spiritual conversation. See S. E. Rosenberg, *Judaism* (Glen Rock, NJ: Paulist Press, 1966), pp. 124ff.

86. Ladd, *New Testament Truth*, pp. 31-33.

87. See Silver, *Where Judaism Differed*, pp. 212-62, ch. XI, "That Men Should Not Enjoy Life."

88. "Judaism is a religion of time aiming at the sanctification of time"—Abraham Joshua Heschel, *The Sabbath: Its Meaning for Modern Man* (New York: Harper & Row, 1966), p. 8.

89. So argues Yaffe, *The American Jews*, p. 21. Will Maslow, in *The Structure and Functioning of the American Jewish Community* (New York: American Jewish Congress, 1974), calls the American Jewish community "aging," based on the fact one out of nine is age sixty-five or older, compared to one out of ten Gentiles (p. 7).

90. Abraham Joshua Heschel, *God in Search of Man* (New York: Harper & Row, 1955), pp. 242-45.

91. Some stress the idea of the Jews looking upon themselves as a *choosing*, rather than a *chosen* people. Hence, the Jews chose God; God did not choose the Jews. Accordingly, Golda Meir (*Time*, Nov. 24, 1975, p. 102) once called the Jews, "The first people in history to have done something truly revolutionary." See also Kertzer, *What Is a Jew?*, pp. 31-32.

92. Heschel, *God in Search of Man*, p. 425.

93. Samuel Sandmel, *After the Ghetto: Jews in Western Culture, Art, and Intellect* (Syracuse: Syracuse University, 1974), p. 20.

94. This position is argued for by Louis Jacobs in *A Jewish Theology* (New York: Behrman House, 1973), pp. 289-91.

95. Milton Steinberg, *Basic Judaism* (New York: Harcourt, Brace & World, 1947), p. 93. Steinberg also states, "To the Jewish traditionalist Judaism is religion *par excellence, the* true faith" (p. 102).

96. Bamberger, *The Story of Judaism*, p. 2.

97. Cf. Seymour Siegel, "Election and the People of God," *Speaking of God Today*, ed. Paul D. Opsahl and Marc H. Tanenbaum (Philadelphia: Fortress Press, 1974), p. 47: "The solution to the tension between the

two faiths can be found, it seems to me, only through a recognition by Christianity that whatever are the truths of that faith it cannot claim to supersede Judaism."

98. This question is raised by A. Roy Eckardt, *Elder and Younger Brothers*, p. 66.

99. Sandmel, *We Jews and Jesus*, p. 119.

100. Samuel Sandmel, "The Jewish Scholar and Early Christianity," *Two Living Traditions* (Detroit: Wayne State University Press, 1972), p. 16.

101. Dagobert D. Runes, *The Jew and the Cross* (New York: Philosophical Library, 1965), p. 89.

102. Eckardt, *Elder and Younger Brothers*, p. 142.

103. Rosenstock-Huessy, *Judaism Despite Christianity*, p. 122.

104. See, for example, Samuel Sandmel, "Christianity and Judaism: Two Articles" (Part II, "A Jewish Reply"), *Jewish Heritage Reader*, ed. Edelman, p. 193.

105. Note the volume by John R. W. Stott, *Christ the Controversialist* (Downers Grove, IL: Inter-Varsity Press, 1970).

106. Littell, *Crucifixion*, p. 33. It is likewise appropriate that Littell has recognized (p. 97) a strong evangelical effort "to recover and reaffirm the essential Jewishness of Christianity as evidenced by the broad student participation in the excellent program of the American Institute of Holy Land Studies conducted by Dr. G. Douglas Young in Jerusalem."

107. Meir Kahane, "Christians for Zion," *Jewish Press* (Jan. 24, 1975), p. 34.

108. A. Roy Eckardt, *Your People, My People* (New York: Quadrangle/ The New York Times Book Co., 1974), p. 115.

109. Abraham Joshua Heschel, "Confusion of Good and Evil," *The Insecurity of Freedom*, p. 146.

110. Hertzberg, *Anti-Semitism*, p. 20.

111. See Jacobs, *A Jewish Theology*, p. 300. It is also pointed out by A. J. Heschel in *Israel: An Echo of Eternity* (New York: Farrar, Straus and Giroux, 1969) that the prophetic or apocalyptic view concerning the coming of the messianic era maintains that "the redemption of Israel and the Messiah will appear suddenly from heaven, and that amid miracles and wonders he will gather the Israelites of the Diaspora to their ancient inheritance" (p. 158).

112. In this connection, George E. Ladd in *A Theology of the New Testament* (Grand Rapids: Eerdmans, 1974) states that "Paul does not speculate when or how the salvation of the Jews will take place, but it is probably an eschatological event to occur at the end of the age" (p. 539).

113. Ibid., p. 538.

114. James Parkes, *Prelude to Dialogue* (New York: Schocken Books, Inc., 1969), p. 188: "I long ago discovered that the question is irrelevant. In St. Paul's day, neither developed rabbinic Judaism nor Nicene Christianity existed."

115. Transcript of "Eternal Light," N.B.C. telecast, February 4, 1973: "A Conversation with Doctor Abraham Joshua Heschel," prepared under the auspices of the Jewish Theological Seminary of America, p. 13.

116. David H. C. Read, *I Am Persuaded* (Edinburgh: T. & T. Clark, 1961), p. 58.

117. Leo Baeck, *Judaism and Christianity* (New York: Antheneum, 1958), p. 166.

2

MICHAEL WYSCHOGROD

Judaism and Evangelical Christianity

A Jewish assessment of evangelical Christianity is no easy task. First and foremost, evangelical Christianity is Christianity, and a Jewish assessment of evangelical Christianity can easily become an assessment of Christianity rather than specifically of evangelical Christianity. Secondly, evangelical Christianity is Reformation Christianity, so that a Jewish assessment of evangelical Christianity requires, at least to some degree, an assessment of some issues raised by Luther, Calvin, and the other Reformers in their dispute with the Catholic Church. The matter is further complicated by the diverse interpretations of Judaism currently extant, each of which might respond quite differently to one or another aspect of evangelical Christianity. Should these complications prove insufficient, there is still another. The Jewish response to evangelical Christianity must necessarily be an external one, the response of one faith to another which is distinct from it and which it can address only from the outside. To some extent this is indeed the situation that obtains between Judaism and evangelical Christianity. But there is also the respect in which Judaism and evangelical Christianity speak to each other from within a common frame of reference provided by the Hebrew Bible (the Old Testament, in Christian parlance) and, as I hope to show, the Jewish dimensions of the New Testament. There is therefore a subtle interplay between fixing the differences between us and the tendency of each side to summon the other to a better understanding of its own tradition from within the common premises of the two faiths. A thorough separation of all the strands mentioned will not be possible within the confines of a short paper. While not overlooking these complications entirely, the focus will be on some basic responses of a Jewish observer of evangelical Christianity in the context of the two-thousand-year-old dialogue between Judaism and Christianity.

The single most important contact between Judaism and evangelical Christianity is the centrality of the Bible in the two faiths. Before proceeding to qualify this point of contact—and qualify it we must—we must first pause to appreciate the significance of this point as a point of contact. Both Judaism and evangelical Christianity would be inconceivable without a Book which is the center of the two faiths. The sacred space of the synagogue centers on the Ark in which the Torah, the parchment on which the Pentateuch is handwritten, is kept and from which it is removed to be read to the congregation during worship. In spite of the significance Judaism attaches to the rabbinic interpretation of the Bible, the reading of the Pentateuch and prophetic portion in the synagogue is not accompanied by the reading of any rabbinic interpretation, though many texts exist whose public reading as an accompaniment to the biblical lection could have been ordained. Instead, the biblical text is read in Hebrew to be heard by the congregation as the Word of God. The study of the Hebrew Bible is the foundation of Jewish education. As the child grows older he is introduced to the study of rabbinic texts to which great weight is attached. But the biblical text always remains in a class unto itself, unapproachable by any other writings, ancient or modern.

The centrality of a text would be a point of contact between Judaism and evangelical Christianity even if the texts central to the two faiths were entirely different texts. But, of course, they are not entirely different texts. To a very large extent they are the same text, the Hebrew Bible. But there is also the New Testament which is sacred to Christians but not to Jews. Reduced to its simplest terms, this is the crux of the difference between Judaism and evangelical Christianity. The evangelical Christian hears the New Testament as the Word of God and it is this basic fact which becomes the foundation of his beliefs. Since Judaism does not hear the New Testament as the Word of God, a deep division between the two faiths becomes apparent. But why does the Christian hear both the Old and the New Testaments as the Word of God while the Jew only the Hebrew Bible? Each side can attempt to justify its obedience to its Scripture by appealing to external validating criteria designed to demonstrate the divine inspiration of its canon. A debate is then conceivable in which each side attempts to demonstrate that its canon is more adequately validated by the criteria which have been agreed upon. The reason that this procedure is not promising in the context of the dialogue between Judaism and evangelical Christianity is that neither Judaism nor evangelical Christianity is prepared to submit its sacred books to any validation other than self-validation. To validate a biblical work by demonstrating that its teachings are in conformity with some preconceived ethical norms (to give one example of the kind of external validation that has been attempted) is to raise the validating criteria, rather than the work being validated, to the status of the ultimate authority. Validated in this way, a sacred text would cease to be what it is supposed to be because it would no longer be the source of all judgment but itself subject to judgment. The difference between those who believe that a given text is of God and those who do not believe that it is, is therefore not easily bridged because it is the mystery of faith that confronts us in such a situation.

But in spite of this difference there is, as we have seen, an important area of agreement. Both Judaism and evangelical Christianity hear the Hebrew Bible as the Word of God. This is surely a matter of decisive significance. The Hebrew Bible is approximately 80 percent (in words) of the Christian canon. It might therefore be thought that Judaism and Christianity agree 80 percent of the time and disagree only 20 percent, but such a conclusion would, of course, be simplistic in the extreme. Because the Christian canon includes the New Testament, the Christian reads the other 80 percent of his canon differently than does the Jew. For the Christian the content of the New Testament sheds a totally new light on the content of the Old Testament and he therefore reads the Old Testament from the vantage point of the New. The events of the Old Testament are taken to foreshadow those of the New; moreover, the significance of Old Testament events would remain shrouded without the vantage point of faith in Jesus as Christ and God. Jews, of course, have traditionally resisted such a reading of the Jewish canon as a retroactive revision of the true meaning of the text, while Christians have accused the Jews of misunderstanding (willfully or otherwise) their own Scriptures. There has therefore grown up an extensive Jewish-Christian polemical literature, much of it focused on certain well-known Old Testament passages which are read Christologically by Christians and otherwise by Jews. It might be pointed out that in connection with this particular issue modern historical scholarship has generally sided with the Jews simply because the historical scholar will not accept that a text written four or five hundred years before the birth of Jesus is in fact referring to him. Lest this support gladden Jewish hearts excessively, it must also be pointed out that the modern historical scholar does not read the biblical text from the standpoint of faith and that his methodology cannot be the ultimate arbiter of meaning for either the Jewish or Christian believer.

What is the Jewish response to the evangelical reading of Scripture? Let us for the moment examine simply the evangelical method of interpretation. I realize that it is not easy to characterize that method and to distinguish it from the fundamentalist and the Barthian, the approaches to the Bible most closely related to it. Without attempting any very fine characterization of the evangelical approach to Scripture, I feel rather safe in defining it as a method that takes Scripture seriously. It is not prepared to allegorize or spiritualize the text nor is it prepared, with Bultmann, to demythologize it to make it palatable to modern man. It does not attempt to penetrate below or above the text, but it assumes that God speaks straightforwardly in the Bible and that he means what he says. The evangelical theologian is aware that the Bible includes various literary forms and that these must be taken into account in properly interpreting the sacred text. He fears above all imposing on the text his own philosophy as an interpreter and then proceeding to extract from the Bible, not what he actually found there, but what he injected into it in the first place. The Catholic doctrine of tradition as a parallel and equal source of authority has little support in evangelical circles because—to the evangelical mind—it amounts to deifying something human, the tradition of the church, instead of what is truly of God, his word in the Bible. How does all this sound to Jewish ears?

In one sense, the Jewish position is closer to that of Catholicism and its doctrine of tradition than to the purer biblicism of evangelical theology. Judaism speaks of the two Torahs, the written Torah which consists of the words of Scripture and the oral Torah which accompanies and elaborates the meaning of the written Torah. Both of these Torahs were, according to Judaism, revealed by God to Moses. Scripture, for example, teaches the law of an eye for an eye. But the oral law, which was revealed to Moses concurrently with the written, interprets this to mean that one who injures his neighbor's eye must pay monetary damages. The verse is interpreted as demanding the value of an eye for an eye. From the point of view of Jewish tradition, we have here not an act of rabbinic legislation but the transmission of the proper meaning of the verse through the oral tradition which, as I have already pointed out, is as divine in its source as is the written law.

Nevertheless, it would be false, I think, to identify the Jewish point of view with the Catholic view of tradition. The essential difference is that tradition in Judaism is a tradition of biblical hermeneutics. The oral law interprets and clarifies the meaning of the biblical text. It is not, as such, an independent Torah. Nor would Judaism apply the term *Word of God* to rabbinic texts. The Vatican II Statement on Revelation asserts that "the task of authentically interpreting the word of God, whether written or handed on, has been entrusted exclusively to the living teaching office of the Church." This makes the expression *Word of God* apply equally to Scripture and tradition. I do not believe it would be proper, from the Jewish point of view, to apply the term *Word of God* to rabbinic texts. After the weekly reading of the prophetic portion in the synagogue, the reader concludes with a blessing that praises God "all of whose words are true and just" and "who is faithful to all of his words." In so doing, the reader expresses the conviction that the text he has just read is the Word of God. No such blessing is conceivable over a rabbinic text. From the halakic (legal) point of view, a Jew who recites a rabbinic text without understanding its meaning has achieved nothing, while one who recites a biblical text without understanding its meaning has performed a mitzvah (commanded act), though it is, of course, preferable to understand the meaning of the biblical text. The biblical text is unique as the Word of God. The oral law elaborates and interprets the scriptural text in such a way that in spite of all the importance Judaism attaches to the oral law, it does not eclipse the primacy of the Bible as the Word of God.

Having established this much common ground in the attitudes of Judaism and evangelical Christianity toward the Bible as the Word of God, we must now turn to the evangelical Christian reading of the Old Testament from the vantage point of the New Testament. That the New Testament is for the Christian the Word of God, while it is not for the Jew, is a point, as we have already said, of primary significance. Nevertheless, this does not solve the question as to how exactly the Christian is to interpret the Old Testament. For the Catholic, it seems to me, this is less of a problem. He interprets both the Old Testament and the New Testament in the light of the tradition of his church and is therefore not under great pressure to take seriously the text in its simple and direct meaning. But presumably this is not so of the evangelical Christian. Nothing intervenes between him and the text of the Old Testament. He is not given to allegorizing or spiritualizing the text or to the many other strategies that human beings have invented to escape coming to grips with the demand that the biblical text makes on man. And yet, while he may firmly reject these hermeneutic maneuvers when it comes to the New Testament, he might slip into them when he deals with the Old Testament. The problem is this: if the Christian is capable of extracting the spiritual kernel of the Old Testament, while rejecting the material dross that surrounds it, is it not to be expected that others will do the same to the New Testament by extracting some sort of spiritual (ethical?) kernel from it and rejecting the Christ-ological incarnation in which these spiritual teachings appear? If the latter is unacceptable, so is the former. No spiritual essence can be extracted from the biblical truth because biblical truth, as the Word of God, is clothed in the form in which God wishes it to be clothed and it is not for man to improve it by separating the essential from the nonessential. But if the Word of God must not be read selectively, then the canonicity of the Old Testament should put a stamp on evangelical Christianity of considerable interest to Judaism.

Let us take as an example the bond between the Jewish people and the land of Israel. It is quite clear that from the initial election of Israel in Abraham the bond with the land is an essential part of the divine promise to Abraham and his descendants. It is equally clear that Israel's disobedience places possession of the land in jeopardy because possession of the land is contingent on the people's adhering to their side of the covenant. And it is further clear that Israel's loss of the land as the result of their disobedience is not a permanent loss but that, because God's promises are not in vain and because man's disobedience cannot cancel God's purpose, it is God's promise that Israel will be restored to their land and will dwell in it in safety. It seems to me that the position I have outlined summarizes the simple meaning of a large number of Old Testament texts strewn over almost the whole of the New Testament. Yet this simple meaning can be undercut by various less-than-straightforward readings of the text. The promised land can be spiritualized and made to refer to a spiritual state which is the reward of all righteous men. Israel can be interpreted to mean the church. The church can be and has been designated the new Israel and the promises made to the old Israel can be and have been transferred to the church. If at the same time the land of Israel retains its geographic reference, the church finds itself promised a territory in which, except perhaps during the crusades, it has expressed relatively little interest. But these less-than-straightforward readings of the text do not recommend themselves to the evangelical mind and, therefore, unless I am badly misinformed, evangelical Christianity has been quite sympathetic to the recent Jewish return to the land of Israel precisely because evangelical ears hear the biblical promises to the people of Israel, the concreteness of which is not dissipated in sophisticated if not sophistical demythologizations but connected with the real world in which the people and land of Israel are existing entities. If this is the result of the evangelical understanding of the authority of the Bible, then, from the Jewish point of view, there must be something profoundly right with that method of understanding.

How about the law? Much of the Pentateuch consists of legislation which Judaism, particularly Orthodox Judaism, considers normative to this day. The commandments in the Pentateuch address themselves to the most diverse aspects of human existence, from the commercial to the sexual, from the ethical to the dietary. Judaism hears these commandments and attempts to obey them. While it is true that in a sense the rabbinic interpretation is interposed between the direct biblical command and its execution, this interposition, except perhaps in the most unusual cases, does not annul the biblical commandments but elaborates and applies them. If the Bible forbids the seething of a kid in its mother's milk, rabbinic law develops and extends this prohibition and so, to this day, meat and milk are separated in the Orthodox Jewish home in accordance with the biblical prohibition. If the Bible forbids the wearing of garments made of wool and linen, Orthodox Jews have their garments examined so as not to be in violation of the biblical prohibition. And the same is true of Jewish religious life in general. Fundamentally, Orthodox Jews attempt to be obedient to the Torah, the commandments and prohibitions of the Pentateuch.

The Jewish observer of the Christian scene, particularly of the evangelical Christian scene, finds it difficult to understand why the legislation of the Pentateuch plays such a relatively small part in the evangelical consciousness. These commandments are there in the Pentateuch, in black and white, for everyone to read. Why does Christianity, including evangelical Christianity, not pay more attention to the Mosaic law? The Jewish observer is, of course, aware that the Christian attitude to the law is conditioned by the New Testament. But it is precisely here that Jewish-Christian dialogue is necessary. Jesus and the apostles were Jews. The New Testament is a book that comes out of the Jewish world and largely presupposes the rabbinic universe of discourse without which much of it is easily misunderstood. Let us focus on the question of the law as one example.

The interpretation that is commonly accepted by Christians is that while it is indeed true that the Mosaic law was of divine origin, its relevance was superseded by the coming of Jesus as the Christ. The justification of the Christian is by faith and not by works of the law. There is no denying that the writings of Paul, particularly in Galatians, can easily be read that way. Yet the Jewish reader of the New Testament finds this reading incorrect. A good example of this is David Flusser's *Jesus* (1969) which portrays the founder of Christianity as a Torah-observant Jew whose disagreements with the Pharisees are very much in the spirit of the perennial intra-Jewish debates so characteristic of rabbinic literature. Evangelical Christians ought not to overlook Matthew 5:17-20:

> Do not suppose that I have come to abolish the
> Law and the prophets; I did not come to abolish,
> but to complete. I tell you this: so long as heaven
> and earth endure, not a letter, not a stroke, will
> disappear from the Law until all that must hap-
> pen has happened. If any man therefore sets
> aside even the least of the Law's demands, and
> teaches others to do the same, he will have the
> lowest place in the kingdom of Heaven, whereas
> anyone who keeps the Law, and teaches others
> so, will stand high in the kingdom of Heaven. I
> tell you, unless you show yourselves far better
> men than the Pharisees and the doctors of the
> law, you can never enter the kingdom of
> Heaven.

And again Matthew 23:2, 3:

> The doctors of the law and the Pharisees sit in
> the chair of Moses; therefore do what they tell
> you; pay attention to their words. But do not
> follow their practice; for they say one thing and
> do another. (NEB)

The Jewish reader cannot help but notice such passages
and they confirm his conviction that the continuity between the teaching of Jesus and rabbinic Judaism is
considerable.

There are those who, while granting a considerable degree of continuity between rabbinic Judaism and particularly the synoptic gospels, draw the line at Paul. He, it is
maintained, broke the bonds that tied Christianity to
Judaism. Did not Paul forbid newly converted Christians
to undergo circumcision and to live in accordance with the
Mosaic law? The commonly accepted interpretation is that
Paul believed the Mosaic law to have been merely a prep-
aration (Gal. 3:24) for the coming of Jesus as the Christ
and therefore to continue obeying the law after the coming of Jesus is to deny the event that was central to Paul's
theology. And yet, there is something that does not ring
true, at least to this Jewish reader. Let us take Acts 15 as
our focus. Here we are told that, after Paul had converted
certain Gentiles to faith in Jesus as the Christ, some Jewish

Christians from Judea presented themselves to the new converts and informed them that "those who were not circumcised in accordance with Mosaic practice could not be saved" (v. 1). This information undoubtedly upset the new converts who had been informed by Paul that no such circumcision was necessary or perhaps even permissible for new Christians. The dissension reached such proportions that Paul decided to submit the matter to the judgment of the Jerusalem church whose leadership consisted of those who, unlike Paul, had known Jesus during his sojourn on earth. In any case, the problem was submitted to the Jerusalem church and "after a long debate" (v. 7) judgment was rendered in favor of Paul. The church in Antioch was so informed in a written communication which demanded of the new Christians not circumcision and acceptance of the whole Torah, but abstinence "from things polluted by contact with idols, from fornication, from anything that has been strangled, and from blood" (v. 20). Paul's position was thus vindicated and the principle was established that Gentile converts to Christianity do not require circumcision and the law.

The Jewish reader, however, is struck by two important points. The first is explicit and the other implicit but nevertheless persuasive. The demands made of the Gentile converts in Acts 15:20 have to be understood in light of the rabbinic view of the obligation that devolves on non-Jews. Because of the covenant made at Sinai with Israel, Jews are obligated to obey the commandments of the Torah. Non-Jews, however, are under no such obligation. Instead, they are obligated to obey the so-called Noachide commandments which the rabbis inferred from Genesis 9. These Noachide commandments, usually said to be seven in number, consist, broadly speaking, of the fundamental moral law and the commandment not to worship idols. From the rabbinic point of view, a Gentile who fulfills these commandments has a place in the world to come. Full conversion of a Gentile to Judaism remains possible. The full convert is circumcised, thus becoming a Jew under full obligation to the whole of the Torah. The predominant rabbinic attitude, however, is to discourage such full conversion because of the dangers involved. Israel has often failed to obey the commandments of the Torah and when it has done so, it has been severely punished by God. Why should a Gentile, reasoned the rabbis, put himself in this danger if he can attain his place in the world to come by adhering to the Noachide commandments? The decision of the first Jerusalem council is to demand the Noachide commandments of the Gentile converts and no more. In so deciding, the Jerusalem church is acting in accordance with the predominant rabbinic thinking of the day.

The second point, as I have said, is rather more implicit but nevertheless persuasive. When the problem presented by Paul—whether or not Gentile converts to Christianity require circumcision and the law—was brought to the Jerusalem church, the decision in favor of Paul ensued only after "long debate" (Acts 15:7). Now—and this is the point—if the Jewish members of the Jerusalem church had been of the opinion that with the coming of Jesus as the Messiah, circumcision and obedience to the Torah were no longer necessary for Jewish Christians, there could hardly have arisen any controversy as to whether circumcision and obedience to the Torah were demanded of Gentile converts. This could have become a debatable issue whose determination required long debate only if it had been generally assumed in Jerusalem that Jews who had come to accept Jesus as the Messiah retained their obligation to the Torah. The debatable question then was whether Gentiles who entered the fellowship of Jesus had to live as the Jewish followers of Jesus did (circumcision and obedience to the Torah) or whether it was sufficient for them to couple their faith in Jesus with obedience to the Noachide law.

The early church, I believe, envisaged itself as being made up of two segments, the Jewish and the Gentile. What they would have in common is what was most important—the faith in Jesus as the Messiah. The difference between them would be that the Jewish portion of the church, the original, cultivated olive tree of Romans 11:24, would remain subject to the Torah, while the Gentile branch, the branch that "against all nature" was grafted into the original tree, would obey the Noachide commandments and not the full Mosaic law. Should this appear strange in view of Paul's repeated assertions that in Christ there is neither Jew nor Gentile (e.g., Col. 3:11), we must remember that while on the one hand Paul teaches that in Christ there is neither man nor woman, he does not hesitate to instruct women to remain silent in the church. In the ultimate sense, before God, men and women are alike in that they have immortal souls and their sins are forgiven in Christ, but in the penultimate sense the role of men and women is not identical. The same is true of Jew and Gentile. Through the coming of Jesus as the Messiah, his death and resurrection, the ultimate difference between Jews and Gentiles has been erased. But just as Paul's teaching about men and women is not to be taken to mean that men and women must begin acting identically, so in the case of Jews and Gentiles a difference remains: Jews are obligated to obey the Torah while Gentiles are not.

Before leaving the topic of the law, we must look at what Paul says about the law, particularly in Galatians. Much of the anti-Jewish tone of some aspects of Christianity can be traced to the Pauline polemic against the law. He speaks of the curse of the law by which no man is justified since justification is only by faith and never by works of the law (Gal. 3:10-12). Such statements have been widely interpreted as expressing the deepest possible rejection of that which is most holy to Judaism—the Torah and its teaching. But as a Jew who proclaimed himself faithful to the traditions of his people, Paul could not have thought of the law as a curse. The truth is that there is something entirely different at stake here. The question is whether Gentiles who wish to enter the church need circumcision and obedience to the law (all those who have been circumcised must obey the law; see Gal. 5:3). Paul's answer to this, as we have seen, is in the negative. Once this is granted, it becomes Paul's duty, in accordance with rabbinic thinking, to discourage Gentiles from circumcision and observing the law. The curse of the law about which Paul speaks refers to the curse (Deut. 27:26) associated with violation of the law. Paul is not saying that the law is a curse. He is saying that Jews have a promise and a threat—the promise of reward if they obey the law of God and the threat of a curse if they disobey it. Because Paul's purpose is to discourage Gentiles from circumcision and observation of the law, he speaks only of the curse and remains silent about the blessing. This is how any rabbi, past or present, proceeds in discouraging Gentile conversion. The potential convert is told of the dangers of becoming subject to the law. Only after he persists and insists on conversion is he told of the blessings which flow from the Torah. It is therefore a profound misunderstanding to read Paul's comments in Galatians as his full evaluation of the law. It is a presentation of the law from one point of view, intended to cool Gentile passions for circumcision and the law. Were Paul writing to Jews, his discussion of the advantages of the law would not be omitted. But, as apostle to the Gentiles, Paul's purpose is to preach Christ crucified and risen to Gentiles and, in view of contrary opinions emanating from Jewish Christian circles in Jerusalem, to dissuade Gentile circumcision and acceptance of the yoke of the Torah.

When Paul says that man is justified by faith and not by works of the law, he is saying nothing that is strange to Judaism. A Jew who believes that man is justified by works of the law would hold the belief that man can demand only strict justice from God, nothing more. Such a man would say to God: "Give me what I deserve, neither more nor less; I do not need your mercy, only your strict justice." If there are Jews who approach God in this spirit, I have never met nor heard of them. In the morning liturgy that Jews recite daily, we find the following: "Master of all worlds: It is not on account of our own righteousness that we offer our supplications before thee, but on account of thy great compassion. What are we? What is our life? What is our goodness? What is our virtue? What is our help?

What our strength? What our might?" The believing Jew is fully aware that if he were to be judged strictly according to his deeds by the standards of justice and without mercy, he would be doomed. He realizes that without the mercy of God there is no hope for him and that he is therefore justified—if by "justified" we mean that he avoids the direst of divine punishments—not by the merit of his works as commanded in the Torah, but by the gratuitous mercy of God who saves man in spite of the fact that man does not deserve it. From this it does not follow that obedience to the commandments of the Torah has ceased to be obligatory for the Jew, just as it does not follow from the Pauline teaching of justification by faith and not by works of the law that the Christian may become a libertine and do as he wishes as long as he retains his faith. It is imperative for the Jew to do everything in his power to live in accordance with the commandments. At the same time, he is aware that he will not succeed fully and that he is therefore in need of divine mercy. It is, then, quite incorrect to distinguish between Judaism and Christianity as if the former puts its emphasis on works while the latter, its emphasis on faith. Both, it seems to me, emphasize works while realizing that the mercy of God is nevertheless essential.

We now come to probably the most difficult point, the question of Jesus. The thinking of Paul and of evangelical Christianity centers on Jesus as the Messiah, the only begotten Son of God in whose death and resurrection man's sins are forgiven and eternal life assured. Here we come to the mystery of the division between Israel and the church. Judaism did not accept Jesus either as the Messiah or as one of the persons in the triune God. For Judaism the Messiah was and is thought of as the legitimate Davidic monarch who will restore Jewish sovereignty and free the people from foreign domination. Since Jesus did not achieve this visible political goal, Judaism continued to hope for the coming of its Messiah. But even if Judaism had accepted Jesus as the Messiah—as Rabbi Akiba later thought of Bar Kochba as the Messiah—it would not have thought of him as God or as an incarnation of God. It is important to recognize that from the Jewish point of view the question whether Jesus was the Messiah is a far less crucial matter than the orthodox Christian teaching concerning the divinity of Jesus. In view of the condemnation of those who worship the works of their hands, Judaism has come to be extremely sensitive about the divinization of any material object, animate or otherwise. But we would be misunderstanding the issue if we rested the matter here. Apart from the question of who Jesus was, an equally important question is what he does for man and in this regard several simple points must be made.

In Judaism, God has two attributes—justice and mercy. At times, he acts as the judge dispensing justice to his creatures. At other times he acts mercifully by forgiving man's transgressions and withholding deserved punishment. There is no discernible rule that determines when mercy displaces justice. If there were such a rule, the application of mercy itself would be ruled by law and it would then cease to be mercy. The point, however, is that in Judaism it is the same God who is sometimes just and sometimes merciful. In Christianity, these two aspects of God are personified by two persons—the Father and the Son. God the Father is the God of justice while God the Son is the principle of mercy. The appearance of Jesus, it seems, assures the triumph of mercy for those who believe in him. In Pauline thinking there is a deeply rooted terror of the justice of God based on Paul's assessment of Jewish experience which he finds to have been an almost unbroken chain of acts of disobedience to the commands of God and the punishment resulting from them. The focus on Jesus is therefore the proclamation of the good news that the rigors of divine justice can be avoided. Through Jesus the mercy of God has triumphed over his justice. Judaism remains under the dialectic of justice and mercy. It is true that in the final analysis the mercy of God prevails over his justice. Israel has been told that it will be redeemed, that its election will never be withdrawn, and that while the anger of God is a passing phenomenon, his love and mercy endure forever. The Jewish people feel themselves so loved by God that they can endure his anger. They know the infinitely deeper love that is only slightly below the surface of the anger. But this requires a great sense of intimacy with God. As the children of adoption, the Gentile Christians are more frightened by the prospect of divine anger than is the Jew, and therefore the total guarantee of mercy in Jesus becomes central in the Christian relationship with the God of Israel. The Jewish relationship is with God the Father, who does for Israel everything that God as Jesus does for the Christian.

It seems to me important both for Jews and Christians to avoid arguing that God could have done what he has done only in the way he has done it. To do so is to convert both faiths into philosophic doctrines which lose sight of the fact that God's freedom is not compromised by restraints of necessity. Each side ought to concede that God could have done what the other faith claims he has done, even as each faith maintains its own belief as to what God has done and how he has done it.

Speaking of Israel, Karl Barth writes (*Church Dogmatics* II. 2, p. 287):

> For it is incontestable that this people as such is the holy people of God: the people with whom God has dealt in His grace and in His wrath; in the midst of whom He has blessed and judged, enlightened and hardened, accepted and rejected; whose cause either way He has made His own, and has not ceased to make His own, and will not cease to make His own. They are all of them by nature sanctified by Him, sanctified as ancestors and kinsmen of the Holy One in Israel, in a sense Gentiles are not by nature, not even the best of Gentiles, not even the Gentile Christians, not even the best of Gentile Christians, in spite of their membership in the Church, in spite of the fact that they too are now sanctified by the Holy One of Israel and have become Israel.

"They too are now sanctified," writes Karl Barth. This, it seems to me, is the challenge to Christianity, particularly evangelical Christianity. Christianity thinks of itself as the new Israel, heir to the election which the old Israel lost because it did not recognize its Messiah in Jesus. If this is so, then, after Jesus there is no longer any theological significance to the existence of the Jewish people. It is still necessary, of course, to bring individual Jews to Jesus because all men need Jesus, but the existence of the Jewish people as such is displaced by the existence of the church.

This has been the view widely prevalent in much of Christianity. The alternative is to see the church as inconceivable without Israel. In this view, Israel remains the people of election; Israel is the nucleus of the cell while the church is the substance that clusters around the nucleus. In this second definition, the church can be understood only as that body of Gentiles that has joined itself to the body of Israel and whose destiny is therefore irrevocably intertwined with the destiny of the people of Israel. Jesus is not, then, severed from his special relationship with the people of Israel but, instead, the people of Israel is seen as the people chosen by God to carry his presence in the world. Since the election of Israel is intended as a blessing for all peoples of the earth, those who are addressed by the God of Israel can join their destinies to that of Israel as adopted sons in the household of Israel. In this interpretation, Christianity becomes the Judaism of the Gentiles.

In view of these considerations, the Jewish reader of the literature of evangelical Christianity finds himself somewhat puzzled by the extent to which Jews and Judaism go unmentioned. For example, the index to Bernard L. Ramm's excellent study, *The Evangelical Heritage*, contains no reference to Jews, Judaism or Israel. And this is not untypical. A recent movie made under evangelical auspices, *The Hiding Place*, focuses with great sympathy on the holocaust of European Jewry during the Nazi period. It depicts the heroic effort of an evangelical Christian family to save as many Jews as possible from the Nazi murderers and the dreadful price that family had to pay for their effort. The film puts its primary emphasis on the heroism of the Christian family whose faith is the source of their strength; some critics have been puzzled by the failure of the film to point to the strength provided by the Jewish faith to the victims of this historic crime. At an early point in the film, as the elderly gentleman who is the head of the heroic Christian family walks the streets of his Dutch city, wearing the star of David which the Nazis had made compulsory for all Jews and which he had adopted voluntarily, he observes a roundup of Jews and exclaims: "They have touched the apple of God's eye." Here recognition of the election of Israel is implicit. Yet the film never connects Jewish suffering with the fact that God elected this people precisely because they are more precious to him than all other families of the earth. The average moviegoer can easily leave with the impression that persecution of the Jews is just another example of man's inhumanity to man rather than an event that can be understood only in biblical categories and in the context of Jewish election. While the suggestion that Jewish suffering is punishment for their rejection of Jesus as the Messiah is tossed out, not much of a parallel is drawn between the crucifixion of Jesus and the historic crucifixion of his people. My purpose is not to be critical of the film, but to voice my impression that the makers of the film were to some degree aware of the election of Israel and the significance of this election for Christianity but not to the degree required. This may be evidence of one reason why dialogue between Jews and evangelical Christians is desirable.

PART 2

The Messiah

3

ELLIS RIVKIN

The Meaning of Messiah in Jewish Thought

The messianic idea was forged in the crucible of crisis. Confronted with mounting evidence that neither Israel nor Judah could withstand the onslaught of such mighty imperial powers as Assyria and Babylonia, inspired prophets sought to understand Yahweh's purpose. Steadfast in their belief that Yahweh is one and omnipotent, and reassured by the mighty acts which Yahweh had performed for Israel in years gone by, prophets like Amos, Hosea, Micah, and Isaiah looked upon the turbulence of events as sure signs of Yahweh's power and as striking evidence of his concern for his people Israel. The ravaging of the land, the despoiling of the people, even the trudging off into exile testified to Yahweh's omnipotence, not his helplessness; to his loving justice, not to the abandonment of his people. Assyria was the rod of his anger, an instrument, not a power in its own right. The devastation and destruction were meted out by Yahweh as punishment—proof of Yahweh's strength, not evidence of his weakness. The prophets stubbornly refused to be swayed either by empirical facts or by necessary inference. Instead of allowing the facts to speak for themselves, these prophets insisted on speaking for the facts.

Their reasoning was simple. Since Yahweh is omnipotent, and since Yahweh's essential attributes are justice, righteousness and lovingkindness, and since the covenant with Israel is a covenant binding Israel to Yahweh's singularity *and* to his attributes, Yahweh would be remiss were he *not* to punish Israel when they flaunted his singularity by worshiping other gods, and when they denied his essential attributes by mocking justice and ridiculing righteousness, by grinding down the poor and humiliating the meek. The destruction of the kingdom of Israel bore stunning testimony both to Yahweh's omnipotence and to his essence, even as the subsequent destruction of Judah was to remove the last lingering doubt that Yahweh is absolutely in control, omnipotent through his proven power to punish his people for the violation of the solemn covenant he had made with their forefathers, a covenant binding them to Yahweh's singularity, omnipotence, and essential attributes.

The prophets thus had an explanation for negative experience, but how were they to resolve the more difficult problem? If Israel was to continue as Yahweh's people, what could they look forward to when they had absorbed their punishment, mended their ways, and dedicated themselves to righteousness and justice? In a world dominated by imperial powers, could they ever enjoy true independence? In a world of rival nations, could they ever enjoy peace? In a world of exploitation and inequity, could the hungry be well-fed, the poor prosperous, the humiliated treated with dignity?

The answer to these questions was found in Yahweh's omnipotence, in his essential attributes—justice, righteousness, mercy, lovingkindness—and in his inviolate covenant with Israel. Yahweh will "on that day"— whenever that day might be—dissolve the old order of relentless war, degrading poverty, rampant unrighteousness, triumphant injustice, and ubiquitous disharmony, and shape in its stead a truly new creation wherein justice will be the line, and righteousness the plummet, and wherein "your covenant with death will be annulled and your agreement with Sheol will not stand" (Isa. 28:17, 18). On that day divine sovereignty will put human sovereignty

to shame as the shoot which has come forth from the
stump of Jesse "judges the poor with righteousness and
decides with equity for the meek of the earth. . . . Righteousness shall be the girdle of his waist, and faithfulness
the girdle of his loins." The very laws of nature will be
suspended as the wolf dwells with the lamb, the leopard
lies down with the kid, the suckling child plays over the
hole of the asp, and the weaned child puts his hand on the
adder's den. "Destruction and hurt will be no more in all of
God's holy mountain, for the earth shall be full of the
knowledge of the Lord as the waters cover the sea"
(Isa. 11:1-9).

How utterly beauteous those latter days will be when

> The mountain of the house of the Lord
> shall be established as the highest of the
>   mountains,
> and shall be raised above the hills;
> and all the nations shall flow to it.
> And many peoples shall come and say,
> "Come. Let us go to the mountain of the Lord,
> to the house of the God of Jacob;
> that he may teach us his ways
> and that we may walk in his paths."
> For out of Zion shall go forth the Law,
> and the word of the Lord from Jerusalem.
> He shall judge between the nations,
> and shall decide for many peoples;
> and they shall beat their swords into plowshares,
> and their spears into pruning hooks;
> nation shall not lift up sword against nation,
> neither shall they learn war anymore."
>   (Isa. 2:2-4)

Indeed, so altered will be the course of history that even
the most congenital of enmities will dissolve into enduring
friendship. Warring peoples will become aware that all are
the chosen of the living God:

> In that day there will be a highway from Egypt to
> Assyria, and the Assyrian will come into Egypt,
> and the Egyptian into Assyria, and the Egyptian
> will worship with the Assyrians.

> In that day Israel will be the third with Egypt
> and Assyria, a blessing in the midst of the earth,
> whom the Lord of hosts has blessed, saying,
> "Blessed be Egypt my people, and Assyria the
> work of my hands, and Israel my heritage.
> (Isa. 19:23-25)

The prophet Isaiah never leaves us in doubt. The very same God who has all the power necessary to punish his people has all the power necessary to transmute nature, society, and the very heart of man. The vision of the perfect king, the shoot of Jesse's stock, was simultaneously the vision of a re-created world built on foundations of economic and social equity, harmony among nations, and creative collaboration between humankind and nature.

Isaiah's vision of "that day" is the most vivid portrayal of the "messianic" idea as developed in the Bible. It is a vision shared by all the prophets who agonized over Israel's pain and believed firmly that God's redemption must be no less impressive than his condemnation. It was, by every worldly measure, a figment of the prophets' imagination, a fantasy of impossibilities, a dream of no substance, a mirage of unrealizable hopes. It was a vision belied by experience, refuted by the facts, and dashed by the subsequent course of events. For in the days that followed, no king ascended the throne of David, much less a perfect king; justice and righteousness did not become the line and the plummet, imperial powers did not desist from warfare, and the lion did not lie down with the lamb. The prophets, so it seemed, had indeed dreamed dreams.

II

The age of messianic scenarios was followed by an age of sober reconstruction. There was a grand sweeping away of the traditional leadership elites. Davidic aspirations were extinguished; expectations of independence were dashed; and the voice of the prophet was no longer heard in the land. With the formal promulgation and acceptance of the Pentateuch sometime between 445 and 397 B.C.E. the immutable written revelation of God dissolved the need for prophets, even as it undergirded the need for firm, decisive, priestly leadership—a leadership with no longings for political independence and no yearnings for a reappearance of divisive, disruptive, and cacophonous prophets. For this priestly class, the law was fixed and eternal; it guaranteed salvation in this world for those who obeyed its injunctions and sought atonement through the sacrificial cult and its expiating priesthood. The altar stood guard over the land, assured certain and abundant harvests, promised the fruitfulness of the womb and long life for all those who hearkened unto the commandments which God had thundered forth on Sinai.

The Pentateuch is down-to-earth revelation. Its promises are in line with realistic possibilities. A land could indeed be fruitful and prosperous if it were at peace. Peasants might indeed anticipate a long and satisfying life, if the rain came in its due season, and dew was plentiful, and imperial powers were benevolent exactors of tribute, not ravaging despoilers. The Pentateuch promised nothing which was not possible, even probable, if the priesthood succeeded where the prophets and kings had failed. Religious autonomy under the single, omnipotent God was far more to be prized than political independence with its warring factions, its loyalties divided between Baal and Yahweh, and its prophets now terrorizing the people with Yahweh's relentless anger and now intoxicating them with visions of nature tamed, nations becalmed, and societies liberated from economic exploitation and social inequity. The triumph of the Pentateuch was a triumph over prophecy and the beauteous vision of "that day" when the leopard would lie down with the kid, when swords would be beaten into plowshares, and when all the peoples of the world would look to Israel for the knowledge of the Lord.

This triumph is poetically confirmed by Ben Sira. Living at the high point of Aaronide-priestly supremacy, and inspired deeply by the revelation of Moses, Ben Sira focuses intently on Aaron and his sons, on the expiating powers of the cultus, and on the everlasting authority which was bestowed on them by God himself, and not on

the prophetic visions of "that day." He, to be sure, vener-
ates the prophets, but he is not intoxicated by their visions.
It is the Pentateuch, not Isaiah's latter days, that he medi-
tates upon day and night, and it is the high priest of his
day, Simon, that he looks to for religious leadership and
inspiration, not Amos, or Hosea, or Micah, or Jeremiah, or
Ezekiel.

III

The messianic idea thus lay dormant for several
hundred years. And for good reason. The Pentateuch
proved to be an incredibly good revelation for years
marked by growing prosperity and relative peace, even as
the Aaronides proved to be effective, judicious, and
statesmanlike rulers who preserved religious autonomy by
forswearing political independence. They were as amen-
able to Alexander as they had been to Artaxerxes. As long
as they were convinced that their God was omnipotent,
they were little concerned with terrestrial potentates—
provided that these potentates reaffirmed the right of the
Aaronides to govern the religious life of the people of
Israel in accordance with the laws of Moses.

But this relative serenity was punctured by a series of
events which quickly toppled the proud tower of
Aaronidism and catapulted the people of Israel into a
searing crisis of leadership. Antiochus Epiphanes rudely
altered the rules of the game when he sent Onias III, the
legitimate high priest, into exile and sold his office first to
Jason and then to Menelaus. Since Jason and Menelaus
had gained the high priesthood illegitimately, and since
Menelaus actually went so far as to turn the Temple over to
the worship of Zeus, there was a desperate need for vital
new leadership to abort seemingly certain disaster.

During those trying days of indecision and uncertainty,
the need for prophetic vision stirred a highly sensitive and
gifted individual to offer just such a vision in the form of
the Book of Daniel. Purporting to be the writings of a
prophetlike figure who had lived in Babylonia during the

exile, the Book of Daniel supposedly foresees the disaster which has now befallen the people of Israel and predicts sure deliverance for those who remain so steadfast that they prefer martyrdom to betrayal of their faith. For such as these, there will be a resurrection made possible and credible by God's omnipotence.

Though the Book of Daniel may have been reassuring, the scholar class which sat in Moses' seat, the scribes and Pharisees, did not revive prophecy to solve the problems of Aaronide collapse and Antiochene persecutions. Instead, they proclaimed a radically new concept of the law and the salvation that awaited those who internalized its teaching. These scribes and Pharisees affirmed that the Father God so loved the individual that he had revealed not one law, but two laws—the written law (the Pentateuch) and the oral law. The individual who internalized this twofold law could anticipate eternal life for his soul in the *olam ha-ba*, the world to come, and the resurrection of his body at some unknown future time. The scribes and Pharisees thus transferred the problem from a focus on a terrestrial solution to a focus on a postterrestrial solution. With one audacious swoop, the scribes and Pharisees brushed aside the empirical world as ultimately unreal and fashioned in its stead the world to come which the soul enters immediately on death, and the resurrection of the body which would come in the fullness of time. By this transference, the scribes and Pharisees rejected a messianic solution for this-worldly problems. All would-be Messiahs were regarded as frauds, for they ultimately were making God's justice and righteousness dependent on the outcome of a terrestrial gamble. The world to come was where God rewarded the souls of the righteous and punished the souls of the wicked. As for the resurrection of the dead, that was a long way off, and would occur when it occurred. That day would indeed usher in a world which would be utterly different from the terrestrial world of our experience.

The scribes and Pharisees thus did not look to a Messiah for the resolution of the problems posed by a collapsing

hierocracy and intense pressures to Hellenize. They supported Judah, Jonathan, and Simon because they offered
inspiring military leadership against the Syrians; they bestowed through their advocacy of the oral law the high
priesthood on Simon even though there was no warrant to
do so in the Pentateuch; they also acknowledged, first,
Salome Alexandra's queenship and, subsequently, Herod's
kingship even though neither was a descendant of David.
Similarly, they admonished the people to pay tribute to
Caesar even as they sought to hold back the people from
rebellion until the very last moment—and beyond. The
scribes and Pharisees simply refused to bend their fundamental teachings to external pressures. This world is a
world of trial and testing. Obedience to the twofold law
does not harvest terrestrial rewards. Pain, suffering,
agony, poverty winnow out the fickle from the steadfast in
faith. Eternal life is stored up not for the frail, but for
sturdy souls who cannot be provoked into disbelief. The
kingdom of God is an internal, not an external kingdom.
As long as kings and emperors do not block the road to
salvation, their terrestrial hegemony must be endured,
however harsh and provocative such rule might be.

IV

The scribes and Pharisees would not budge and could
not be lured by the prophetic visions of "the latter days."
They knew all these prophecies, but they refused to apply
them to the solution of terrestrial problems. These visions
were for a distant day when the dead would be resurrected, not for the here and now. Such prophecies had no
bearing on the sweeping away of Roman rule by some Son
of Man, some Messiah, who would fulfill the prophecies in
actual history.

But there were those who imagined otherwise. They
could not reconcile their belief in God's omnipotence with
the reading which the scribes and Pharisees had of the
messianic prophecies. The promise of the world to come
and of the resurrection of the dead at some distant time

was not enough. God would make manifest his saving power now, if only the people would show themselves worthy. The kingdom of God was not only a kingdom within, but a terrestrial kingdom as well—a kingdom swept free of evil, a kingdom as envisaged in the most glowing of prophetic visions. Even as the Pharisees brushed aside messianic claims as fraudulent, messianic claimants insisted on making their bid for recognition. Of these messianic claimants, only one, Jesus of Nazareth, so impressed his disciples that he became their Messiah. And he did so after the very crucifixion which should have refuted his claims decisively.

But it was not Jesus' life which proved beyond question that he was the Messiah, the Christ. It was his resurrection. It was only when his disciples were convinced that Jesus had indeed risen from the dead that they were stunned into awareness that Jesus was the Christ. It was not by virtue of any signs that attended his earthly ministry, but by his resurrection. He was thus like no Messiah foreshadowed in ancient prophecies; he was not like any Messiah the Israelites had anticipated. For in all the speculation with respect to a Messiah, there had been no premonition that the Messiah would prove himself to be the Christ *after* his death, not before, and by his resurrection, not his life.

And it is precisely with respect to the resurrection that we are confronted with a startling paradox. The scribes and Pharisees had resisted Jesus' claims to being the Messiah on the grounds that he had given no convincing signs, that he had not been preceded by Elijah, that he had defied the authority of the Pharisees. As far as they were concerned, his terrestrial evidences were unimpressive. But now the claim had been elevated to a new level. Jesus' disciples bore witness that he had been resurrected and that it was his resurrection which proved beyond question that he must necessarily be the Messiah, the Christ. The belief that resurrection was not only possible, but fundamental, was among the core teachings of the Pharisees. Jesus' disciples were thus predisposed to his resurrection not by the prophetic teachings, but by Pharisaic teachings.

The very Pharisees who had developed a strictly defensive concept of the Messiah—a concept that effectively blocked any would-be Messiah from meeting the necessary criteria—were the very ones who, by teaching the resurrection of the dead as a vital dogma, opened the eyes of Jesus' disciples to the possibility that what they had seen could indeed be true. The issue, then, was not whether resurrection was credible, but whether Jesus' resurrection had indeed occurred.

This is precisely the question which so agitated Paul. As a zealous follower of the Pharisees, Paul was certain that the world to come and the resurrection were the ultimate rewards for those who were "as to the law blameless." Jesus had defied the Pharisees; he could not then have been resurrected if the twofold law of the Pharisees was the road to salvation. Little wonder, then, that Paul's immediate reaction was violent opposition to the claims that Jesus had been resurrected. The very notion was both absurd and dangerous and should be rooted out. After all, resurrection was for the steadfast followers of the twofold law, not its detractors.

The more, however, Paul sought to eradicate the claim, the more the question persisted. Was Jesus' resurrection fact or fancy? Resurrection was credible—there was no impossibility—but was Jesus' resurrection factual?

We know the outcome. There came a stunning moment of realization, a moment of transmutation, when the non-fact was translated into the fact. Jesus had indeed been resurrected. If he was resurrected, then the twofold law of the Pharisees cannot be the road to salvation. The road to salvation must be the road of the risen Christ. Not the law, but Christ's saving grace was the path to eternal life. The law was a snare and a delusion. It was the *agent provocateur* of sin. It masked the power of sin, for it created the illusion that obedience to the law dissolved the primordial regenerative sources of sin within us. Sin skillfully manipulates the law; the law thus arouses the very passions which it was meant to still. Notice the words of Paul in the Epistle to the Romans:

While we were living in the flesh, our sinful passions, aroused by the Law, were at work in our members to bear fruit for death. . . . What shall we say? That the Law is sin? By no means! Yet, if it had not been for the Law, I should not have known sin. I should not have known what it is to covet if the Law had not said "You shall not covet." But sin, finding opportunity in the commandment, wrought in me all kinds of covetousness. Apart from the Law sin lies dead. (Rom. 7:5-8)

So I find it to be a law that when I want to do right, evil lies close at hand. For I delight in the Law of God, in my inmost self, but I see in my members another law at war with the law of my mind and making me captive to the law of sin which dwells in my members. Wretched man that I am! Who will deliver me from this body of death? Thanks be to God through Jesus Christ our Lord! So, then, I of myself serve God, but with my flesh I serve the law of sin. (Rom. 7:21-25)

For God has done what the Law, weakened by the flesh, could not do; sending his own Son in the likeness of sinful flesh and for sin, He condemned sin in the flesh, in order that the just requirements of the Law might be fulfilled in us, who walk not according to the flesh but according to the spirit. (Rom. 8:3, 4)

Now what is striking about Paul's concept of the Christ is that it is rooted exclusively in the resurrection. It was not what Jesus had taught when he was alive, but what his life meant in the light of the resurrection. For Paul, Jesus is the Messiah because he was resurrected, and he was resurrected so that all might know that the power of sin can be dissolved only through God's grace as made manifest through Jesus Christ. Paul's concept of the Messiah is thus a highly original one, one which is not rooted in biblical prophecy, and which is not dependent on any radical transformation of the terrestrial order. What is to be transformed is the individual. Through Christ's grace, he becomes a new creation. He sloughs off sin as he draws in

Christ; and as sin falls away, he glimpses the eternal life which his faith has earned.

It was Paul's Christ that, in retrospect, was the vitally living Christ. Those followers who had anticipated that Christ would soon return to usher in the kingdom of God on earth were harshly disappointed. For the fact is that Jesus did not fulfill, either during his lifetime or at any time thereafter, the biblical prophecies of "that day." If wars continued, economic and social exploitation remained the norm, and human degradation and humiliation went on apace, this did not mean to Christ's followers that he had not come and that his power was illusory. Far from it. The more distant the day of his second coming, the more vivid was his immediate presence. Christ was overcoming sin in each individual who internalized him. One did not have to await Christ's return, since Christ had never gone away. The Christ within was the real Christ whose continuous saving grace was always transforming the very nature of a true and believing Christian.

V

In retrospect, some revealing patterns had emerged by the third century. The Pharisaic and tannaitic teachers had assigned the messianic hope a subordinate status in the hierarchy of beliefs. The decisive defeat of Bar Kochba's messianic pretensions had all too clearly exposed the danger lurking for Judaism and the Jewish people in a misreading of prophetic visions. The messianic belief was, to be sure, not abandoned, but it was not elevated to the status of dogma. Such a status was reserved for the belief in *olam ha-ba*, the world to come, and *tehiat ha-metim*, the resurrection of the dead. "All Israel had a share in the world to come" is the crisp affirmative declaration of the Mishnah. "He who denies that the resurrection of the dead is articulated in the Torah," warns the Mishnah, "is deprived of any share in the world to come" (Sanhedrin 10:1). The condemned criminal was admonished, as he drew near to the place of stoning, that he should confess, "for whoever confesses has a portion in the world to come" (Sanhedrin 6:2). "These are the things," according to the Mishnah, "the fruits of which a person eats in this world, even as the principle is set up for him in the world to come; honoring father and mother, the doing of gracious acts, and bringing about peace between a person and his neighbor; but the study of Torah is equal to all of them (Peah 1:1)."

The focus was clearly on the world to come for the soul immediately on death, and on the resurrection of the body at some unknown and unstated time. The coming of the Messiah is never interlinked with either the world to come or the resurrection. The passages referring to the days of the Messiah are not associated with either of these vital dogmas. And never in the Mishnah is the messianic age held out to the believer as the reward for his righteousness. Whatever the days of the Messiah meant to the tannaitic sages, they were neither identified with nor fused with either *olam ha-ba* or *tehiat ha-metim*. This needs especially to be stressed, since the fact that the resurrection was to occur at some point in time allowed for a melding of the two concepts. But such a melding is not attested in the Mishnah.

For the Christians a similar pattern had crystallized. Though the belief in the second coming was not abandoned, the focus was on the internalized Christ and the salvation which awaited the soul and ultimately awaited the body. The Christian leaders were no more eager to court disillusionment than were the tannaitic sages. Just as in Pharisaic teaching obedience to the internalized law would yield immediate salvation for the soul when the body died, so in Christian teaching faith in the internalized Christ would yield immediate salvation for the soul. Resurrection might be a long way off, but the soul could scarcely become impatient as long as it lived alongside God the Father.

The belief in the world to come and in the resurrection was thus for most Jews and for most Christians a sturdy shield for warding off the batterings of fate and the bludgeonings of chance. The outside world might be bleak, dreary, and convulsed with pain, but the inner world was warmed with the golden glow of God's loving concern for the individual, a concern so deep and tender that he had made possible for the truly faithful eternal life for the soul and resurrection for the body. This inner world was a reality so precious that the seductive snares of the outer world could not dissolve it nor could the pain, agony, humiliation, and death inflicted by external forces undermine it.

But even believing Jews and faithful Christians could not so flee their human frailty as not to wish that it were otherwise. If only the inner and the outer would meld. If only the vivid prophecies of the latter days were ushered in, then, as God had promised, justice, righteousness, and mercy would go hand in hand with a harmonious nature and with a prosperous and joyous humankind. If only Christ would come again in all his glory, then there would be simultaneously a kingdom of God within and a kingdom of God without. And since such hopes were deeply rooted in Scripture, Jews and Christians would have been less than human had they not, from time to time, responded to the tumult of wars, the ravaging of pestilence, the ceaseless poundings of disaster, and the relentless pressure of tragic happenings, with illusions that the Messiah must be coming, or coming again. For Jews this was, at times, some leader of promise who was ready to gather armies to regain the Holy Land; at other times it was some charismatic personality who anticipated that God himself would remove all obstacles, break down all barriers, as his Messiah led the people back to the land for "that day" which Isaiah had foreseen.

We now know that the signs must have been misread, the meaning of the prophecies not deciphered. The Messiah neither came for the Jews nor came again for the Christians. Each and every claimant misled himself even as he misled others. Neither simple piety, impressive strength, stunning erudition, nor mystic intoxication yielded a Messiah for the Jews even when, as in the case of Sabbetai Zevi (1626-1676), an impressive array of re-

spected scholars and vintage cabalists convinced themselves and the masses at large that the sacred texts were
clearly being fulfilled.

VI

Judaism entered the modern world with a highly confused concept of the Messiah. Unlike the twin dogmas of
the world to come and the resurrection of the dead, the
belief in the coming of the Messiah—a belief which Maimonides had elevated into a principle of faith—was highly
vulnerable to empiric disaster, as the Sabbatian debacle
had so shockingly revealed. The coming of the Messiah
was thus, for all intents and purposes, a noncoming. It was
elevated into the realm of dream, fantasy, and illusion.
Indeed those who like the followers of the Baal Shem Tov,
the Hasidim, were so transported by vivid imaginings of
the Messiah and his coming that they broke forth in dance
and song, were the most scrupulous in keeping his real
coming a faroff event. The more ardent the belief, the
more remote the actualization.

The belief, however, had become a dogma and, as such,
had to be dealt with by those Jews who became advocates
of a westernized, modernized Judaism. The more radical
among them, such as Abraham Geiger, who fathered the
Reform movement, were embarrassed by what was for
them the naive belief in a personal Messiah, and transmuted this dogma into the concept of a messianic age. This
age they visualized as the outcome of the modernization
and westernization process which must, so they believed,
press on inexorably till all the major problems of humankind would be resolved. Judaism, so they taught, was itself
a religion of progressive revelation, which, in its highest
stage of development, made manifest to all humankind the
pure monotheism which was the essential message that
prophets had proclaimed. They were confident that there
would come a day in which God would be one, his name
one, and his children drawn to one another with bonds of
love. On that day, swords might indeed be built into plow-

shares, poverty might be overcome, and exploitation might vanish.

There was, however, an ironic aspect to their thinking. Convinced that Judaism was the bearer of universal truths and that the Jewish people were designated to spread these truths among the nations of the world, these leaders rejected any national aspirations for the Jewish people. For them, such aspirations would be a throwback, a betrayal of the divine mission of Israel to be a light to the nations, a beacon to the peoples. For them, the diaspora was evidence that Israel was a transterritorial, transnational, transpolitical people—a people not by might but by spirit.

Yet these same ardent spokesmen of Israel's transnational mission were no less ardent in their devotion to the nation states in which they lived. Their zeal for their fatherland frequently took on a religious fervor, as they offered, week in and week out, heartfelt prayers for the well-being of their nation and its governors. Indeed, patriotism was deemed to be a positive commandment as long as it was not dedicated to the restoration of a Jewish polity in the Holy Land.

VII

The coming of a messianic age proved to be as illusory as the coming of the Messiah. Westernization seeded total war, not total peace. The modern nation state became the breeding ground of irrational hatreds, devastating weapons, rapacious ambitions, and insatiable greed. Its moment of glory was on that day when the guns of August launched eager and joyous armies to kill, ravage, and despoil. Its moment of truth dawned four years later when peace settled over a Europe in shambles, when the inexorable march of progress bogged down in the muck of disaster, and when a star of ominous portent reddened on the eastern horizon. Propped up by a peace treaty recrowning the sovereign nation state, the peoples of Europe stumbled from economic stagnation to economic collapse, revealing as never before in human history the awesome power of sin to demolish all barriers, break through all dams, and tear down all fortresses devised by humans to block the primordial lust of evil. And it was the fate of the Jews to illustrate this gruesome truth. Civilization was, it seemed, the *agent provocateur* of sin, not its master. The holocaust, not the messianic age, was human destiny; Hitler, not the Son of David, was the Messiah. Or so it must have seemed to those whose road ended at Auschwitz and whose path broke off at Belsen.

VIII

Paralleling the trajectory of the European nation states was the emergence of a novel concept of what the messianic age for Jews might be. Disturbed by the first signs of re-emergent anti-Semitism in the West, and convinced that the Jews of eastern Europe would never be liberated, gifted leaders transmuted the messianic hope. The redemption of the Jews was to be a national redemption. The people of Israel were not pre-eminently a people of God with a divine mission, but the manifestation of a powerful national spirit which refused to die. The prophets may have expressed the nation's yearnings and hopes in the religious images appropriate for their unenlightened age, and sages may have fortified the national spirit with the reassurance that God's anointed would some day restore his nation to their land. But however obscured it might be by religious language, the essence of the people of Israel was the national, not the religious, spirit. The nation had donned a religious mantle for self-preservation during the centuries of naive faith and superstitious beliefs. Now, however, the protective covering might be stripped away as an enlightened sophisticated generation revealed nationalism to be the eternal underpinning of Jewish existence and a restored homeland the cornerstone of security, serenity, and reborn self-esteem. Pious Jews who prayed thrice daily for the restoration of Zion, but looked upon secular Jewish nationalists as sinners who were holding God back, were regarded by the brave new breed of nationalist leaders as unwitting betrayers of the essence of the Jewish people, the national idea or spirit.

This leadership shaped a radically novel concept of Jewish peoplehood and of the messianic hope. And this concept proved to be, in its own way, redemptive, for it stirred Jews with a vision of self-liberation and self-redemption and energized them to build the foundations for a modern viable society which was ready, willing, and able to offset the holocaust with rebirth and the on-rush of evil with a mighty fortress of fortitude, determination, and constructive growth. And the state of Israel still stands firmly as the beacon of development in the Middle East and as the light which may yet illumine the way for their Arab brothers.

IX

Let us pause briefly, on the edge of today and tomorrow, to get our bearings. We have come a long way from Isaiah's vision of "that day." We have chartered the ebbs and flows of messianic ideas and hopes. We have noted how they have not only waxed and waned, but how they have been transmuted. For the Aaronide priests, these were hopes of a bygone era; for the scribes and Pharisees, they were subordinated to the more reassuring anticipation of the world to come, and the distant certainty of the resurrection. For medieval Jews, they were longings which, on infrequent occasions, could blind the eyes of even the clear-sighted so that they stumbled after would-be Messiahs, but which for the most part were consoling imaginings of the impossible. For strident spokesmen of Reform Judaism, they were the intimations of a messianic age which lay at the end of the road of progress, the summit of humankind's climb to redemption. For Jewish nationalists, they were the mandate to build a secure and prosperous nation.

Are, then, the prophetic visions limited to what Jews have interpreted them to mean? Is their fulfillment limited to what has thus far been attained—an Israeli state with secure and recognized borders serving as a beachhead of development in the Middle East? Or do the prophecies hold within them yet unfulfilled possibilities? Is the security of the state of Israel the fulfillment or simply a reliable sign that fulfillment must be on its way?

If we seek to penetrate to the deepest meaning of Isaiah's prophecies, we discover that he was affirming that God has the power to do the seemingly impossible. God is not limited by the seeming imperatives of empirical experience. If God were limited in this way, then Israel itself could not have survived the obvious conclusion which any thinking person would have drawn from the destruction of the land, the gutting of the Temple, and the tossing of the people into exile. The empirical evidence revealed an impotent, not an omnipotent God. Yet, in response to the prophetic insistence that defeat was victory, destruction rehabilitation, exile redemption, the people of Israel simply denied the facts and persisted in their belief that their God is singular, omnipotent, and utterly committed to the creative survival of his people. Hence the first impossibility, Israel's ongoing creative existence, turned out to be a stubborn, irreducible fact.

What were the other impossibilities? Isaiah foresaw a time when nature would be so transformed that the lion would lie down with the lamb; when peoples would be so transmuted that they would live in harmony with one another; when congenital hatreds would dissolve as Egypt, Assyria, and Israel all recognized that each was God's chosen; when justice and righteousness would displace economic exploitation and social inequity; when human worth and dignity would be the norm; when the knowledge of the Lord would undergird a new creation.

What of these impossibilities? Is the empirical reading of reality to be triumphant? Are the brute facts to be decisive? Is evil so powerful that God's omnipotence is to be put to shame? Is there to be only a kingdom within and not without? Is humankind doomed to eternal warfare? Are nature and humankind to strive forever for destructive mastery? Are poverty and degradation to be the tragic destiny of the wretched of the earth? Is the holocaust to be the ultimate achievement of sinful man? Is "that day" to be a day of all-consuming terror as God's claims to sovereignty are mocked, and as his glowing attributes of promise are snuffed out one by one?

As a believing Jew, I have deep faith that just as God has accomplished the impossible by preserving Israel despite the facts, so he has the power to shape a new creation. And the signs abound if we but have the eyes to see and the ears to hear. For at that very moment when the demonic seemed to have gained decisive mastery, we began to latch onto the mind of God. And, ironically, the latching occurred as we strove to develop a weapon of such overwhelming power that Naziism would be doomed. The Manhattan project ushered in a new age, for it revealed that it is possible to take an abstract, mathematical law of nature—a thought in the mind of God that holds together, sustains, and regenerates his creation—and use it to create an end product which otherwise would have been impossible. And this tapping of the mind of God did not end with lethal weapons of destruction. Drawing on abstract laws, immaterial formulae, invisible interconnections, we burst through our terrestrial limits. We rove through space, land men on the moon, explore the host of emergent possibilities as the realm of the impossible shrinks before the knowledge of God's eternal laws. We erase pestilence at its core, eradicate illness in its womb, and banish for all time immutable killers of yesteryear. With weightless thoughts, we create miracle rice; with abstractions we develop hardy new strains; with mental formulae we seed the abundance of the world to come. Indeed, as God's laws become known and prove true and steadfast, the impossible recedes. There, indeed, can come a day when nature and humankind are reconciled, when the lion may indeed lie down with the lamb, and when even death will die.

And if we turn to the international arena, we can glimpse in the very depths of the strife and in the very core of the raging violence the first seedlings of harmony among the nations. And one of these seedlings, sown in the furrows charred by the holocaust, is already beginning to bear fruit. The European Economic Community has proved that nation need not lift up sword against nation, even if such lifting up belongs to its most cherished memories of national pride and aspiration. Germany and France will go to war against each other no more. Evil can be barred from demonic intrusions on the emergent good. Collaboration among the nations can diminish the lure of sovereignty even as it can foster the pursuit of national diversity.

And no less reassuring a sign, one plucked out of the distressing pressures now besetting Israel in the wake of the United Nations resolution, is that on the very eve of the vote, the fifth and sixth ships with Israeli cargoes passed through the Suez Canal and docked at Israeli ports. The settlement with Egypt is holding—with all of its implications for the possibility of the impossible, that is, the day on which all the nations of the Middle East will be one with each other, as Isaiah predicted.

The crucial signs are here. They can be found by anyone who looks beneath the surging surface of events. They proclaim that Isaiah was right. God has the power to overcome the impossible if only we tap the mind and spirit of God. There can indeed be a new creation. Nations can live in harmony. Poverty can be overcome and exploitation end.

But these are as yet only the signs that the prophecies could come true. They are not in themselves the fulfillment. They signal to us that we can create a new kind of world, one which is the very negation of the world we have so long taken for granted as eternal. But for such a creation, we need not only the mind of God, but the spirit of God. Our awareness of the steadfast laws of nature gives as much power to destroy this world as to build the world to come. The kingdom of God without must be patterned on the kingdom of God within. Without those divine attributes of goodness, mercy, justice, and love, even the most impressive of worldly societies will be without life. The affluent individual will not be liberated by his affluence from the need for salvation. Only the divinely implanted hierarchy of enduring values can displace the alienation, ennui, and despair which sear the souls of those who have "liberated" themselves from God's justice, graciousness, and love.

We are, I am convinced, going through the convulsions which the prophets always associated with the eve of "that day." They never promised an easy transition. And they had no illusions that God would shape a new creation without human collaboration. The messianic age is within our grasp, the prophecies are true prophecies, and their fulfillment is awaiting our decision—for God.

4

WILLIAM SANFORD LaSOR

The Messiah: An Evangelical Christian View

The assignment which I was given was "to present a paper on the concept of the Messiah from the historic evangelical perspective." I must begin with a mild disclaimer. I shall present my own understanding of the subject, with the hope that there will not be too wide a divergence from the assigned topic. I know that among evangelicals there are some rather strong differences on certain points. Some will probably feel that my viewpoint does not represent the historical position of evangelicals. This is understandable, and I take no offense; I simply hope that in turn I shall not give offense.

I would like also to offer a word of explanation to my Jewish audience. As a Christian and a professor of the Old Testament, I shall make extensive use of the *Tanach*. Since I have both studied in Jewish institutions and engaged in extensive dialogue with Jewish scholars, I know that my understanding of passages from the Hebrew Bible does not always agree with the understanding of my Jewish friends. (I might also add that, since I have had the benefit of dialogue with Jews, my understanding of the Old Testament does not always agree with that of my Christian friends.) Therefore, I do not present this paper as a definitive treatment of the subject, but rather as a personal testimony. This is the way that I, as an evangelical Christian, understand the concept of the Messiah.

The Method of Approach

Basically, there are two ways to approach the subject of the Messiah as seen by Christians. The one looks back from our present position to the Old Testament accounts. The other looks at the Old Testament accounts from within their own context.

From the present position

If we approach the subject from the present position, we follow a procedure somewhat like this. We have a rather full notion of the Christ (Messiah) from what the New Testament tells us about Jesus as well as from what the creeds of the church have said about the scriptural passages. By this last statement, I mean such things as philosophical and theological definitions that go beyond the language of Scripture, such as the "pre-existence" of the Messiah, "persons" in the "Godhead," and "the second person of the Trinity." I am not denying the truth in such statements. They were formulated in the postapostolic period by a broad representation of the church which was seeking to formulate the truths which it found in Scripture in language that was meaningful to its day. But such things do have their influence on our inquiry.

Working backwards from our present full notion of the Christ,[1] we look for passages in the Old Testament that appear to furnish details of the life of Jesus. If we are patient and persevering we can put together a large number of passages—sometimes referred to as "proof texts"—which combine to give us a rather complete picture of Jesus. The Christ-Messiah is the "everlasting Father" (Isa. 9:6 [5 MT]), whose "goings forth" have been "from everlasting" (Mic. 5:2 [1 MT]). He is "the seed of the woman" who was to come to crush the serpent's head (Gen. 3:15), the "Shiloh" who was to be the culmination of the rule of the tribe of Judah (Gen. 49:10).

He would be born in Bethlehem (Mic. 5:2 [1 MT]) of a virgin (Isa. 7:14), and his name would be Immanuel, which means "God with us." He would be "called out of

Egypt" (Hos. 11:1) after Herod's attempt to get rid of "the king of the Jews" by killing the male babies in Bethlehem. He would grow up "like a tender plant" (Isa. 53:2), and "the Spirit of the Lord" would rest upon him (Isa. 11:2). He would "bring good tidings to the afflicted" and "bind up the broken hearted" (Isa. 61:1). He would come to Jerusalem "humble and riding on an ass" (Zech. 9:9). There he would be "despised and rejected by men" (Isa. 53:3), and as a result of giving his "back to the smiters" and his "cheeks to those who pulled out the beard," hiding not his face "from shame and spitting" (Isa. 50:6), "his appearance was so marred, beyond human semblance" (Isa. 52:14). "Like a lamb he was led to the slaughter, and like a sheep that before its shearers is dumb, so he opened not his mouth" (Isa. 53:7).

On the cross he cried, "My God, my God, why hast Thou forsaken me?" (Ps. 22:1). He was "scorned by men, and despised by the people," and could say, "All who see me mock at me, they make mouths at me, they wag their heads" (Ps. 22:6, 7). In his agony, he could also say, "I am poured out like water, and all my bones are out of joint" (Ps. 22:14). Since he was crucified with evildoers and buried in a wealthy man's tomb, we can, with a slight rearrangement of the text, say that "they made his grave with the wicked and with a rich man in his death" (Isa. 53:9).

But he knew that this was not the end of God's purpose, and could therefore say, "Thou wilt not abandon my soul to Sheol, neither wilt Thou allow Thy holy one to see the pit" (Ps. 16:10). After the resurrection there would be an exaltation, for "he shall be exalted and lifted up, and be very high" (Isa. 52:13), and the Lord would say to him, "Sit at my right hand, till I make your enemies your footstool" (Ps. 110:1). There, as "a priest for ever after the order of Melchizedek" (Ps. 110:4), he makes intercession as our great High Priest, going into the very presence of the Lord to make atonement for our sins (Lev. 16:12-14). In this manner, he ratifies the "new covenant" (Jer. 31:31-34).

He shall come "on the clouds of heaven" "like a son of

man" (Dan. 7:13), like "a stone cut out by no human hand" (Dan. 2:34), to "break in pieces" the kingdoms of this world, and "set up a kingdom which shall never be destroyed" (Dan. 2:44; cf. Isa. 9:7). "In that day the Lord will extend his hand yet a second time to recover the remnant which is left of his people, from Assyria, from Egypt, from Pathros, from Ethiopia, from Elam, from Shinar, from Hamath, and from the coastlands of the sea" (Isa. 11:11). "Righteousness shall be the girdle of his waist, and faithfulness the girdle of his loins. The wolf shall dwell with the lamb, and the leopard shall lie down with the kid, and the calf and the lion and the fatling together, and a little child shall lead them" (Isa. 11:5, 6). In those days "the mountain of the house of the Lord shall be established as the highest of the mountains . . . and many peoples shall come, and say: 'Come, let us go up to the mountain of the Lord, to the house of the God of Jacob; that he may teach us his ways, and that we may walk in his paths' " (Isa. 2:2, 3).

Many more passages could be added to this already long list. According to one count, as many as seventy-five allusions to Christ can be found in the Old Testament.[2] Somewhere, I came across the figure of 333 prophecies that were "fulfilled" in Christ. In several periods of the history of the church strong emphasis was placed on the evidential value of these prophecies.

Now, I do not wish to leave the impression, by this treatment, that I reject the notion of prophecy and fulfillment. Quite the reverse. I believe in the fulfillment of prophecy, and I believe that the Old Testament is fulfilled in Jesus Christ. But, speaking for myself, I find the prooftext method of studying the Old Testament to be unsatisfactory. As I say this, I am aware of the fact that this method has been used by many of the great minds of the church. Indeed, it was used by the New Testament writers themselves, particularly Matthew. But in my opinion it opens the door to too many sectarian interpretations. Moreover, it fails to give us a view of how the messianic idea developed, and how the Jews of the first century had come to a messianic hope, what that hope was, and how the life and death of Jesus raised serious problems because he did not quite fit into the current notions of the Messiah.

From the historical perspective

I therefore have come to look upon the Christian messianic view as the end product of a long development of ideas. By using the word *development*, I am not denying the doctrine of inspiration. I believe that God revealed his will in stages to his servants—to Abraham and the other patriarchs, to Moses, and to the prophets. I believe that this revelation was distributed over two thousand years, and was so involved with the historical situation that men of God were led to view his revelation in the light of the historical situation. They formulated their faith in conflict with and in contrast to the religious thoughts and practices, as well as the historical situations, among which they dwelt. Gradually their faith became larger and more complex. Their God YHWH, who may once have seemed to be only a tribal deity, was seen as the creator and ruler of all the earth, who holds the destinies of the nations in his hand. The simple idea that an ideal "Son of David" would occupy the throne in Zion and bring the nation into an age of peace and prosperity and religious leadership among the nations had become quite complex. Divine intervention was necessary. God himself would be the shepherd over his vicegerent David (Ezek. 34:11, 12, 22, 23). It would take the divine Spirit to bring the nation to life (Ezek. 37:11-14). The destruction of Gog and the forces that sought to destroy God's people could be accomplished only by God himself (Ezek. 38:21-23). Or, to change the figure, the terrible beast that arose out of the sea and the other satanic beasts could be finally subdued only by the "Ancient of Days" (Dan. 7:22-27). And someone—he is not clearly defined in the Old Testament—would accomplish for his people the redemptive work that would heal them by taking their chastisement and sin upon himself (Isa. 53:4-12).

In the balance of this paper, I shall attempt to describe

the development of these various strands that are woven together to form the Christian idea of the Messiah.

The Redemptive Revelation of YHWH

The soteriological purpose

From the very beginning it was God's purpose to reverse the satanic[3] deed that resulted in the sin of our first parents. When God pronounced the curse on the serpent in the garden, he declared this purpose in the words, "I will put enmity between you and the woman, and between your seed and her seed; he shall bruise your head, and you shall bruise his heel" (Gen. 3:15). This is a soteriological or redemptive promise, rather than a "messianic" prophecy.[4] Throughout the Old Testament we find promises of ultimate redemption from sin. Properly speaking, these are not "messianic prophecies," but promises of salvation. The messianic hope is part of this larger soteriological hope.

The Abrahamic covenant is part of this soteriological purpose. When God called Abram, he stated the promise that "by you all the families of the earth will bless themselves" (or "be blessed," Gen. 12:3). From this point on, the Old Testament is concerned principally with the people of God's choice, Israel. But at the same time, the nations of the world are not forgotten. Abraham was "the father of a multitude of nations" (Gen. 17:5), and ultimately the kings of the earth who have set themselves against YHWH and his anointed (Ps. 2:2) will come to Jerusalem to bring gifts to God (Ps. 68:29).

The Mosaic covenant is part of God's soteriological purpose. The nation Israel was to be YHWH's "own possession among all the peoples," and YHWH added, "for all the earth is mine, and you shall be to me a kingdom of priests and a holy nation" (Exod. 19:5, 6). The expression *a kingdom of priests* suggests the role of mediator. Israel was established by God to have a redemptive role among the nations of the world. This redemptive role is integrally bound up with the Torah revealed at Sinai—the instruction designed to produce the "holy nation." For a long period of time we hear little about the universal purpose of the Torah, but when we come to the prophetic period, it is clearly expressed. At last, when "the mountain of the house of the Lord" is established "as the highest of the mountains," "all the nations" are to flow to it. The redemptive purpose of the Torah is set forth in these words: "For out of Zion shall go forth the law, and the word of the Lord from Jerusalem," and as a result the nations "shall beat their swords into plowshares, and their spears into pruning hooks; nation shall not lift up sword against nation, neither shall they learn war any more" (Isa. 2:2-4).

The Davidic covenant, likewise, is part of God's redemptive purpose. The eternal throne which YHWH promised to David and to his son (II Sam. 7:13-16) is ultimately to have "the nations of the earth" as its heritage, and "the ends of the earth" as its possession (Ps. 2:8). And while the punitive nature of this kingdom is stressed in Psalm 2 (cf. vv. 9-11) and elsewhere (cf. Ps. 68, 110, etc.), ultimately the "shoot from the stump of Jesse," that is, the king that shall come from the redeemed remnant of Israel, is to bring righteousness and peace into the world, and be the object of the quest of all nations (Isa. 11:1-10). But this leads to our next point.

The king-messiah concept

The Israelite nation considered God to be its king. This is inferred from the Sinaitic (or Mosaic) covenant, where God calls the nation "a kingdom of priests" (Exod. 19:5, 6), and again from the words of YHWH to Samuel, when the people demanded "a king to govern us like all the nations" (I Sam. 8:5), and Samuel was reluctant to comply with their demand. The Lord said to Samuel, "They have not rejected you, but they have rejected me from being king over them" (I Sam. 8:7). With the establishment of the Davidic covenant, as we have seen, God promised an eternal dynasty for the seed of David (II Sam. 7:12).[5]

This is the beginning of the "messianic hope" (using the expression in its strictest sense). It is important that we recognize that we are using a term that conveys to us more than its original meaning. The word *Messiah* comes originally from the Hebrew word *māšîᵃḥ,* a simple adjective meaning "anointed," which can also be used as a noun meaning "the anointed one(s)." It occurs thirty-nine times in the Hebrew Bible, usually with reference to the king.[6] With the possible exception of Daniel 9:25, the word is never used as a technical term meaning "the Messiah."[7] There is therefore a "messianic idea" in the Old Testament, without the use of the term *Messiah.* How can this be?

A great deal has been written about the Israelite concept of the king. Thus we have "divine kingship," "sacral kingship," "charismatic kingship," "sacerdotal kingship," and other theories. According to these views, the Israelite concept of the king was derived from Babylonian, Canaanite, or Egyptian (or other) views, and the king was conceived of as a god, a "son" of the god, a priest-king, or the recipient of a divine charism. There are cultic acts that depict the divine marriage, the dying-and-rising-god theory, the New Year's festival, or the royal enthronement, and many other elements. In each of these views there are kernels of truth, but I find far too much hypothesis and too little attention to the scriptural passages that clearly refute the theories that have been spun.[8]

But when we have distilled these various theories and gone back to the Scripture for further understanding, we find that there are a great many statements that refer to the king in such a way that we must conclude that the concept goes far beyond simply that of a reigning monarch or a dynastic succession. Let us look at some of these statements.

The name *David* is to the kingship what *Abraham* is to faith, *Moses* is to the law, and *Elijah* to the prophets. We never hear any prophecies concerning "the Son of Solomon" or "the Son of Hezekiah." It is always "the Son of David." When God's wrath is poured out on the faithless kingdom and its king is cut off, the coming ruler, whose origin is from of old, will come from Bethlehem, the ancestral home of David. The child who will assume the burden of a government whose characteristics are peace, righteousness, and justice, will occupy the throne of David (Isa. 9:7 [MT 6]). When the tree is felled and only a stump remains (Isa. 6:13), it is the stump of Jesse (Isa. 11:1) from which a "shoot" shall come forth, a "branch" shall grow, and he shall judge with righteousness (Isa. 11:1-4). When God himself comes to search for his sheep, which the false shepherds have not cared for, he "will set up over them one shepherd, my servant David" and "my servant David shall be prince among them" (Ezek. 34:11, 23, 24). "Son of David" therefore becomes a messianic title.[9] When the crowds greeted Jesus on his ride into Jerusalem with the words, "Hosanna to the Son of David!" (Matt. 21:9 and parallels), they were hailing him as the awaited Messiah.

The king is sometimes addressed in terms that seem to ascribe divinity to him. These expressions need careful study. For example, we read, "I will tell of the decree of the Lord: He said to me, 'You are my son, today I have begotten you' " (Ps. 2:7). It is important that we read no more into this than was understood by those who first heard the words. David's son, whom YHWH would raise up and whose throne he would establish forever, was to be YHWH's son (II Sam. 7:12-14).[10] It is easy for us Christians to jump to the conclusion that this passage refers to the Messiah, but note carefully the context. Immediately after YHWH says, "I will be his father, and he shall be my son," he goes on to say, "When he commits iniquity, I will chasten him . . . but I will not take my steadfast love from him, as I took it from Saul" (II Sam. 7:14, 15). It is clear that the immediate reference is to a human descendant of David, specifically Solomon. But there is in the entire passage a *sensus plenior*, for it refers to an eternal kingship. The Christian, therefore, may see in this passage, and in the expression *Son of God*, a prophecy that was "fulfilled"—that is, it took on its fuller meaning—in Jesus Christ.

The king is also referred to, it would seem, as "God." Psalm 45 is clearly "addressed to the king" (v. 1 [2 MT]). It seems to be a psalm written on the occasion of the marriage of the king's daughter (v. 10 [11 MT]; cf. "the princess" in v. 13 [14 MT]), although we need not press this detail for we are concerned only with the first half of the psalm. In verse 6 (7 MT) we read, "Your throne, O God, is for ever and ever; a scepter of equity is your royal scepter" (lit. trans.). The Revised Standard Version translates, "Your divine throne"—but this cannot be supported by the Hebrew *kissăḵā 'ĕlôhîm*. To complicate matters for the Christian, this passage is quoted in Hebrews 1:8, 9, where it is commonly translated, "Thy throne, O God." Now if this translation is supported, we must recognize that the king is called by the title *'ĕlôhîm*. While this word is commonly translated "God," there are places in the Old Testament where it must mean something significantly less, as when it is used of judges (Exod. 22:8, 9) or angels (Ps. 8:5 [6 MT]).[11] It is therefore not impossible that the term *'ĕlôhîm* was used with reference to the king. Certainly, we may reason, if the king of the throne in Zion was the "son" of God, ruling over God's people and destined to have a universal dominion, it is conceivable that he could be addressed as "God." However, we note that in the verse that follows, these words occur: "Therefore God, your God, has anointed you . . ." (Ps. 45:7 [8 MT]). We might therefore translate the preceding verse, "Your throne is God for ever and ever."[12] In any event, it is easy to see how the early Christians could find scriptural support for the concept of the divine sonship of Jesus Christ.

In fact, we must go beyond this moderate statement. According to the New Testament accounts, one of the crucial points in the trial of Jesus concerned the claim of divinity which Jesus is alleged to have made. According to Mark, the high priest asked Jesus, "Are you the Christ, the Son of the Blessed?" (Mark 14:61). The question in Luke is phrased, "Are you the Son of God, then?" (Luke 22:70). In John the tradition is presented somewhat differently. When Pilate was consulting the Jewish leaders concerning the crime of which Jesus was accused, they told him, "We have a law, and by that law he ought to die, because he has made himself the Son of God" (John 19:7). At this point, I am not concerned with the problem of whether these accounts record *verbatim* what the Jewish leaders said, or whether this is the language of the later Christian *kerygma*. It is enough for us to accept the fact that many, if not most, of the Christians at that time were Jews, as indeed was Paul. For these Jews, the concept that Jesus could be the Son of God as well as the Messiah simply had to be reconcilable with the Scriptures. To the extent that Paul and the early Christians proclaimed the divine sonship of Jesus, they must have been able to reconcile their belief with their understanding of the Old Testament. No less could be expected of any Jew who was faithful to the law of the Lord.

In Psalm 110 we find the concept that the king of Zion (v. 2) is "a priest for ever after the order of Melchizedek" (v. 4). Since the name *Melchizedek* occurs only here and in Genesis 14:18, we could skip over this, except for several significant facts. Melchizedek was, as we know, both a king and a priest (Gen. 14:18). Therefore, the advocates of the theory that the Israelite king was a priest-king find some support in this psalm. Further, the mention of Zerubbabel the king and Joshua the high priest in the prophecies of Haggai and Zechariah, particularly the passage in which Joshua the high priest is crowned and called by the messianic title *the Branch* (Zech. 6:9-12), seems to give some support to the priest-king theory. We might further mention that a "priestly Messiah" or a Messiah from the house of Levi is found in later Judaism and possibly in the Qumran writings.[13] To complicate the problem for the Christian, the author of Hebrews says that Christ (the Christian Messiah) was "designated by God a high priest after the order of Melchizedek" (Heb. 5:10, cf. v. 6).

The Son-of-Man concept

The expression *Son of Man* is used frequently in the New Testament, almost exclusively on the lips of Jesus. He used the expression, for example, in Mark 13:26: "They will see the Son of Man coming in clouds and with great power and glory" (cf. Matt. 24:30). It seems clear that he drew the figure from Daniel 7:13. To the Christian, therefore, the term *Son of Man* is a messianic title.

When we turn to the Old Testament, however, we find that, with the exception of the verse in Daniel, the expression *Son of Man* is never found with any messianic frame of reference. Ezekiel is often called "Son of man," but the title simply means "man, human being." In fact, the expression *son of man* in Aramaic (which is the language of Dan. 7:13) simply means "human being."[14] In Jesus' use of the term, "Son of Man" sometimes means simply "I"; for example, "Foxes have holes, and birds of the air have nests; but the Son of Man has nowhere to lay his head" (Matt. 8:20). Certainly the term was not equated with the idea of the Messiah in the popular mind, for Jesus charged his disciples to tell 'no one that he was the Messiah (Mark 8:30), even though he was constantly referring to himself as "the Son of Man."[15]

In the intertestamental period a strongly apocalyptic element developed. Possibly it was the result of a dark pessimism. The throne of David had disappeared, and with it had gone the hope that a "Son of David" would be raised up to lead the nation into an age of peace and prosperity. Instead, some men looked for an irruption of God into history. This position could be supported by passages from the Old Testament, particularly those which have been labeled by scholars as "apocalyptic." The smashing of the powerful pagan kingdoms could be accomplished, to use Daniel's language, only by a stone that "was cut out by no human hand" (Dan. 2:34), a kingdom that God himself would set up (2:44). The "Day of YHWH," mentioned by several of the prophets,[16] was to be a time of the "coming" of YHWH to fight against and destroy the enemies of Israel, and also to judge his people. In the later intertestamental or early Christian period, the "apocalyptic Son of Man" concept was formulated. We find it first in Book II (the Similitudes) of Enoch, and in view of the fact that this portion is completely lacking among the Qumran fragments of Enoch, we may tentatively conclude that Book II was a later (i.e. post-Christian) addition.[17]

Judaism—meaning the main stream, or what G. F. Moore called "normative Judaism"—never embraced the apocalyptic notion, although the concept of the two ages, *hā'ôlām hazzê* ("this age") and *hā'ôlām habbā'* ("the age to come"), certainly could have accommodated a divine irruption. There were Jewish apocalyptic movements, as we know from their writings.[18] The Qumran sect, in spite of the complete absence of a Son-of-Man concept, could be characterized as apocalyptic, for they expected God to intervene, particularly through the agency of Michael (1QM 17:4-8; cf. 1QH 3:31-36). At the same time, the Qumran community was clearly looking for a Messiah of the line of David.[19]

The early Christians took up the apocalyptic ideas to a considerable extent. With the doctrine of the return of Christ (or the second coming, the parousia) they incorporated a considerable number of passages from Ezekiel, Daniel, Zechariah, and other Scriptures that speak of divine intervention and the end of the age or the coming days. But this also serves to underscore the difficulty of distinguishing "apocalyptic" from the soteriological thread of the Old Testament, as well as from eschatology in general. The very notion that God has determined to redeem his creation, that the blessings which he promised to Abraham were intended one day to extend to all the nations of the earth, assumes an *eschaton*, an "end" when the redemptive purpose will be complete. How is that to be accomplished? What lies beyond that point? If it is accomplished by divine intervention, rather than by human means, it is called "apocalyptic." If the new age lies beyond history, it is "eschatological." On these points there is much difference of opinion.

In the Christian view, as I see it, the first advent of Christ has already introduced the end of the age (cf. I Cor. 10:11). The blessings of the messianic age have already begun. But the old age has not yet ended. With the second advent of Christ, the Davidic reign shall once again be established in Jerusalem. The idyllic conditions of the coming age, which were foretold by the prophets, will become realities. During the days of his first advent, Jesus, by his teachings, his example, and his wonderful deeds, gave a little sample of what we may expect in the messianic age. But with the apocalyptic advent of the Son of Man, the messianic age in all its beauty will be inaugurated.

The Suffering Servant

One of the most difficult teachings of Jesus, one that his disciples resisted right up to the resurrection, was the necessity of his suffering and death. If I have analyzed the accounts of his earthly life correctly, the first announcement of his suffering came around the mid-point of his ministry. At Caesarea-Philippi, when Jesus asked his disciples who men said he was and who they thought he was, Peter made the announcement, "You are the Messiah, the Son of the living God" (Matt. 16:13-16). From that time on Jesus began to tell the disciples "that he must go to Jerusalem and suffer many things from the elders and chief priests and scribes, and be killed, and on the third day be raised" (Matt. 16:21). Peter's immediate reaction was typical of every reaction that we find to such a suggestion: "God forbid, Lord! This shall never happen to you" (16:22). The crucifixion of Jesus was a major stumbling block to his disciples. The disillusionment that they felt is expressed by one of the disciples on the Emmaus road after the crucifixion and before the fact of the resurrection had become known: "We had hoped that he was the one to redeem Israel" (Luke 24:21). "We *had* hoped"—but the hope died when he died on the cross.

But when the fact of the resurrection became known to the early Christians, and probably as a result of the post-resurrection teachings of Jesus (cf. Luke 24:26, 27), they began to search the Scriptures. They fastened on the subject of the Suffering Servant, particularly as he is set forth in Isaiah 53.

Now, we know that there is little if any evidence that the

Jewish people ever understood Isaiah 53 as a messianic prophecy. Judaism knows nothing of a suffering Messiah. But it does know of a Suffering Servant. I cannot even begin to enter into the long and complicated study that would be necessary, if we were to consider this problem. I have done it elsewhere.[20] Here I can say only that the concept of suffering as part of God's redemptive purpose is clearly taught in the prophets. The problem is not to find the Suffering Servant but to identify him. Is the servant Israel? There are certainly enough passages to establish this identification beyond question. It is regrettable that Christians have been so blind as not to see that the sufferings of Israel have been, and still are, part of God's redemptive work. Is the Suffering Servant the righteous remnant of Israel? We would all agree, I think—Jew and Christian alike—that it is the righteous remnant that has redemptive value for the rest of the religious community. Without a righteous remnant the knowledge of the Lord would long ago have disappeared from the earth. They have suffered to preserve it and to make it known. For the Christian, the Suffering Servant is seen most clearly in Jesus.

Part of the reason for this, it seems certain, is to be found in the fact that Jesus chose to use the servant image. I don't mean that he announced, "I am the servant of the Lord." Rather, he said simply, "The Son of Man came not to be served, but to serve, and to give his life as a ransom for many" (Mark 10:45). He stressed the point that he was a servant, not so much in word as in deed. He tried to impress upon his disciples the truth that the first in the kingdom is the one who is the humblest servant (Matt. 20:26, 27). And he connected this servanthood with a redemptive act, by which his life was offered for the salvation of others.

The Synthesis of the Messianic Idea

We have examined three Old Testament concepts—the messianic king, the apocalyptic Son of Man, and the Suffering Servant. To the best of my knowledge, no one prior to the time of Jesus ever attempted to bring these three concepts together in one person. Jesus did. While he did not go about publicly claiming to be the Messiah, he did admit to the identification. At Caesarea-Philippi, after Peter's statement, "Thou art the Christ," Jesus replied, "Blessed are you, Simon Bar-Jona! For flesh and blood has not revealed this to you, but my Father who is in heaven" (Matt. 16:17); and again, before the high priest, when he was asked under solemn oath, "Are you the Christ, the Son of God?" (Matt. 26:63), he replied, "You have said."[21] The high priest's reaction ("You have heard the blasphemy") indicates that he took Jesus' reply to be affirmative.

There is no question that Jesus took upon himself the title *Son of Man*, and by associating with it the idea of his return at a future time, he accepted the term with its apocalyptic significance (cf. Mark 13:26; 14:62). But he also added to the concept by associating the title with his suffering (Mark 8:31). Furthermore, he joined the title *Son of Man* with the concept of the servant who was to give his life as a ransom for many (Matt. 20:28).

The Christian concept of the Messiah, in the light of the claims of Jesus, is a synthesis of the Old Testament concepts of the messianic King, the Son of Man, and the Suffering Servant. But to reconcile all the various Old Testament teachings on these concepts with the Christian concept of the Messiah is a rather complex problem for Christians—and we have not yet reached full agreement.

As far as the kingdom is concerned, we have the word of Jesus that his kingdom "is not of this world" (John 18:36). When his followers attempted to take him by force and make him king, he simply withdrew to another place (John 6:15). The early church rarely, if ever, referred to Jesus as "King," and the title *King of kings* is found only in Revelation (17:14; 19:16). Still, there must have been some preaching to the effect that Jesus was the messianic King, for the charge brought against the apostles in Thessalonica was that they had said, "There is another king, Jesus" (Acts 17:7). Furthermore, in early apostolic preaching which set forth Jesus as the Messiah there were quotes from Psalms 2, 16, 45, and 110[22]—this implies that he was recognized as the messianic King.

Still, there is considerable disagreement over the way the Old Testament passages are to be understood. If the kingdom is "spiritualized," then the promises of material prosperity, the return of Israel to the land, the king on the throne in Jerusalem (or Zion) ruling over his people while the Gentiles (or nations) come to Jerusalem for instruction and blessing, all have to be spiritualized. It was against this Christian interpretation that Klausner was protesting when he said that Christianity has attempted to remove the political and nationalistic part of the hope.[23] There are Christians who approach the subject from another direction, and I count myself among them. With the clear teachings from Jesus and the apostles that he is coming again, and against the background of Paul's discussion of the Jews in Romans 9-11, I am led to the conclusion that there will indeed be a literal fulfillment of the political and nationalistic elements of messianic prophecy. There is a very brief reference to a millennium in Revelation (20:1-3), and it raises a number of questions; but such a period, during which Satan is bound (20:2), provides the opportunity for the re-establishment of Israel and Judah under the messianic king in Jerusalem, and for the instruction of the nations in the law of the Lord. The regathering of the people of God is foreshadowed in Ezekiel 36-37. The "loosing" of Satan "for a little while," which takes place after the millennial period (Rev. 20:3), provides the opportunity for Gog of the land of Magog to attempt once more to exterminate the people of God, Israel, who "are dwelling securely" (Ezek. 38:14-16; cf. Rev. 20:7, 8). That sets the stage for the final intervention of God and the final destruction of the satanic forces (Ezek. 38:21-23; Rev. 20:9, 10). The details of Zechariah 9-14 must likewise be set into this picture.

Conclusion

I do not wish to leave the impression that I, as an evangelical Christian, have all the answers. Nor am I convinced, from studying the works of my fellow evangelicals, that they have all the answers. There are many pieces of the Old Testament King/ Son of Man/ Servant-complex that either do not fit or do not fit very well. Personally, I believe that we need a great deal more exegetical study of the Old Testament passages, taken in their contexts, without forcing them into a New Testament mold. In addition, I believe that we must listen more to what the Jew says about his understanding of these passages. Just as I refuse to believe that God has rejected his people (Rom. 11:1) and that there is no longer any place for Israel in God's redemptive work or in the messianic hope, so I refuse to believe that we who once were not his people, and who have become his people only through his grace, can learn nothing from those who from of old have been his people.

It is my hope that this conference will be just the beginning of a series of studies in which we evangelical Christians will learn more about the messianic King and his kingdom from those whose Bible is God's word both to them and to us.

NOTES

1. Although both Messiah and Christ mean "anointed," the New Testament term *Christ* contains several more ideas than are contained in the term *Messiah* as it is understood by the Jews. This will become clear in the development of this paper.

2. John L. McKenzie, *Myths and Realities* (Milwaukee: Bruce, 1963), p. 233. Orville J. Nave, *Nave's Topical Bible* (Lincoln, NE: Topical Bible Publishing Co., 1905), pp. 1009f., lists 62 OT passages and the NT passages in which the fulfillment is found.

3. I use the word *satanic* in its basic meaning, namely, that which is adverse or opposed to the divine will. Later the substantive form *adversary* (*śāṭān*) became a proper noun—*the Adversary* or *Satan* (*haśśāṭān*).

4. Joseph Coppens, *L'Attente du Messie* (Paris: Desclée de Brouwer, 1954), pp. 35-38, distinguishes three perspectives in Israel's hope—the soteriological, the eschatological, and the messianic. I have discussed this in "The Messianic Idea in Qumran," in *Studies and Essays in Honor of*

Abraham A. Neuman, ed. Meir Ben-Horin, Bernard D. Weinryb, and Solomon Zeitlin (Leiden: Brill, 1962), pp. 347-51.

5. RSV reads "your son," but the Heb. reads *zār' ăḳā,* "your seed."

6. For a complete list, see my article, "The Messianic Idea in Qumran," p. 345, notes 4-7.

7. The expression in Dan. 9:25 lacks the definite article, and furthermore places the "adjective" before the noun, *māšîᵃḥ nāgîd;* hence it is probably to be translated, "an anointed one, a prince."

8. For a lucid discussion, see D. J. A. Clines, "The Psalms and the King," *Theological Students Fellowship Bulletin* 71 (Spring 1975), 1-6.

9. Cf. Ps. Sol. 17:23; Matt. 9:27; Sanhedrin 97-98.

10. It is sometimes stated that the sonship of the king was by adoption. While it is true that the words *bᵉnî 'attā* ("you are my son") are used in the adoption formula, the words that follow rule out this possibility. *'ănî hayyôm yᵉliḏtiḳā* could be translated either "today I have begotten you" (as the result of an act of procreation) or "I have caused you to be born" (by divine causality). Whereas the former is the common expression for human paternity, we must hesitate to use it here, since it would suggest the divine-marriage idea (a god mates with a human female and produces a god or demigod). Once again we can see a possible *sensus plenior,* and can understand how the early Christians found a fulfillment in Jesus.

11. Heb. 2:7 supports the translation "angels."

12. The Greek of Heb. 1:8 is capable of the same alternate translation.

13. Particularly in the Testaments of the Twelve Patriarchs; cf. Joseph Klausner, *The Messianic Idea in Israel* (New York: Macmillan, 1955), pp. 310-16; cf. Millar Burrows, *The Dead Sea Scrolls* (New York: Viking Press, 1955), pp. 265-66.

14. In the post-Christian dialect of Aramaic which we call Syriac, there is a clear-cut distinction between *bar nâšâ* ("man, human being") and *bᵉrêh dᵉnâšâ* ("the Son of Man").

15. Cf. Harold Henry Rowley, *The Relevance of Apocalyptic,* Second edition (London: Lutterworth Press, 1947), pp. 30-31.

16. Isa., Jer., Ezek., Amos, Obad., Zeph., Zech., Mal., and especially Joel—about twenty references in all.

17. Eleven different MSS of Enoch are represented in the Qumran fragments, representing all parts of Enoch except Book II. There is little likelihood that Book II was in the Qumran library.

18. Cf. Robert Henry Charles, ed., *The Apocrypha and Pseudepigrapha of the Old Testament,* 2 vols. (Oxford: Oxford University Press, 1913).

19. Cf. William Sanford LaSor, *The Dead Sea Scrolls and the New Testament* (Grand Rapids: Eerdmans, 1972), p. 103.

20. In the first chapter of *Israel, A Biblical View* (Grand Rapids: Eerdmans, 1976).

21. I understand this to be a strong affirmative (like "You said it!"), and not an attempt to dodge the question.

22. Cf. Acts 2:25-28, 34-36; 4:25, 26; Heb. 1:5, 8, 9; 5:5, 6, etc.

23. Klausner, *The Messianic Idea in Israel*, p. 10.

PART 3

The Meaning of Israel

5

SEYMOUR SIEGEL

The Meaning of Israel in Jewish Thought

For faith he gave us land and took the land,
Thinking us exiles of all human kind.
Our name is yet the identity of God
That storms the falling altar of the world.

Karl Shapiro, "The Synagogue"

Blessed art Thou, O Lord our God, King of the universe who hast chosen us from all peoples, and hast given us Thy law.

Daily Prayerbook

In a chronicle from the years of the holocaust entitled *Kiddush Hashem* (*The Sanctification of the Name*) the following is told:

> Thousands of people, living, healthy, life-loving people are marching with shuffling feet, apathetic, indifferent. The shadow of death already hovers over all of us ... near me there stands out a figure of a tall, old Jew with a patriarchal grey beard.... He carries his talith (prayer shawl) and tefillin (phylacteries) under his arm.... Nothing more.... He jumps up with a strong and confident voice: "Jews do not be troubled. Do not be melancholy! Why do you look so sad. God forbid! If I would have something to drink I would propose a *lechayim*. Do you not see that we are going to greet the Messiah?"

What did the old Jew mean when he said, "We are going to greet the Messiah?" Did he believe that the unspeakable suffering of his fellow Jews was in some way redemptive, and would thus bring the Redeemer? Did he mean, perhaps, that the awful suffering would shame God into releasing the Redeemer and permitting him finally to come? I do not really know. But it is clear that this old Jew in our chronicle was expressing the self-understanding of Jews as the people of the covenant. This self-understanding gives some meaning and substance to Jewish existence—even when it is existence leading to the gas chambers. As such the covenant and the Torah (which is its outward expression) have been, in the words of the traditional liturgy, "our life and the length of our days."

This self-understanding of Jewish existence has not been without its price. The rabbis—in a bitter pun—point out that Sinai and *sinah* (hatred) sound very much alike—with Sinai came hatred of the Jew. From ancient times Jews were seen as being exclusivistic and arrogant. "From olden times," wrote Philostratus in the third century, "the Jews have been opposed not only to Rome but to the rest of humanity." "The most notorious historical example of idolization of an ephemeral self," writes the late Arnold Toynbee in *A Study of History,* "is the error of the Jews. . . . They persuaded themselves that Israel's discovery of the One True God had revealed Israel itself to be God's chosen people." "The arrogance of a people thinking themselves to be chosen has introduced racism into the Middle East," averred recently the distinguished representative of Saudi Arabia to the United Nations.

There is undeniably a tension between the people of Israel and the nations of the world—a tension which has embittered the lives of Jews from time immemorial, and which has impeded the progress of the redemption of the world.

As many theologians have pointed out in recent years—both Jewish and Christian—the misunderstandings and long traditions embedded in various levels of Christian memory and teaching have been partially responsible for the horrors visited upon the children of Israel (and others) during the twentieth century. If nothing else these experiences should cause us to re-examine ourselves anew and to make radical changes if necessary.

We will, therefore, attempt to schematize briefly the filament of theological concept and living reality with which the self-understanding of the Jew is inextricably webbed.

The Biblical Pattern

The whole of the biblical story describes the attempts of the Creator to realize his purposes on earth. He has chosen man as his instrument to so perfect and guard creation that it will return to him. At first the Creator relied on Adam and Eve. However, God's "experiment" was unsuccessful. The earth was filled with violence and sin. God even regretted that he had begun the whole project. He decided to start all over again, this time focusing on Noah and his family. However, they too sinned and were thus unable to be the instruments of God's will. Therefore, the Almighty turned to a family among the children of Noah—the sons of Abraham, Isaac, and Jacob. This family was destined to be God's family. "For I have known him, that he may charge his children and his household after him to keep the way of the Lord by doing righteousness and justice" (Gen. 18:19).

The covenant made with Abraham is a prelude to the great covenant made with the descendants of Abraham, Isaac, and Jacob after the Exodus. As Martin Buber and John Courtney Murray have both pointed out, the name of God revealed to Moses at the burning bush (*Ehyeh asher ehyeh*) has as one of its meanings, "being-with-people." The faithful presence of God among the people is the "banner" of Israel, the rallying cry around which the tribes "realize their religious and national unity as a people."[1] This promise is of tremendous significance—this people would not live out their existence like other peoples—isolated, subject to the inexorable laws of nature and history. But they would have the presence of God with them always. This would mean deliverance; it would also mean chastisement and punishment.

The Hebrew root *bacar*, which means to "choose," in addition to its secular meaning (Gen. 13:11), is used to indicate the choice of persons by God for a particular role or office, such as a priest ("For the Lord your God has chosen him and his descendants to come out of all your tribes, to be in attendance for service in the name of God forever" [Deut. 18:5; I Sam. 2:28]), or a king. It also can indicate the setting aside of a place for a sanctuary (Deut 12:5). Moreover, we read in Deuteronomy 7:6: "For you are a people consecrated unto the Lord your God; of all the peoples of the earth the Lord your God chose you to be His treasured people." God not only chooses Israel, he also knows (*yada*) Israel—the wording implies an intimate relationship with his people.

The making of the covenant with Israel does not mean that other nations are ignorant of God. "For from the rising of the sun even to its setting, my name is great among the nations, and in every place incense is offered in my name, . . . my name is great among the nations, says the Lord of hosts" (Mal. 1:11, RSV). The pact with Israel is not the first in history. God had established a covenant with Noah and with the forces of nature (Gen. 9:8-17). But this is the first one with a particular people. There is no parallel among other ancient covenant treaties.[2]

It is this covenant loyalty of God toward Israel and Israel's turning to God in loyalty which create *shalom*, which means more than peace. It often means prosperity, completeness, tranquility, welfare, even friendship. The covenant secures *shalom*, for the people are confident that they are under the rule of the loving God.

All of this is familiar territory. But there are two aspects of covenant theology which are of crucial importance in our discussion.

There are two metaphors that are cherished in biblical speech to describe the relationship between God and Israel—father-son and husband-wife.

In the father-son metaphor what is being expressed is

the indissolubility of the covenant. A son may be unfaithful to his father; he may even hate his father, or curse
him—but he does not as a result cease to be the son of his
father. Israel may be unfaithful to the covenant—but the
sonship remains. Citing Deuteronomy 14:1, "You are the
sons of the Lord your God," Rabbi Meir says, "Whether
you act as sons or do not act as sons, you are still the 'sons
of the Lord your God'" (Kiddushin 35b).

The husband-wife metaphor describes the passion and
the intimacy of the relationship. Again a striking rabbinic
saying is worth noting:

> The Holy One, praised be He, said to Hosea,
> "The Israelites have sinned." His reply should
> have been: "Sovereign of the universe, they are
> Thy children, the offspring of Thy chosen ones,
> Abraham, Isaac and Jacob, extend them mercy";
> not only did he fail to say this, but he spoke thus:
> "The entire world is Thine, exchange them for
> another people." Said the Holy One, praised be
> He, "What shall I do with this old man? I will tell
> him to take a harlot for a wife and I will tell him
> to send her away. If he should be able to send
> her away, then I will reject the children of Is-
> rael." After she bore him two sons and a daugh-
> ter, the Holy One, praised be He, said to Hosea:
> "Should you not have followed the example of
> your master Moses who separated from his wife
> after I began speaking to him (Exodus 18:2)?
> Separate yourself from her." Hosea replied,
> "Sovereign of the universe, I have children
> borne by her. I cannot divorce her." The Holy
> One, praised be He, then said to him: "If you
> feel thus about your wife who is a harlot and
> whose children were conceived in harlotry, shall
> I not feel similarly about the children of Israel,
> My children, the offspring of My chosen ones,
> Abraham, Isaac and Jacob? And yet you said,
> 'Reject them for another people!'" When Hosea
> realized that he had sinned, he began to plead
> for mercy on his own behalf. The Holy One,
> praised be He, then said to him: "Instead of
> pleading for mercy on your own behalf, plead
> for mercy on behalf of Israel." (Pesachim 87b;
> Yaikut Shimoni on Hos. 2:1)[3]

The intimacy of God with his people is a guarantee of their continued relationship, come what may.

This is the theological root of the doctrine of messianic redemption. Since God is the protector of Israel, under all circumstances, he will, in his good time, redeem Israel when it is in straits. The coming of the Messiah will not therefore establish a new covenant. It will fulfill the eternal one.

There is another important aspect of the covenant idea as the key to the self-understanding of the people of Israel. The people of Israel is not defined by ethnic origin or geographic propinquity alone. It is a people formed around an idea—an obligation, a relationship with God. Therefore, it was possible for some who were not born into the covenant to become part of the chosen people. This was accomplished by re-enacting the Sinai event, that is, by baptism, circumcision, and acceptance of the command-ments. Of course, the covenant had been made with those who stood at Mount Sinai and their descendants. The sign of the covenant was sealed in the organ of generation to symbolize that the privileges and obligations of the *berith* are passed down from generation to generation. But the idea that an individual who was not part of the covenant by birth could enter into it by an act of free will had an immense influence on the subsequent history of Judaism, and even more on Christianity. It gave an interior mean-ing to Jewish consciousness.

The lasting quality of the covenant meant the inevitabil-ity of punishment when there were breaches of the cove-nantal obligations. As a matter of fact the punishment of the people by the other partner of the *berith* was in itself a sign of the permanence of the *berith*. For if the agreement had been dissolved, there would be no justification for punishment. "Only you have I known of all the families of the earth, therefore I will visit upon you all your iniquities" (Amos 3:2).

The doctrine of the covenant also led to what Walter Eichrodt called "the factual nature of the divine relation." God's existence and character are not grasped through speculation or mystical contemplation. His existence and will are disclosed through the overwhelming events of history. The mighty acts of the Lord in bringing the people out of Egypt to Mount Sinai and then to the Promised Land are the confirmations of the "theology" of the biblical man. That is why his "theology" is one of "recital."[4] All prior history is seen as leading up to the moment of covenant and all subsequent history is interpreted in its light. The great anxiety of ancient man was a result of his understanding of his gods as capricious, subject to the whims and passing fancies that human flesh is heir to. The idea of the covenant created an air of trust and security for Israelite life, even when they were faced with tremendous crises. Their Lord was a Lord characterized by *chesed* ("covenant loyalty"). This led to an affirmation of earthly life and an air of confident existence.

Covenant and Law

The human obligation entailed in the covenant is expressed on the level of observing the law of the Torah. ("Law" is, of course, not an appropriate translation of Torah.) The covenant is made concrete and sustained through the Torah. The Torah is the sign of God's grace to Israel, for it is the vehicle through which the people relate themselves to their covenant partner. The observance of the law is an expression of the *da'at elohim*, knowledge of and intimate relationship with God. When this *da'at elohim* is forsaken, there occur the breaking of the law and the outbreak of horrible immorality.

The relationship between the covenant and the law is expressed in the liturgy of the synagogue: "With everlasting love hast Thou loved the house of Israel. Thou hast revealed to us a Law and commandments, statutes and judgments. They are our life and the length of our days." The law embodies the signs of the covenant—special remembrances of the covenant throughout the liturgical year as well as the *otot*, observances such as the Sabbath and circumcision. The *berith* without the law is an idea without expression.

Covenant and Land

The covenant promises always involve the land of promise. Thus, the confession of faith which is found in Joshua 24 consists of a recital of the great deeds of the Lord, a renewal of the covenant, and a reminder that the Lord had delivered to the Jews the land of promise.

Professor Abraham J. Heschel has movingly described this relationship.

> There is a unique association between the people and the land of Israel. Even before Israel becomes a people, the land is pre-ordained for Israel. Even before there was a people, there was a promise. The promise of a land. The election of Abraham and the election of the land came together. The promise of the land to the patriarchs is the leitmotif of the five books of Moses. Beyond the promise of the land and increasing prosperity, the promise to Abraham was a blessing for all the families of the earth. The gift of the land is an earnest of a greater promise.[5]

This concept and this dimension of the idea of chosenness and covenant are of crucial importance. Covenant does not involve merely spiritual dimensions. The promises are tied to earth, life, land. The Hebrew Bible is not a book about heaven—it is a book about the earth. The word *erets* (land), Heschel points out, occurs at least five times as often in the Bible as the word *shamayim* (heaven).[6] Of course, the people will have to learn to live without the land in the future. They will have, in the words of a famous Zionist spokesman, a portable homeland. But always there will be the hope for a return to the land and its fruits.

Exile and Return

The concrete history of the people of the covenant involved *galut* (exile). The promises had been fulfilled; the people inherited the land—but they lost it to foreign foes. This did not mean that God had forsaken them. He could be worshiped even without Temple and cult. This led to the creation of the most remarkable institution in the history of religion—a sanctuary for prayer without visible tokens of sacrifice or worship. The *mikdash me-at* (miniature sanctuary, synagogue) is the progenitor of the church and the mosque. Thus before the Temple was rebuilt, the people had contact with God through their prayers and study.

Instead of seeing exile as the end of the covenant, the rabbis believed that God also went into exile. Everywhere the Israelites suffered exile, the *shechina* (the divine presence) went with them. A remarkable passage in *The Zohar*, the classic work of Jewish mysticism, is worth quoting.

> It is written: "On that day the Lord shall be one and his name one" (Zech. XIV, 9). It may be said: Is He not now one? No; for now through sinners He is not really one; for the Matrona is removed from the King and they are not united, and the supernal Mother is removed from the King and does not give suck to Him, because the King without the Matrona is not invested with His crowns as before. But when He joins the Matrona, who crowns Him with many resplendent crowns, then the supernal Mother will also crown Him in fitting manner. But now that the King is not with the Matrona, the Supernal Mother keeps her crowns and withholds from Him the waters of the Stream and He is not joined with Her. Therefore, as it were, He is not one. But when the Matrona shall return to the place of the temple and the King shall be wedded with her, then all will be joined together without separation, and regarding this it is written, "On that day the Lord shall be one and his name one." Then "saviours shall come up on Mount Zion to judge the mount of Esau" (Obad. I, 21), as it has been taught: R. Simeon said, The Matrona will not enter her temple in joy until the kingdom of Esau has been brought to judgement and she has taken vengeance on it for causing all this. Therefore "they shall judge the mount of Esau" first, and then "the kingdom shall be the Lord's" (*Ibid.*), the kingdom being the Matrona. (*The Zohar* V)

What is being said here is that as long as the Israelites are in exile, the processes of the universe are out of focus. Not only are the people estranged from their land, but the cosmos is estranged from its Creator. Even more boldly, the Godhood is estranged from itself. This means that all peoples have a stake in helping to bring harmony back to the universe and to God. This is symbolized by the Jews' return from exile and recovery of their patrimony.

Kiddush Hashem (Sanctification of the Name)

Being part of the covenant means that the chosen people have the responsibility of *kiddush hashem* (the sanctification of the name). This means "to bear witness to the God of Israel, amidst the idolatries of the world, to proclaim in word and deed, in life and thought, there is no real God but the Transcendent One and to give the world no rest until it acknowledges the sovereignty of the Lord."[7] The ultimate test of *kiddush hashem* is martyrdom—testifying with one's being to the faith which gives life. The idea of *kiddush hashem* reaches its apex in the prophetic idea of the Suffering Servant. Though there are many interpretations of this concept, it is clear that the prophetic assertion is that Israel bears the pain and the suffering which an unredeemed world inflicts upon those who represent by their very being the divine demand for justice.

In sum, the biblical understanding of the nature of the Jewish people is based on the idea of covenant and chosenness which involves *destiny, duty, and hope.*

The Rabbinic Elaboration

The rabbinic Midrashim on the concept of *berith* and election were worked out in a historical period which presented a unique crisis for Judaism. The doctrine was being challenged by the sophisticated Greeks, by the new Christian community, by growing sectarian movements, and most of all by the catastrophes of history—the beginning of the exile, the loss of national independence, the destruction of the Temple, and the growing isolation of the people from the processes of history.

"There is not a single endearing epithet in the language such as brother, sister, bride, mother, lamb, or eye which is not, according to the rabbis, applied by Scripture to express the intimate relationship between God and His people."[8] Regardless of what has happened, Israel remains the foundation stone of the divine plan for the world:

> The matter is to be compared to a king who was desiring to build, but when he was digging for the purpose of laying the foundations, he found only swamps and mire. At last he hit on a rock, when he said: Here will I build. So too, when God was about to create the world, he foresaw the sinful generation of Enosh; and the wicked generations of the flood, etc. He said: How shall I create the world whilst these generations are certain to provoke me? But when he perceived that Abraham would one day arise, he said: Behold I have found the *petra* on which to build and base the world. The patriarch Abraham is called the rock (Isa. 51:1, 2) and so Israel are called the rocks (Num. 23:9). (quoted in Yalkut, No. 766)

The universalist character of God's providential concerns was expressed through the notion of the Noachide commandments by means of which the righteous of the world would have a share in the world to come.

When the catastrophes of national disaster occurred, the rabbis taught that God's covenant was not abrogated. Indeed he was even closer to them than he had been before, for he suffered along with them. Sufferings were seen not as a rejection of the people, but rather as a testing of them. "Flax," it was said, "improves when threshed, but only when it is of good quality; the potter does not tap a cracked vessel, lest it break. He tests. He tests only the perfect vessel. God tries the righteous."

The destruction of the Temple and its cult was assimilated into Pharisaic Judaism, which had, in any case, not been so dependent upon Temple worship. The Halakah was to be the Jewish bulwark. They would live their holy life, as best they could, in exile. Under foreign domination they would keep themselves ready for the final redemption when all would be set right.

The debacles of the Roman war and the Bar Kochba revolt convinced the rabbis that Israel should have as little as possible to do with the comings and goings of empires and the rise and fall of ambitious military leaders. The Israelites took an oath, says the Talmud, that they would not wage war ("they would not storm the ramparts") and that they would not rebel against the nations of the world.

The withdrawal as a people from active participation in the geopolitical events in the world did not, of course, mean the end of corporate existence or the enjoyment of autonomy. The covenant was still in force; God was still with the people. But the main duty now was to wait patiently for the coming of the redemption of the world.

The Challenge of Christianity

More serious, as it turned out, was the challenge to the self-understanding of the Jewish people by the new Christian Midrash. Christianity came unto the scene with a totally different Midrash on the Hebrew Scriptures which negated a good part of the Pharisaic Midrash. It negated the law, gave strange interpretations to familiar texts, and worst of all claimed to have superseded the normative views about the status of Judaism and Jews in the divine economy. It is beyond the competence of this writer to judge what is the correct interpretation of the gospels and the epistles. I have been impressed by the recent work of Rosemary Ruether, *Faith and Fratricide*, in which evidence is marshaled that the result of the new Christian Midrash was not only a rejection of the people of Israel, but a casting of them in the role of sinners, rejectors of the truth, who had never really understood their own faith. This validation of Christianity by the negation of Judaism represents what Ruether calls "the left hand of Christology." She takes as normative the statement of Justin Martyr: "Those who follow Christ are the true Israel; the children of the promise; they are the true successors of those Jews who found justification in times past."

The Jewish messianic idea which expected concrete results from the messianic fulfillment—results that would lead to the recovery of national independence and the reign of peace and justice throughout the world—did not seem to apply to the work and achievements of Jesus of Nazareth, and the Jews could not understand how anyone could take his messianic pretensions seriously. The messianic idea, as Gershon Scholem points out,

> is totally different in Judaism and in Christianity; Judaism in all of its forms and manifestations has always maintained a concept of redemption as an event which takes place publicly, on the stage of history, and within the community. It is an occurrence which takes place in the visible world and which cannot be conceived apart from such visible appearances. In contrast Christianity conceives of redemption as an event in the spiritual and unseen realm; an event which is reflected in the soul, in the private world of each individual, and which effects an inner transformation which need not correspond to anything outside.[9]

The rabbis did not as a rule directly confront Christianity. Though the growing church and its assumption of secular power made it necessary to encounter the Christian claim, most of the teachings of Christianity's Midrash (especially those which led to the abrogation of the law and the assertion of the arrival of the Messiah) were not conceivably true. The great historian Graetz observed that although the Mishnah devotes a special tractate to the laws concerning the heathens, there are no laws specifically regarding Christians. The rabbis emphasized repeatedly that the purpose and goal of the election of Israel was to observe the Torah, which was a sign of God's grace. "Judaism responded to Christianity by strongly consolidating itself around its rabbinic leadership and re-affirming its basic self-understanding. The idea that the gentiles were elected while Israel was rejected, was not even discussable as far as the rabbis were concerned."[10]

The rabbis were sensitive to the argument that the fall of

the Temple was a sign of God's wrath. They interpreted it as a punishment for sins—not for the sin of rejecting Jesus, but for not being obedient to God's commandments. The remedy was obedience to the Torah. There is no contemporary evidence of reaction to Jesus' ministry. It is not even accurate to say that Judaism *rejected* Jesus. Accepting Jesus was simply not a real theological option for believing Jews. The Christians (or anyone else) who were observant of the Noachide commandments were in the opinion of the Jews already following a religion which would result in their inheriting a share in the world to come. But claims that Christianity had superseded Judaism and had made a new covenant to replace the "older" ones were not openly discussed in the rabbinic writings. There are, of course, hints of anti-Christian polemics—but there are no clear-cut references to Christians.

In the Middle Ages, leading Jewish thinkers, especially the great philosophers such as Yehuda Halevi and Maimonides, acknowledged Christianity to be a *preparatio messianica* while the church regarded Judaism to have been a *preparatio evangelica*. There is a divine plan evident in the rise of Christianity and Islam. Halevi wrote:

> The wise providence of God towards Israel may be compared to the planting of a seed of corn. It is placed in the earth, where it seems to be changed into soil and water and rottenness, and the seed can no longer be recognized. But in very truth, it is the seed that has changed the earth and water into its own nature, and then the seed raises itself from one stage to another, transforming the elements, and throws out shoots and leaves. . . . Thus it is with Christians and Muslims. The Law of Moses has changed them that come into contact with it, even though they seem to have cast the Law aside. These religions are the preparation and the preface to the Messiah we expect, who is the fruit himself of the seed originally sown, and all men, too, will be fruit of God's seed when they acknowledge Him, and all become one mighty tree. (Kuzari III)

A similar view is set forth by Maimonides in his authoritative code:

> It is beyond the human mind to fathom the designs of the Creator, for our ways are not His ways, neither are our thoughts His thoughts. All these matters relating to Jesus of Nazareth and the Ishmaelite who came after him, served to clear the way for King Messiah, to prepare the whole world to worship God with one accord as it is written. Zeph. 3:9. Thus the messianic hope, the Torah, and the commandments have become familiar topics—topics of conversation among the inhabitants of the far isles and many peoples. (Mishne Torah, Hillchort Melakhim)

Until the advent of the modern period, the Jewish people held fast to their self-understanding as the people of God, serving him as best they could, prisoners of the hope that eventually the Messiah would come to bring the truth to all men. Meanwhile, the other biblical religions were preparing the way for King Messiah.

The Modern Times

Two great challenges to the self-understanding of the Jews as the people of God arose in modern times—modern liberalism with its stress on universalism and the holocaust.

As in so many other areas, Benedict Spinoza is the spokesman for the new turn in thinking which is characteristic of modern times. Spinoza viewed the past as a series of enslaving superstitions which were the cause of the persecutions so characteristic of religious communities. He wanted to establish a new religion not founded on revelation, a "church whose rulers were not priests or pastors, but philosophers and artists. The millennial antagonism between Judaism and Christianity was about to disappear." The new church would transform Jews and Christians. Chosenness was absurd in a world ruled by reason—all men who are reasonable are chosen, and in any case, a God that is equivalent to nature can choose only in a metaphorical sense. It was Spinoza who inspired the notion of the birth of a new universalism either based on reason, or on the victory of the proletariat which would abolish the existing religions and usher in a new era of brotherhood and enlightenment. Needless to say, this dream proved to be worthless and illusory. Universalism could be bought only at the cost of ruthlessly suppressing the natural impulses at self-expression. The abstract God of rationalism gave way to the more vivid God who could enter into dialogue with human beings. As soon as one admits the possibility of dialogue he is caught up in a form of particularism, for one does not dialogue with an abstraction, but only with another person who has chosen him as a partner.

It was the horrible holocaust of the forties that shook Judaism and Christianity to their foundations. How can one expect to believe in God and the God of the covenant, when unspeakable acts were perpetrated against his children? A gifted Yiddish poetess of our time wrote:

Merciful God, choose another people.
We are weary from dying.
We have no more prayers.
Choose another people;
we have no more blood to shed as a sacrifice.
Merciful God, give us ordinary clothes of
   shepherds of flocks,
and do us one more kindness, merciful God:
Take away your shechina from us.

However, it is the experience of the holocaust which seems to have confirmed, perhaps in a perverse way, the uniqueness of Israel. The very fury and the irrationalism which were unleashed seem to confirm that the tyrants of history cannot abide what the Jew stands for. They cannot endure the fact that he has a special relationship to the source of value. The holocaust moved many Christians to re-evaluate their own traditions, to see whether they have in any way contributed to this unspeakable crime. The injustices and pogroms inflicted on the Jews by Christian nations over the centuries, writes Gregory Baum, often in the name of Christian principles, did not stir the conscience of theologians until fairly recently. It was the advent of Hitler's anti-Semitism that produced uneasiness in some church circles and made theologians take a new look at their Christian past.

These events form the background of the rise of Zionism and underscore the importance of Israel for both contemporary Jews and Christians. Though the roots of Zionism are many, its main thrust is the result of the understanding that whatever improvements the modern world may have wrought, the soul and the body of the Jewish people are in grave danger. According to traditional teachings the return of the Jews to their homeland under conditions of independence awaited the coming of the Messiah. Zionism signaled an abandonment of the passive stance toward history which had been the hallmark of rabbinic Judaism. The oaths made in the wake of the Bar Kochba debacle, referred to earlier, were revoked. Israel would wage war for its own survival. Zionism thus made a benign but slightly heretical thrust. It would now use *secular* means to effect the Jewish return. Zionism's most thoughtful pamphlet was "Autoemancipation" by Leon Pinsker. Zionism was born out of the feeling that the Jews could depend neither on the nations of the world nor even on God to free them. When Zionism first appeared it was strongly opposed by many Jews. There were those who dreamt of a bogus universalism and denigrated all nationalisms, especially Jewish nationalism. There were those who clung to the old beliefs that only a miraculous redemption brought about by God would save Israel. There were those who believed that somehow it was not proper for Jews, dedicated to things of the spirit, to dirty their hands with politics and state-building. The great Protestant theologian, Reinhold Niebuhr, understood the crucial issue that stood at the heart of the Zionist effort: "I do not see how it is possible to develop this prophetic overtone of high religion in the Jewish community if the nation does not have a greater degree of political security."[11] Jewish consciousness did not give up the whole traditional messianic idea. It still looked forward to universal peace and cosmic harmony. It decided, however, to begin through secular means to implement at least part of the vision. Perhaps this would shame God into bringing about the total redemption.

Zionism was not concerned only with the physical survival of Jews. It was also concerned about Judaism. Jewishness was threatened by assimilation—a painless form of death, but death nevertheless. Everywhere Jewishness represented a minority culture. There is a certain grandeur in being in the minority. But the demands of the covenant, the central concept of Jewish self-understanding, must be fulfilled under conditions of autonomy. Martin Buber, in a letter to Mahatma Gandhi expressed this idea eloquently:

> We went into exile with our task unperformed; but the command remained with us. We need our own soil in order to fulfill it; we need the freedom to order our own life—no attempt can be made on foreign soil and under foreign statute. We are not covetous, Mahatma. Our only desire is that at last we may be able to obey.

The Jewish spirit needs to be released from bondage in order to flourish anew. The ancient idea of chosenness finds new meaning in Zionism. So when Zionism was created it was based on an intuition that messianic redemption and chosenness would have to be transmuted in order to rescue the Jewish body and the Jewish soul. The nations of the world would not allow Jacob to dwell securely.

The horrible events of the twentieth century confirmed the Zionist ideas. The withdrawal of the Jewish people from active participation in history resulted in unimagined destruction, degradation, and holocaust. Though Zionism is based on messianism, it should not be confused with it. The Jews in Israel live in an unredeemed world. They know this every single day. They still share the human predicament of sin and anxiety. Israel is not the messianic kingdom, though the messianic vision was largely responsible for the founding of the state. The recognition that the Messiah has not come forces Israel, like all other states, to find a way to secure itself, using the means employed by others.

The Jew, by his very existence, outrages all those who seek to dominate men, to claim total sovereignty over their mind, body, and soul. The Jew is the eternal protester against the idolatries of the world, even when he himself participates in them—his very being reflects the divine imperative. This is partly the reason for the fury of anti-Semitism again raising its head. However it may express itself, at bottom anti-Semitism reflects the revolt of man and society against the God of the Bible. "Hatred of Judaism is at bottom hatred of Christianity. Whenever the pagan within the Christian soul rises in revolt against the yoke of the Cross, he vents his fury on the Jew" (Maritain).

Jews and Christians

The story of the relationship between Judaism and Christianity is a painful one to contemplate. The elder and younger brother have sown hatred instead of love. The solution of the tension seems to me to lie on the theological plane—at least in the beginning. Christianity must reinterpret itself so that its important role in the economy of salvation not bring with it the claim that the Jews and their faith have been superseded. This kind of work is going on in all areas of Christianity. Jews must have a new awareness of the importance of Christianity. For several decades, the Jewish community has been pondering over the views of Franz Rosenweig.

> Our recognition of Christianity rests, in fact, upon its recognition of us. It is the Torah, ultimately, which is spread abroad by Bible societies to the most distant lands. No one comes to the Father—except through him (that is, through Jesus). No one *comes*, but the situation is different when one need no longer come to the Father because he is already with Him. That is the case of the nation of Israel.

What Rosensweig is saying is that there may very well be a new covenant and an "old one." But the new one does not abrogate the old one. It is the additional covenant for the Gentiles to become part of the people of God. It is, as Michael Wyschogrod has said, the "Judaism of the Gentiles."

If we are indeed younger and older brothers, it is the duty of the Christian to share in the protection of the Jewish people from their enemies. Precarious is Jewish existence—who can be at ease in Zion?—for God is beckoning us to be restless until his fulfillment comes.

On the other hand, we as Jews should feel a responsibility for Christianity, which is under attack by the idols of the world. We have a stake in the continuation of Christianity and its vigor. The ways of providence are beyond our ken. It was decided that in large areas of the globe it would be the Christian church which would preserve and teach the truths of creation, revelation, and redemption. We cannot, as Jews, allow the church to be replaced by those forces which seek to destroy it—and with it the human spirit.

Jewish self-understanding still rests on the doctrine of chosenness and covenant. It affirms that the Jewish people is not an ordinary people like all other peoples, but one called into being by God to serve his purposes in the world. This is a summons and a sending—an obligation to witness to justice and truth amidst the cruelties and hypocrisies of the world. This task we share with men of good will, especially our Christian brothers who read the same Scriptures and who look to the same God.

Ernie, the hero of André Schwartz-Bart's novel, *The Last of the Just*, says as he is shepherding a group of children into the gas chamber, "O God, O Lord, we went forward like this thousands of years ago. We walked across arid deserts and blood-red seas, through floods of salt-bitter tears. We are very old, we are still walking. Oh let us arrive finally."

Consciousness of uniqueness, persistence of trust, eternal hope—this is Israel's covenant with the God of us all.

NOTES

1. John Courtney Murray, *The Problem of God* (New Haven, CT: Yale University Press, 1964), p. 11.

2. Dennis McCarthy, *Treaty and Covenant* (Rome: Oxford, 1963).

3. See also the text in H. Cohen, *The Commentary of Rabbi David Kimchi on Hosea* (New York: Columbia University Press, 1929), pp. 11f.

4. G. E. Wright, *The God Who Acts* (London: SCM Press, 1952).

5. Abraham J. Heschel, *Israel* (New York: Farrar, Straus & Giroux, 1969), p. 100.

6. Ibid.

7. W. Herberg, "The Chosenness of Israel and the Jews of Today," *Midstream*, Vol. 1, No. 1 (Autumn 1955), 88.

8. Solomon Schechter, *Some Aspects of Rabbinic Theology*, p. 46.

9. Gershon Scholem, *Major Trends in Jewish Mysticism* (New York: Schocken, 1947), p. 314.

10. Rosemary Ruether, *Faith and Fratricide* (New York: Seabury Press, 1974), p. 167.

11. Reinhold Niebuhr, *The Jews and the Gospel* (Westminster, NJ: Newman Press, 1961).

6

CARL EDWIN ARMERDING

The Meaning of Israel in Evangelical Thought

Introduction

To imagine that one can deal with the subject "Israel in Evangelical Thought" in a forty-five minute paper is itself an example of incredible *chutzpah*. It would require much longer than that fully to define what an evangelical is; and if that task seems difficult, it is nothing compared to the difficulties inherent in defining "Israel." It is not enough to become party to the debate on the level of traditional Judaism or even modern Israel. When the question of a Christian view of Israel is introduced, the discussion is necessarily moved to the level of historic and contemporary exegetical and theological concerns that are unique to Christian consciousness as a community which has derived its major identity from its continuity or discontinuity with the Israelites of the old covenant. But the difficulties inherent in the topic do not remove from us the necessity of dealing with it. Especially in the evangelical wing of Christianity, the traditional seedbed of the movements that have been called "Christian Zionism," and even more in light of the presence of a modern state of Israel, the concern must be addressed. Indeed, no conference of Christians and Jews could be conceived apart from such a discussion. If, as I am going to suggest, the primary concern of Christians has usually (but not always) been theological, and the primary concern of Jews has usually

119

(but not always) been social and economic, the concerns of the one in relation to the other cannot be ignored.

First, then, what do I mean by evangelical? I shall use the term to describe a movement of North American and European Christianity identified not only with the Reformation but with certain movements of renewal and reawakening in North America, in England, and on the continent. Perhaps the earliest movement was the Great Awakening in the early eighteenth century amongst Colonial Reformed Churches, a movement associated with the names of Jonathan Edwards and the English Anglican George Whitefield. In the British Isles the period from 1750 through 1815 can be seen as formative[1] and the names associated with the movement would include members of a wide variety of churches. The Wesleys and Methodism were central to the movement as were men such as George Whitefield, whose greater commitment to Calvinism led him to separate from the Wesleys. Also involved were Protestant conformists in the Church of England, such as John Newton, William Wilberforce, and Charles Simeon. Evangelicals today draw also on a heritage of German pietistic Lutheranism, sing hymns written by Count Zinzendorf of the Moravians, and count among their numbers descendants of similar movements throughout all of northern Europe both within and outside of established churches.

Latourette describes the various awakenings as having certain distinctive features, some of which may still be determinative in creating a distinctly "evangelical" view of Israel today.[2] Basic was a fervent commitment to the authority of Scripture, a commitment that would make possible in some of the later stages of the evangelical movement the rise of millenarian groups which had as their cornerstone the conviction that prophecies of Israel's return to the land were to be taken literally and were as yet unfulfilled. Second among these characteristics was zeal for spreading a gospel which demanded personal response and an evangelical experience for every person who would know the salvation of God. This emphasis on "new birth" (in contrast to traditional Roman Catholic ideas of salvation through participation in the community of grace or even Reformed views of the church as covenant community) led to many of the great missionary movements of the nineteenth century, and had as one of its earliest manifestations the London Society for Promoting Christianity Among the Jews.[3] It may also be germane to note that it was the Evangelical Awakening, particularly in its British form, that brought to an end much of the injustice in British society, although it had some ambivalence in its attitude toward restrictions on full freedom for the Jews.[4] Its concerns in the social and political field were a clear translation of its theological concerns, a precedent that may give direction to our practical response at the close of this paper.

Turning to the second question we ask: What does an evangelical mean when he speaks of Israel? Again, it must be stressed that his primary point of reference is theological. The evangelical, with his intensely biblical orientation, is accustomed not only to reading in the Scriptures about Israel, but in some general fashion identifying with Israel (the high water mark in this area was undoubtedly the Puritan period). While there remain great exegetical and hermeneutical differences among evangelicals about the meaning of the term *Israel* in the New Testament, it is probably true to say that most identify the people of God in the Old Testament as the same ethnic-national-religious community they see in Judaism today. That evangelical Christians, in common with almost all Christians, see themselves having some kind of continuity with that people is one of the greatest reasons why a dialogue such as the present one can and must take place.

When we move to the New Testament the question becomes immediately more difficult. Israel, in the New Testament, is a theological concept as well as a national or ethnic reality, and Christians through the years have by no means agreed on the direction Christian theology should take regarding the question. The central concern of the New Testament is not, of course, national Israel but spiritual Israel. National Israel, up to a point, was an accepted fact of life, but whether writers like Paul or teachers like Jesus saw national Israel as having become anachronistic in light of the calling of a new people is still much in debate.

In light of the remarkable continuing role of the Jewish people and the rise in our own time of a national state of Israel, Christians can no longer afford to discuss the question with an armchair mentality. There are political, economic, and social issues that call for consideration, indeed have called for Christian response (often without much satisfaction) for many years, and I would not want to denigrate their importance. But when it comes to Israel there is an added dimension. To the Christian church the Jews are not simply another minority group striving for full civil rights, nor is modern Israel Biafra. The issues are so inextricably tied to the theological concerns of the church that no realistic discussion of the matter can avoid that dimension, though many Jews might wish to omit it. Professor Jakob Petuchowski certainly expressed the ambivalence of many Jews when he wrote, "I am still of a divided mind on the question of whether a special concern with the Jews on the part of the church would necessarily be desirable."[5] But he, like other thoughtful Jews, realizes that the two communities which feel some identity as the saving remnant or people of God cannot afford to be isolationists. And if there is to be an ongoing recognition of our common heritage there must be freedom for each community to discuss the question within its own natural boundaries. If for the Jew the question of modern Israel has been primarily one of economic, political, and social survival, the Christian church must respond to those kinds of concerns. Likewise, if for the Christian the question has always been one of theological identification, Jews must permit us to consider our response in those terms as well. I, for one, am of the opinion that neither community is presently as convinced that the problem is purely secular or religious as it might have been even ten years ago. Christians are realizing that for the Jew modern Israel is a matter of survival and identity and that means politics and economics, while Jews themselves are turning away from the purely secularist model of the new Jerusalem that was too often put forth in the early days of Zionism.

What then are the dimensions of contemporary Christian concern? I would like to follow an outline that sets the question in a theological framework, for I think that will always be the starting point for Christians. We need to look briefly at the exegetical questions raised by the New Testament and its attitudes to Israel. First, do the New Testament writers allow any significant theological role for an Israel separated from the church? I realize that this is a concern of Christians and not of Jews, but it has been a Christian concern for so long that we shall not be able to carry on dialogue together unless Jews understand something of the question. Second, is the New Testament anti-Semitic, in the sense that it actually rejects Israel and condemns that entity to continuing disgrace?

The question is not merely exegetical, however. I think it will be valuable to see how Christian tradition has treated the question of Israel, particularly within that heritage I have described as evangelical. Is there special precedent within the evangelical church either for avoiding or responding to contemporary Judaism and the state of Israel? It may also be helpful to review the rather extensive and widespread movements within evangelicalism that have been called "Christian Zionism" and to evaluate them in light of both Jewish and Christian concerns of the present day.

Finally, I should like to ask of ourselves some questions that have both theological and practical relevance. How does the evangelical Christian view Israel (particularly modern Israel) in light of his commitment to Scripture, his sense of identification with God's work in both the old and new covenants, and his conviction that in Jesus God's final word was spoken? Is there still room for a Jewish national Israel in our scheme of things? And inasmuch as a Jewish national state is now an entity, with or without our theological approval, do we recognize in it some special redemptive working of God, or is it merely another evidence of general providence, not unlike bringing the Philistines from Caphtor and the Syrians from Kir? I think there are also purely human questions that arise, such as what response is appropriate from Christians whose tacit approval permitted the pogroms and the holocaust. I do not mean to avoid these issues, but I do intend to ask first and foremost the kind of questions that separate the Jewish situation from that of Biafra. Perhaps then we can get back to the kind of questions that deal with both the Jewish situation and Biafra.

Israel in the New Testament

I have argued earlier that it is appropriate in such a discussion for Christians to use the New Testament as a starting point. If the Old Testament is taken in isolation, there is little upon which to disagree. Furthermore, there is little value in a purely historical discussion of a people living before the common era.

It must be admitted at the beginning that the New Testament has its own system of hermeneutics with regard to the Old Testament. Christian scholars have long recognized that neither the system nor its conclusions were arrived at by some kind of purely objective study of the Old Testament. Rather, it was the conviction in the early church that in Christ the kingdom had come and the new age of the spirit had descended upon Israel. From that conviction they felt free to read the Scriptures Christologically, following the leading of their Master (cf. Luke 24:27: "Beginning with Moses and all the prophets, he interpreted to them in all the scriptures the things concerning himself"). It should be recognized that this way of looking at the Old Testament was not entirely subjective or removed from a biblical theology. It was the conviction of the apostolic fathers that they were being true to the Scriptures, and C. H. Dodd has argued forcefully that their method had a biblical and theological sophistication that goes well beyond the mere "proof-texting" that we sometimes hear described.[6]

If Christology was the basic concern of the New Testament writers, they were never able to separate that concern from what became their ecclesiology. Ultimately their attitude toward Israel is a reflection of their attitude toward Jesus. As a community of Jews who owned Jesus as Lord, with a postresurrection theology that increasingly directed all of Israel's promises to its one seed, Jesus (Gal. 3:16), the apostolic band naturally wrestled with their own identity in relation to the larger community of which they were a part. In what is probably the finest survey of the material, Professor Peter Richardson of Toronto has concluded that, during apostolic times, the church never actually saw in itself a real *tertium genus*; rather it was constituted a band within Israel, conscious of its function as a purifying remnant and aware of its special status but never appropriating to itself terminology of identity relating to the whole.[7] According to Richardson, not until Jesus was clearly seen as personally embodying all of the corporate character of Israel, a tendency perhaps implicit in Johannine theology but not made explicit until the mid-second century (Justin Martyr, A.D. 160), was the church itself identified with the "Israel of God."[8]

If it be true that the New Testament writers never explicitly see the church as having replaced Israel, what then is their view? Again, Richardson provides the best survey of the evidence available, although the question has called forth many and varied responses. That there is an anti-Jewish polemic in some parts of the New Testament is readily apparent. It is not clear, however, that this is anything more than an "in-house" debate amongst various parties of Judaism. Charges of a developed anti-Semitism in the New Testament seem to presuppose a higher degree of Gentile influence on the sources than is warranted,[9] and may be reading backward into the first century a phenomenon that was, in its presently understood form, not apparent until somewhat later. Jesus is pictured as having been rejected by Jewish leaders, but the gospels are always careful to show that he himself does not reject out of hand either Jewish institutions or his own Jewishness.

Synagogue and the Temple, the Jerusalem leadership and the law—all are in their own way both upheld and yet superseded.[10] What then is the picture? Jesus the Jew is seen as having collected a band of followers, twelve in number, a kind of nucleus of a new people within Israel. There is no clear evidence at the earliest stage that anything extra-Israelite was intended and indeed Jesus even went so far as to restrict his own message to the "lost sheep of the house of Israel" (Matt. 10:6; 15:24).

There were, nevertheless, the seeds of separate development even within the apostolic period. In addition to the very basic question of whether Jesus' claims and mission were compatible with first-century Judaism,[11] there is the problem of the early progression of Christianity from a Jewish to a Gentile mission with all of the implications that move had for the status of the community and its self-understanding.

It was in full light of the Gentile mission that Paul wrote his *magnum opus*, the letter to the Romans. And if there was one burning question that dominated the whole it was the need to render Paul's Gentile gospel compatible with the promises and covenants to Israel. His response stands as the basic New Testament passage in the debate. The charge is clear: if Paul's gospel, increasingly going out to non-Jews, is true and in fact Judaism has become a stumbling block to the acceptance of the gospel, then it follows that all of the promises and covenants of the Scriptures directed toward Israel have now been set aside. His response is equally clear: the Word of God (to Israel) has not failed (Rom. 9:6) because true election is a spiritual rather than a national matter. The reason why natural Israel has not grasped this has nothing to do with the validity of the promises; rather it has to do with a wrong method of approach to the question (Rom. 9:31—10:21). The psalmist, Joel, Isaiah, and Moses are called as witness to the essential obduracy of the nation. If Paul were to stop at this point, certainly the charge that he had relegated Israel to the scrap heap would be justified, and there have never been wanting those within the Christian community who have stopped at the end of chapter 10. But to admit such a conclusion would be self-defeating and the entire apologetic of the epistle would have failed. Paul, as a committed believer in the Scriptures, must justify the ways of God with Israel and so chapter 11 follows.

In reading Romans 11 we are struck with the fact that Paul feels there is still a discernible plan for God's overall redemptive history, and that Israel figures in that plan. The familiar concept of the remnant is introduced, with the apparent conclusion that within the overall election of Israel there is a further election of a particular remnant, a remnant of which Paul saw himself a part. But it goes beyond that. Israel has stumbled, it is true, but not with ultimate rejection as the result. Rather, Gentile inclusion will cause jealousy amongst the larger Jewish group, with the ultimate result of their turning to Christ.[12]

In such a situation, what really is the Christian view of Israel and her place? The argument concludes (vv. 12-36) with a strong affirmation that the future will see, in place of failure, an Israel returned to fullness and life. Far from being through with Israel, even God's present outworking of Christianity to the Gentiles is but a step in completing his great plan whereby "all Israel will be saved" (v. 26). In light of this, Paul can affirm with confidence that "the gifts and calling of God are irrevocable" (v. 29).

In the New Testament, then, Israel occupies a somewhat ambivalent role. Certainly there is movement in the direction of the later Christian position that equated the church with Israel and reduced national Israel to the status of vestigial anachronism, but it does appear that the line was never completely crossed. Richardson argues that the final break was not made until historical factors in the late first and early second century forced the two communities apart. It was the Bar Kochba rebellion, rather than the theology of Paul or the synoptics, that created the climate in which Christians saw themselves as a new and isolated group.

In light of the above, what theological position regarding Israel is normative for the contemporary evangelical

Christian? First, I would join with H. Berkhof in calling for evangelicals of all camps to put away language that defines the church as "the new Israel."[13] There are now enough exegetical data so that both Reformed and dispensational apologists can agree on the fact that national Israel does have some continuing relevance. Furthermore, since the term *Israel* cannot be shown to be a biblical designation for the church, it should be avoided in that context. This will help us to avoid any kind of a priori reasoning that reduces theological discussion with Jews to the level of discussion with pagans. Even in the most negative reading of Paul one is forced to the conclusion that Israel (admittedly disobedient, but only in the same sense that Paul predicts the Gentile church will disobey) is still beloved of the Father. We must admit that we do not yet know just what is meant by the expression *all Israel will be saved*; at the very least it means there is a continuing role for God's original covenant people. If they now appear as "partially hardened," that can be no cause for dismissing them, for the one who spoke of this mystery concentrated his concern on the possibility of Gentile hardening and made it clear that in no event did God's unconditional election depend on the response of the elect, important as that might be. The same one spoke of God's grafting in again the natural branches, reminding the Gentiles that they were the wild branch and should not boast against the tree or its natural branches. And further, he concluded his discussion with the stern reminder that the ways of the Lord are unfathomable and his judgments unsearchable. I fear we are all too prone, in the matter of Jewish identity, to forget Paul's poignant and searching question (quoted from Isaiah), "Who has known the mind of the Lord, or who has been his counselor?" The fact is, we are dealing with a mystery, the depth of which would require the mind of God himself to plumb. Any evangelical scheme which sets forth in absolute terms a Christian understanding of the place of national Israel in God's plan of salvation, whether discarded as in Reformed theology or revived as in various millenarian schemes, arrogates to itself an

awareness of God's counsel that not even the great apostle
dared to presume.

In saying all of this I no doubt appear more concerned
with the lack of understanding of Israel's meaning within
the Christian community than outside of it. I realize that
many of these issues are simply not those of a people who
have been struggling for millennia to preserve a visible
presence in an often bitterly hostile world. If the discussion so far sounds hopelessly removed from the issues
facing contemporary Jews, I would like to beg for consideration of its implications. Returning to some of the considerations that opened this paper we can perhaps see that
this position, which I believe to be consistent with the New
Testament *kerygma*, does provide a theological framework
in which the concerned Christian can and must view
Judaism as different from the rest of the non-Christian
world. We will be forced back to what was, for the earliest
Christians, a given: our identity with the older people of
God. We will, while never forgetting that the person of
Jesus Christ still stands between us, realize again something of the sense that God's redemptive history involves
his nurturing of both "branches" and we will not boast
against the root that now feeds and supports us. I think,
too, although this may be an extrapolation from the
present argument, that we must view present-day Israel as
different from Biafra and Bangladesh. While I would prefer to leave to the Jewish community the question of
whether, how and in what way the present state of Israel is
the "spiritual center" of Judaism, there is no question but
that the present state is a part of Israel in the broadest
sense, and a very important part at that. As such it is first
and foremost a remarkable witness to the continued existence of God's ancient people, but for the Christian it is
more. If there is, in the mysterious outworking of God's
total plan of redemption, still more to be revealed, who is
to say that the land of Israel will not again be the focal
point of his activity? I do not mean, thereby, to eliminate
human political and economic considerations. Nor do I
mean in any sense that Christians (or Jews) must blindly

support the policies of the state of Israel. We are all too close to the politics of pragmatism, self-interest, greed and exploitation to expect that our Israeli friends should somehow be immediately freed from such motives. Christians (and Jews) can make common cause against social and political evil and oppression wherever they appear, but Christians can also stand in a special way alongside of that portion of God's ancient people in their struggle to remain a continuing and free people in a world that has all too often tried to remove their candlestick. Our record in the past (particularly in North American evangelical circles) has tended on the one hand to a brand of reductionistic theology that is offended by any nationalist presence of Israel, and thus almost automatically supports the enemies of the state.[14] On the other we have a kind of simplistic futurism that romanticizes all that is done in modern Israel,[15] though we usually see our role as observer rather than participant.[16] I believe that neither extreme is consistent with the view of Israel I have outlined above. The *via tertia* I have presented should provide opportunities not only for practical help in political and economic concerns, but will, I trust, open the way for further dialogue between us. This position takes Israel seriously enough to be concerned with her role in the redemptive plan of God, but does not attempt to fit Israel into a preconceived scheme of Christian prophecy. Such a position can take an interest in the political and social aspects of the question, for it avoids a passive apocalyptic that would detach it from all worldly concerns and simply await the end. Israel's practical existence is like that of all other people struggling for identity and security, but it is different from other struggles because we can identify with the people struggling.

Israel in Evangelical History

Christian attitudes to Judaism, Jews and Israel have, needless to say, not always been a model of ecumenical relations. Perhaps because there is so much we would rather forget, we often hesitate to look at what may be constructive approaches to the problem for fear of awakening the ghosts that still sleep somewhat lightly. I would like, however, to look now at some of the attitudes and approaches to Judaism and Israel that have been expressive of the mainstream of evangelical thought, particularly in Britain where concern for the question dominated whole generations. Hertzel Fishman's *American Protestantism and a Jewish State* (1973) reflects much of the thinking of liberal Protestantism toward the modern idea of Israel, but it is a bit deficient in its treatment of the evangelical heritage, especially that which has its roots amongst evangelical British political leaders as far back as the early nineteenth century. While I am not personally in agreement with some of the theological romanticism of that era, I do feel that contemporary evangelical views on the subject cannot be understood apart from this heritage. The ethos of evangelicalism, while it may not partake of their particular eschatological schemes, is better explained by looking at the diaries of the Seventh Earl of Shaftesbury and Lord Balfour than by perusing the pages of the *Christian Century.*

British identification with the people of Israel may not have been as complete as claimed by Barbara Tuchman in *Bible and Sword*, but it certainly held its place in the national psyche. Mrs. Tuchman's survey of the evidence, as charming as it is enlightening, identifies the high points of Hebraic influence as the Puritan period and the Victorian revival following the years of Restoration and secularism in the eighteenth century. While it is no doubt true that in the Commonwealth there was a clear attempt to recreate the theocracy of the old covenant, what is less well known is the exact nature of Puritan influence on the later Evangelical Awakening. At any rate, the concerns of the nineteenth-century evangelicals with regard to Israel were very different from those of the seventeenth-century Puritans. One could imagine Cromwell feeling that the true Zion was to be built in "England's green and pleasant land" but we would be surprised to see that same worthy involved in a scheme to build a Zion in Palestinian Jerusalem. Not so with that band of noble and highborn evangelicals who arose from the Awakening of the nineteenth century. England is no longer blithely equated with Israel; rather it is recognized that there still are real Jews, that they did have a land of their own once (if not as green and pleasant as England, at least flowing with milk and honey), and that they still identify with much of their old heritage. It is in this atmosphere that the phenomenon often called "Christian Zionism" took root and for a time flourished.

Ben Halpern's *The Idea of a Jewish State*[17] traces briefly the development of this idea, drawing heavily upon the aforementioned work of Barbara Tuchman and the classic *History of Zionism* by Nahum Sokolow.[18] He rightly sees that the motive for such activity was primarily theological. It was a movement of upper class Englishmen, few of whom were particularly close to Jews needing a homeland but whose reading of Holy Writ convinced them that Zion still had a future. As I have said above, this was foreign to typical Puritan hermeneutics and it was certainly at wide variance with what became the motives of Jewish Zionism a generation later. It is significant that debate occurred in which the major representative of Judaism was the respected Sir Moses Montefiore, hardly the underprivileged or wandering Jew of the Eastern ghettos. In fact, the evangelical revivals occurred in countries where the Jews tended to be both scarce (partly because they had been banned in an earlier age) and liberated. Where the Jews were numerous and persecuted there was little evangelical fervor of any kind, and certainly no major Christian moves to return the people to Palestine. However, it was in this second sphere, a generation later, that political Zionism began to flourish.

Unlike Christian Zionism, with its intensely religious and theological orientation, political Zionism was largely a movement of the secularist forces within the Jewish community. My colleague, Guenter Strothotte, in an unpublished thesis entitled "The Relation Between Religion and Nationalism in Early Zionist Thought" cites example upon example to show the essentially nonreligious outlook of the early Zionists. Perhaps a few quotations will serve to demonstrate the distance between such men and evangelical Zionists such as Shaftesbury and Oliphant. From the Cologne lawyer Max Bodenheimer comes the statement: "It had nothing to do with religion. Rather I remained a godless atheist—if a man can be so designated who regards the idea of a personal God as the superstition of a primitive people."[19] And from Theodor Herzl himself comes evidence of the same strain. Concerning Herzl's religious convictions, Strothotte writes:

> Herzl never made a secret out of the fact that there really was no religious motivation behind his plan. He told later Chief-Rabbi Guedemann of Vienna and Chief-Rabbi Adler of London that he was not obeying any religious impulse in his project. This was not to mean that he was antireligious. Herzl assured them: "But I certainly honor the faith of my fathers, at least as much as I would honor other faiths.[20]

How far this is from the ethos of British evangelically-inspired Zionism of an earlier generation is evident from a typical statement from that period. The Seventh Earl of Shaftesbury, about whom we shall say more later, wrote in his diary of his conversations with the then Foreign Secretary, Lord Palmerston:

> How singular is the order of Providence! Singular, that is if estimated by man's ways! Palmerston had already been chosen by God to be an instrument of good to His ancient people, to do homage, as it were, to their inheritance, and to recognise their rights without believing their destiny. And it seems he will yet do more. But though the motive be kind, it is not sound. I am forced to argue politically, financially, commercially; these considerations strike him home; he weeps not like his Master over Jerusalem, nor prays that now, at last, she may put on her beautiful garments.[21]

Quotations like the above could be multiplied from countless diaries of those whose high station in life combined with an evangelical piety to drive them into a kind of romantic Christian Zionism very different from the Zionism of our own day and yet not entirely at one either with the millenarian movements of contemporary North America.

No figure better represents the movement of which I speak than Anthony Ashley Cooper, the Seventh Earl of Shaftesbury, a man called by Tuchman "the most influential nonpolitical figure, excepting Darwin, of the Victorian age."[22] He was a man whose entire acceptance of the Bible and its message drove him to act on behalf of the poor and wretched in every corner of England and he is credited with a major role in forcing through Parliament the most progressive legislation of the day, including the Factory Act, the Mines Act, the Lunacy Act and the Lodging House Act. Though a frequent guest in the homes of both Tory and Whig parliamentarians, Shaftesbury felt he could best influence his generation by remaining outside the government.

In the matter of Israel, Shaftesbury maintained the same steadfast devotion to a cause and drew on the same source, the Bible, for his inspiration. What made him a Zionist half a century before the publication of Herzl's *Der Judenstaat* (1896) was his intense conviction that the Jews were destined by God to return to their own land as part of the fulfillment of biblical prophecy. Although the motives were not primarily humanitarian (and Jews have always been understandably nervous about schemes which made them pawns in an essentially Christian eschatological myth), it should be noted that these schemes were the work of great Christian humanitarians. Shaftesbury and his colleagues felt no compunction about using the Foreign Office's political interest in the Eastern question, or the desire of Sir Moses Montefiore to protect Eastern Jews, but their ultimate motive was the ushering in of the kingdom of Christ. To that end they not only gave themselves to creating openings within the Ottoman Empire for resettlement of Jews in Palestine, but just as fervently argued for the establishment of an Anglican bishopric in

Jerusalem as the first step toward the millennial setting promised in Holy Writ. The efforts toward creating a Jewish-Christian commonwealth in Palestine were a notable failure, as Tuchman points out, chiefly because the Jews were not then interested either in Palestine or Christianity. Nevertheless, the influence of the London Society for Promoting Christianity Among the Jews was felt in Eastern Europe to a degree not recognized by most Jewish historians. At any rate, the idea of a new Jewish-Anglican Jerusalem as a precursor to the return of Christ was never to materialize, but the political and social result of Shaftesbury's work did open the way for British control of the land and sea lanes to India as the Turkish Empire progressively came apart.

I have purposely recited some detail of the life and work of Lord Shaftesbury for he was the archetypical evangelical leader of his day.[23] Some of his visionary expectations may appear to later generations a bit silly, but the tone of Victorian evangelicalism cannot be understood apart from an awareness of men like him. It remained for a later generation of British statesmen, more pragmatic but less evangelical, to give substance to the dream of Zionist hopes at a time when the one indispensable ingredient, the Jews, were ready to return. A long line of travelers, soldiers, philanthropists, and statesmen, from Colonel Charles Henry Churchill (a contemporary of Shaftesbury) to Arthur James Balfour were concerned with the practical realities of Jewish resettlement, but none were free from the evangelical heritage left by the dreamers whose interest in Jerusalem was attached to biblical imperatives.

Perhaps I should draw the discussion to a close at this point. I have purposely focused my attention on the British evangelical contribution to the idea of a modern Israel for two reasons. First, I believe this British contribution has had an incalculable influence on all evangelical history since the days of the Evangelical Awakening. Even those evangelicals who have been ill disposed toward the notion of God's restoration of a redemptive purpose amongst Jews have had to interact with the ideas of the

British evangelicals. Secondly, the British evangelical ethos in the time of Shaftesbury was never divorced from the practical political implications of its doctrine, and therein lies perhaps its greatest importance for our own thinking. Even the cool and skeptical Balfour, whose concern for the Jewish return was certainly not imbued with the eschatological fervor of Shaftesbury, never considered divorcing his biblical commitments from his political concerns. It was the evangelical faith of these men, never seen as inconsistent with the practical realities of British political and economic life, that gave direction to much of their concern for Israel. If the result was not always as pure and as enlightened as later generations might wish, we have only to consider what European politics from 1830 to 1919 might have been without this influence to shun the alternative.

Summary and Conclusions

First, it should be apparent that there are varying evangelical views of "Israel," both as a collective term describing Jewry and as a modern state in the Middle East. For evangelical Christians these views reflect long-held exegetical and theological traditions rather than concern for the exigencies of a people seeking a continuing self-identity. The evangelical revivals and the theologies they have spawned, whatever their attitudes toward a continuing role for the Jews, have usually taken place in a context somewhat removed from the center of the Jewish problem.

I have suggested, largely for my fellow evangelicals, a theology that takes more seriously Paul's Jewish concerns than have many American Christians of the Reformed tradition. On the other hand, I have suggested that some of the millenarian schemes of evangelical origin have attempted far too explicit an expression of the mystery of God regarding the Jews and their future. I must confess to not knowing what God has in mind for the Jews, except in the general terms in which the New Testament outlines the ultimate triumph of the kingdom of God. As a Christian, I cannot view that kingdom apart from Jesus as its King, but to suggest that this makes me party to secrets concerning Jewish-Gentile participation seems to me a serious overextension of the evidence.

But because I do not see Jesus or Paul rejecting his Jewishness, and because I find in the New Testament a recognition that God still loves and is working with his ancient people, my attitude can in no way approximate studied neutrality, Even as I would hope Jews are open to the implications of the Jewishness of Christianity, I feel we must as Christians be open to the reality of the role of this other "People of God" in our theology and corporate life.

Finally, I have cited some of the basic practical concerns of the early British evangelicals. It must be granted that many of them were born to power in a way that is not true of contemporary evangelical North American leadership, but the essential difference is one of outlook rather than situation. Men like Shaftesbury, Laurence Oliphant, and Arthur James Balfour espoused an evangelical faith that led them to action. Whether it was in relieving the slum conditions of Victorian London or enabling the Jews to return to their ancient land, these men were committed to a faith that worked. I think it was because of this that their contribution to the discussion will always stand as much more significant than the records of countless prophetic conferences in our own day.

I believe we need an evangelical community that recognizes its debt to Israel and sees the modern state of Israel as an important part of the very existence of God's ancient people. Such a community can and should make common cause with Jews in opposing the kind of unjust and selective condemnation of one brand of nationalism that we have recently seen in the United Nations. It can and should actively consider the political and economic needs of modern Israel, if for no other reason than that Israel is an expression of a people beloved of God. It cannot, on the other hand, give blanket approval to the actions of any one government, any more than we might expect Jews as a community blanketly to endorse the actions of a government predominantly made up of Christians.

In closing I shall quote the words of H. Berkhof on the question of whether the Christian approach to the Jews should be characterized as "dialogue," "mission," or something else:

> Paul points in a different direction when he considers it the duty of the church "to make Israel jealous" (Rom. 11:11, 14). This is a category different from both missions and ecumenical dialogue. It is not ours to convert the Jews to Christ by our words, but to offer the "demonstration of the Spirit and power."[24]

I would like to think that evangelical Christianity, admittedly and unashamedly committed to Jesus Christ and the scriptural message, is the kind of concerned, loving, caring, and thinking community to which, like the house of Mary, Martha, and Lazarus, our Jewish friends would seek to repair. As one who has spent much time in the Jewish community and is aware of both the good and the bad, I can say that there are times when I am jealous of friends who are Jewish. But eating Levy's rye bread isn't the same as being one of the family. I would like to think that we also belong to the kind of family which would arouse a bit of jealousy on the part of our friends. I think that may be what Paul had in mind.

NOTES

1. Kenneth Scott Latourette, *A History of Christianity* (New York: Harper, 1953), pp. 1022ff.

2. Ibid., p. 1019.

3. Barbara Tuchman, *Bible and Sword* (New York: Minerva, 1968 reprint), p. 183.

4. Ibid., p. 189.

5. Jakob J. Petuchowski, "Jewish Response to 'Israel as a Theological Problem in the Christian Church,'" *Journal of Ecumenical Studies*, VI (Summer 1969), 348.

6. Charles H. Dodd, *According to the Scriptures* (London: Fontana, 1952).

7. Peter Richardson, *Israel in the Apostolic Church* (Cambridge: University Press, 1969), p. 204.

8. Ibid., pp. 205f.

9. George Kilpatrick of Oxford has recently argued that even Luke is an intensely Jewish treatise (unpublished lecture at Regent College, Nov. 1975).

10. Richardson, *Israel*, pp. 53-56.

11. This is a still-debated issue. While not wishing to smooth over the real difficulties, I do not think it helpful for Jewish scholars to attach themselves to the radical interpretations of Jesus by men like S. G. F. Brandon and then to present these interpretations in an apologetically minded student periodical as "A Jewish Approach" to the Synoptic Jesus. See the article by Zev Garber, *Davka*, II (March-April, 1972), 19-49.

12. For an even stronger statement of this position, see Johannes Munck, *Paul and the Salvation of Mankind*, trans. F. Clarke (Richmond: John Knox, 1959). Munck sees Paul's Gentile mission as a conscious device to provoke the Jews to jealousy and thus bring them to Christ.

13. Hendrikus Berkhof, "Israel as a Theological Problem in the Christian Church," *Journal of Ecumenical Studies*, VI (Summer 1969), 335.

14. See remarks by James L. Kelso in *Christianity Today* (July 21, 1967), p. 1052.

15. See the Billy Graham film "His Land" or Hal Lindsey's *The Late Great Planet Earth*.

16. I recall a lecture given in Israel in 1968 by Yonah Malachi in which he attempted a Jewish explanation of the curious phenomenon observed within dispensational Christianity. Never was a people so involved in the theory of Israel's growth and victory, but still able to remain almost totally uninvolved in making it happen.

17. Ben Halpern, *The Idea of a Jewish State*, second edition, in *Harvard Middle Eastern Studies* (Cambridge, MA: Harvard University Press, 1969).

18. Nahum Sokolow, *History of Zionism, 1600-1918*, 2 vols. (London: Longmans, Green, 1919).

19. Guenter Strothotte, "The Relation Between Religion and Nationalism in Early Zionist Thought," unpublished thesis (Simon Fraser University, 1971), p. 69.

20. Ibid., p. 79.

21. Quoted in Halpern, *Jewish State*, p. 255.

22. Tuchman, *Bible and Sword*, p. 176.

23. For more detail, see the authoritative biography by Edwin Hodder, *Life and Works of the Seventh Earl of Shaftesbury*, 3 vols. (London: Cassell, 1886).

24. Berkhof, "Israel as a Theological Problem," p. 340.

PART 4

Interpretation of Scripture

7

ASHER FINKEL

Scriptural Interpretation:
A Historical Perspective

A proper approach to interpretation dictates a transference to a historical past of the Near East, to an axial period which gave rise both to Christianity and to postbiblical Judaism. The emergence of two distinct biblically-oriented faith communities, which shared a common scriptural tradition of the past, resulted from critical events and cultural changes while being colored by theocratic and eschatological outlooks on life. Although the critical events, the crucifixion of Jesus for Christianity and the destruction of the second Temple for Jamnian Judaism, were viewed differently by the respective communities, their significance and meaning were rooted similarly in biblical exegesis. For biblical exegesis comes to resolve the tension between scriptural promises and salient history, as well as to effect accommodation with and resistance to cultural changes.[1] Biblical exegesis in the form of creative and integrated interpretation[2] becomes an extension of past revelation (the Scriptures viewed as God's words), an extension which reflects the community's self-understanding as an embodiment of that revelation.

The Jewish people who lived at the time of the destruction of the second Temple and in the following century (this corresponds with early Christian history) attached meaning to persons, events, actions and experiences from their relationship with God, as his will and acts are expressed in the Scriptures. They had already accepted the Pentateuch as the basis for their society. In the Pentateuch, God's will appears in the form of commandments; God's acts are narrated in the form of the history of salvation. The former affects human life in four areas of relationships: the transpersonal (between person and God), the interpersonal (between persons), the subpersonal (between person and nature) and the intrapersonal (between person and himself). The latter offers not only the models, the principles, and the understanding for living a theocratic life, but also a perspective on the evolution of human life in history—individually, collectively and universally—with a resultant view on life beyond history. The Jewish people saw in the prophetic traditions and in the words of the succeeding generations of teachers a further expression of the Pentateuchal revelation. These traditions and teachings came to define God's demands and to translate them in concrete situations, as well as to continually develop the recital in terms of meaning and significance for the ongoing history which was marked by crises and catastrophes in a changing world.

At this time, the rabbinic exegesis developed along the above delineations of Halakah (the way of life) and Haggadah (the recital about life).[3] The former, with its translation of God's demands in concrete situations, found expression in Midrashic and Mishnaic forms,[4] which evolved into later authoritative editions. The latter, with its recitative approach, found expression in expositional and homiletic forms,[5] which evolved into standard Aramaic and Greek Targums and Midrashic anthologies. For later generations the Halakah became binding while the Haggadah did not. Before the destruction of the Temple various forms of postbiblical Judaism were emerging with their own particular expressions of revelation.[6] These expressions included allegorical presentations (such as the Philonic works and IV Maccabees), rewritten Scriptures (such as the apocryphal writings of Jubilees and Testaments), manuals and Pesharim (such as the Dead Sea Scrolls), and apocalyptic literature.[7] The apocalyptic literature encompassed theosophy and cosmosophy (e.g., the Enochic material) as well as historiosophy and eschatology (from Daniel to IV Ezra). Even though after the destruction of the Temple this literature was relegated to mystical and esoteric circles,[8] the Haggadic material remained colored by a similar eschatological consciousness.[9]

This development illustrates the dynamics of biblical exegesis, offering a religious expression on three levels—the synagogical, the academic, and the communal. The synagogical level relates to all segments of the worshiping society. It finds expression in the public readings of Scriptures, in the Targums, in the homily and in the liturgy. The lections from the Pentateuch on consecutive Sabbaths and on designated festivals, concluding with a prophetic selection, were governed by a correlative principle.[10] To introduce the current religious terminology and to relate to contemporary views and practices, the readings were rendered into the vernacular in elaborated or more literal forms.[11] The public reading with the translation was followed by proemical or didactic homilies which respectively presented a lesson from stringing verses together or an interpretive solution to a religious problem.[12] The liturgy consisted of private recitations and benediction-like petitions, recalling key biblical texts and phrases with their interpretive theological meaning, as well as incantational, numinous and spontaneous forms.[13] The synagogical expression reflects popular religious vocabulary, ethical values, eschatological ideas and principles of faith. It demonstrates the unity of the Scriptures, a synthetic view of the Scriptures and sacred history, and the actualization of the Scriptures or their relevance to contemporary situations.

The academic level relates to judicial bodies and successive Tannaitic schools, which preserved the court decisions and opinions of the schools, oral traditions and customs, quantitative definitions and religious measures, ceremonial and Temple matters. The academic religious expression reflects a rabbinic vocabulary, hermeneutical principles, and the *seyag* (hedging) approach in the form of *Taqqanah* (repairment of scriptural proscription) and

Gezerah (enactment of precautionary measures).[14] It demonstrates the continual effort to harmonize the Scriptures with real life situations.

The communal level relates to a translation of the biblical ideal of a holy nation or the eschatological model of a fellowship with angels into a configuration of initiated members, such as the Pharisaic *Haburoth* (associations) and Essenic *Yahad* (Togetherness).[15] Their Halakic interpretation became restrictive for and exclusive to the community. The Pharisaic associates lived by regulations that spell out the realization of the priestly kingdom on earth. In the Pentateuch it is synonymous with "holy nation" (Exod. 19:6). Thus, in Leviticus 19:2 "holy," the governing theme for such a nation, was rendered "Pharisee"[16] in the Sifra. The Dead Sea covenanters saw themselves as the chosen members of the eschatological community. They even prepared themselves for the final battle (cf. the War Scroll) and the new Temple (cf. the Temple Scroll).

This dynamic religious expression can be seen in the contemporary literary works and later rabbinic editions which preserve traditions that can be traced historically to earlier periods.[17] The task for the modern exegete is not only to inquire into the linguistic, historical, and literary aspects of the available material, but mainly to enter the world of thought and religious psyche of first century Judaism. It is imperative to gain a proper understanding of the hermeneutics as related to the three levels of Jewish religious expression we have discussed. Modern exegesis must focus on the evolved religious vocabulary and imagery as well as on the organic relationships of value concepts and of symbols with events or persons. It must study the theocratic and eschatological models with their respective determining principles. It must note the relationship between worship and ethics as well as the relationship between worship and the dramatization of the history of salvation.

The same approach must be taken by the modern exegete in his exploration of the emergent Christian expression. For the New Testament texts, in effect, are religious works produced by Jews. They preserve traditions and interpretations emanating from Jesus and his followers in a Jewish world of thought. Even though the investigator has painstakingly examined the horizontal cross section of this religious tradition, he cannot neglect examining the extra dimension that makes this religious expression viable and meaningful in its particular way. To be able to see this clearly, he must study the vertical cross section of the historical religious tradition. For there is a straight line running from the Old Testament through the intertestamental times up to the events recorded in the gospels, including the formative years of the church. This development, which indeed affects the Christian message, reflects dynamics of Jewish scriptural interpretation that must be fully comprehended in order to present a proper New Testament exegesis. This approach, which can be described as interpretation criticism,[18] must accompany the modern critical results of literary (form, source, and redaction), historical and textual investigations. Furthermore, this approach is not concerned with traditional or new hermeneutics, valuable though that may be for understanding how the theologian or the preacher in different ages made the Christian message relevant and meaningful to his day. It aims at a journey back in time in order to see how first century hermeneutics in an experiential and dynamic sense gave rise to the gospel in the first place. Once the fuller meaning of this literature in its proper liturgical setting becomes evident, it may lead to new directions in our contemporary exegesis, as well as to conscious efforts to dispel existing anti-Jewish notions.

The New Testament exegete must refrain from simply drawing on parallels from early materials, no matter how suggestive they may be, without first evaluating the system in which they appear.[19] Where an Old Testament text has been cited in isolation, he must be cautious not to interpret it without evaluating the fuller implication derived from the lection in its liturgical setting.[20] He should not develop a thesis from preconceived positions without testing them out in their organic relationship to the total religious expression.[21] Furthermore, he should not judge Jesus' message simply by a criterion of dissimilarity, thereby defining its authenticity in terms of departure from contemporary Judaism.[22] For he may be ignoring in his study the appearance of similar expression in different Jewish circles. The significance of Jesus' message relates to particular stresses placed on the Jewish tradition and reflects a peculiar structure of thought governed by given principles.[23] The exegesis cannot develop solely from a reliance on secondary literature, without assaying closely the primary Jewish sources.

The well-defined disciplines of contemporary scholarship are only necessary preliminary approaches to the study of the gospels. They offer a critical view on the separation of the units of Jesus' tradition from the complexes in which they appeared, whether in oral or written forms, and from the final redacted works reflecting the theology of the evangelists. The results of this investigation relate to the history of transmission as well as to the historical settings for the evolved tradition, from Jesus through the disciples to the gospel writers. However, the proper evaluation of the gospel message, including both the teachings of Jesus and the preaching about Jesus, can be made only from a fuller understanding of early Jewish scriptural interpretation. Such an evaluation will show that the gospels relate heavily to the liturgical expression of the Jewish community.

Jesus' ministry is associated with the synagogical Jews, the country folk and the sinners of the society, whose religious knowledge came from a liturgical world. Jesus' disciples were not members of academic circles. The religious terminology (e.g., "Kingdom of God," "Father [in Heaven]"), the introductory formulas ("Woe," "Happy is"), the proverbs ("measure for measure," "physician heal thyself") and principles ("a disciple is not above his teacher"; "Elijah does come . . . so also the Son of Man") are all true reflections of liturgical expression.[24] The followers of Jesus, who continued to preach in the public forum of the Temple or synagogue, developed the *kerygma* from a liturgical setting.[25] This development can be seen in the primitive sermons preserved in Acts and in the gospels. They reflect the use of texts indicating fulfillment in preaching, lectionary structures, midrashic principles and motifs, Jewish homiletic forms and a recital. The academic expression affects the Pauline epistles more than the gospels. In the latter, only Jesus' interpretations of the Pentateuch reflect halakic hermeneutics or the application of the *seyag* principle.[26] The communal expression governs Jesus' reaction on matters of concern to the Pharisaic *Ḥaburoth*: tithes, purities and vows. Jesus' teachings on the Sabbath, divorce, and money suggest also a knowledge of the way of life of the Essenic *Yaḥad*.[27]

Jesus' didactic ministry should be evaluated as an extension of the liturgical and communal expressions, introducing both a theocratic and an eschatological model for living in God's presence. A proper view of the ministry draws on a complex of relationships and combination of forms. The gospel account is based on how Jesus related to and was understood by the different disciples and the people, the scribes and the Pharisees, Jewish and Roman authorities, as well as how he was compared with John the Baptist, the prophets and existing messianic views. The gospel account reflects the time of Jesus in addition to the later apologetic and polemical interests of the church. The historical Jesus does not conform to one description, either as a rabbi, an Essene, a charismatic miracle worker, a zealot, or a magician. Different expressions and various forms can only add to the understanding of his own consciousness. In any case, his ministry does not suggest a radical departure from Judaism.

Let me conclude with illustrations taken from the didactic ministry of Jesus and the subsequent gospel tradition about him. The theocratic teachings of Jesus are usually interpreted as opposing those of the rabbis. In essence, his teachings relate to conflict situations confronting those who live by God's demands. Such situations occur when interpersonal obligation comes into conflict with a transpersonal proscription. An example is the didactic parable of the Good Samaritan (Luke 10:30-35). The priest and the Levite, on their way back from Jerusalem to their peer groups, do not take care of the fallen person, as demanded by the interpersonal law of "love thy neighbor as thyself" (Lev. 19:18). They cross over to the other side in order not to be contaminated by what appears to be a corpse, a transpersonal proscription (Lev. 21:1). Ordinary Israelites are not mentioned, for they indeed are not faced with this dilemma. Another example appears in Mark 7:9-13 (Matt. 15:3-6). "Honor thy father and thy mother," an interpersonal obligation in terms of support, was canceled out by dedicating food items to the Temple in the form of a gift-vow (qorban). The food was then forbidden to all, including the parents, by a transpersonal proscription. For Jesus the concomitant commandment of love, which governs in many ways his eschatological program, dictates the resolution to these theocratic conflict situations. Note that the post-Jamnian rabbis solved them in similar fashion.[28] However, Jesus in his teaching is not introducing a messianic Torah, which comes to alter the former covenantal demands.[29] But he is making eschatological demands on those transformed individuals in whose life the "evil inclination" has been uprooted. In similar fashion the Haggadic material on messianic times refers to the elimination of the "evil inclination," a fulfillment of Ezekiel 11:19. In this light, the rabbis suggest that given transpersonal demands, such as sin sacrifices, will not be applicable.

The passion narrative is influenced by early Christian *kerygma* and recital. Not only liturgical texts (such as Ps. 22 and Hallel Psalms 116-118) but also basic motifs of atoning sacrifices in addition to the sacrifice of Isaac govern the narrative.[30] The passion story, an early Christian work, is not merely a journalistic record of events but a recital history of believers. The ritualistic background of Tamid sacrifice, paschal lamb, red heifer, the scapegoat and the beheaded heifer serves to explain the expiatory death of Jesus. (Compare the interpretive development in the Letters to the Hebrews and of Barnabas.) The last two sacrifices mentioned determined the inclusion (within the gospel tradition) of far-reaching statements affecting Jewish-Christian relations throughout the ages. Jesus and Barabbas were presented to the crowd and they demanded Jesus' death. So the scapegoat was chosen from two identical goats on the Day of Atonement. The crowd hastily sent the scapegoat to a rock (compare Golgotha) to be killed as a sign of total remission of sins (Lev. 16:22; Mishnah Yoma 6). The beheaded heifer absolved the community from the sin of homicide committed by an unknown person. The elders of the people washed their hands over the heifer, declaring, "Our hands did not shed this blood." The priests responded, "Do not let guilt for the blood of the innocent be upon your people Israel." Similarly Pilate washed his hands, saying, "I am innocent of this man's blood." The people responded, "Let his blood be upon us." A counterpart to this tradition in Matthew is Luke's account of Jesus' statement, "Father forgive them." The ceremony of the beheaded heifer ended with the awareness that the Holy Spirit affirmed, "The blood [of the heifer] causes their forgiveness" (see Deut. 21:6-9; Mishnah Sotah 9). Alas, the reader of the passion narrative has lost sight of the original ritualistic background and as a result misunderstandings have occurred.

NOTES

1. See Daniel Patte, *Early Jewish Hermeneutic in Palestine*, SBL Dissertation Series 22 (Scholars Press, 1975). Compare the review in Richard Longenecker, *Biblical Exegesis in the Apostolic Period* (Grand Rapids: Eerdmans, 1975).

2. See Menachem Elon, "Interpretation," *Encyclopedia Judaica*, Vol. 8 (Jerusalem: Keter, 1971); the Hebrew works of I. Heinemann, *Darke Ha'aggadah*[2] (Jerusalem: Magnes, 1953); Ezra-Zion Melamed, *Bible Commentators* (Jerusalem: Magnes, 1975). Compare the review of "Bible and Midrash" by G. Vermes in *The Cambridge History of the Bible*, ed. P. R. Ackroyd and C. F. Evans, Vol. 1 (Cambridge: University Press, 1970).

3. On definition and studies consult Hermann L. Strack, *Introduction to the Talmud and Midrash* (New York: Meridian, 1959 reprint) and the additional bibliography by John T. Townsend, "Rabbinic Sources" in

The Study of Judaism (New York: Anti Defamation League, 1972). Compare the sample study of J. Bowker, *The Targums and Rabbinic Literature* (Cambridge: University Press, 1969).

4. On forms consult Jacob Z. Lauterbach, "Midrash and Mishnah" in *Rabbinic Essays* (New York: Ktav, 1973 reprint) and the discussion in his articles on "Midrash Halakah" and "Mishnah" in *Jewish Encyclopedia*, Vol. 8 (New York: Funk and Wagnalls, 1910).

5. See H. Albeck's edition of L. Zunz's classical study of *Die gottesdienstlichen Vorträge der Juden historisch entwickelt* (Jerusalem: Mosad Bialik, 1954).

6. See the bibliographical review by Richard Bavier, "Judaism in New Testament Times" in *The Study of Judaism* (New York: Anti Defamation League, 1972). In addition consult S. Sandmel, *The First Christian Century in Judaism and Christianity* (New York: Oxford University, 1969); S. Simon, *Jewish Sects at the Time of Jesus* (Philadelphia: Fortress, 1967).

7. See D. S. Russell, *The Method and Message of Jewish Apocalyptic* (Philadelphia: Westminster, 1964).

8. Similar literary categories appear in mystical literature: theosophic works such as Merkabah and Hekhaloth works (discussed by G. Scholem, *Major Trends in Jewish Mysticism* [New York: Schocken, 1954]); cosmosophy in *The Book of Formation*, ed. L. Goldschmidt (Darmstadt: Wissenschaftliche Buchgesellschaft, 1969 reprint) and neo-apocalyptic writings collected and edited by J. Ibn-Shemuel, *Midrashe Ge'ulah* (Jerusalem: Mosad Bialik, 1954).

9. Compare P. Volz, *Die Eschatologie der jüdischen Gemeinde in neutestamentlichen Zeitalter*[2] (Tübingen: Mohr, 1934); George F. Moore, *Judaism*, Vol. 2 (Cambridge: Harvard University Press, 1950); E. Urbach, *The Sages*, ch. 17 (Jerusalem: Magnes, 1969).

10. See the classical presentation of J. Mann, *The Bible as Read and Preached in the Old Synagogue*, Vol. 1 (New York: Ktav, 1971 reprint), Vol. 2, ed. I. Sonne (Cincinnati: Hebrew Union College, 1966).

11. See M. McNamara, *The New Testament and Palestinian Targum to the Pentateuch* (Rome: Institut Biblique, 1966) and *The Targum and Testament* (Shannon, 1972).

12. See A. Finkel, *The Pharisees and the Teacher of Nazareth*[2] (Leiden: Brill, 1974).

13. See I. Elbogen, *Der jüdische Gottesdienst in seiner geschichtlichen Entwicklung* (Hildesheim: Olms, 1962 reprint); J. Heinemann, *Prayer in the Period of the Tanna'im and the Amora'im*[2] (Jerusalem: Magnes, 1966).

14. See J. Doeve, *Jewish Hermeneutics in Synoptic Gospels and Acts* (Assen: Van Gorcum, 1954), and A. Finkel, *Pharisees*, part D:6.

15. See Ch. Rabin, *Qumran Studies* (New York: Schocken, 1975), and J. Neusner, *Fellowship in Judaism* (London: Vallentine, Mitchell, 1963).

16. On definition and the related primary sources see E. Rivkin, "Defining the Pharisees: The Tannaitic Sources" (Hebrew Union College Annual, 1970); J. Neusner, *From Politics to Piety* (Englewood Cliffs, NJ: Prentice-Hall, 1973); J. Bowker, *Jesus and the Pharisees* (London, 1973).

17. Compare the study of G. Vermes, *Scripture and Tradition in Judaism*[2] (Leiden: Brill, 1973).

18. This approach is applied by G. Vermes, *Scripture*, and A. Finkel, "The Passover Story and Last Supper" in *Root and the Branch*, ed. Zeik and Siegel (Williston Park, NY: Roth, 1973).

19. On rabbinic material see S. Sandmel, "Parallelomania," *Journal of Biblical Literature* (March, 1962). On Essenic writings, see W. S. LaSor, *The Dead Sea Scrolls and the New Testament* (Grand Rapids: Eerdmans, 1972).

20. On Hallel in its liturgical setting and Christian *kerygma*, see A. Finkel, *Passover*. Other examples include: (1) Mark 15:34 refers to Ps. 22, chanted at sunrise, the time of morning sacrifice; (2) Matt. 4:6 (Luke 4:10, 11) refers to Ps. 91, a psalm for the afflicted; (3) John 10:34, 35, in connection with the Levitical Tuesday Psalm 82.

21. See H. Odeberg, *Pharisaism and Christianity* (St. Louis: Concordia, 1943). He reviews the erroneous conceptions of Pharisaic Judaism presented in Strack and Billerbeck, *Kommentar*. A. Finkel in a forthcoming article, "Jabneh's Liturgy and Early Christianity" (to be published in a collection of papers by the National Conference of Christians and Jews) criticizes the accepted view that Jamnian Judaism developed an anti-Christian liturgy. This untenable position determines the Matthean study of W. D. Davies, *The Setting of the Sermon on the Mount* (Cambridge: University Press, 1966).

22. This approach is followed closely by J. Jeremias, *New Testament Theology* (New York: Scribner, 1971), and N. Perrin, *Rediscovering the Teachings of Jesus* (New York: Harper and Row, 1967).

23. "Abba" is an address to God in private prayer and is used in charismatic circles. See D. Flusser, *Jesus* (New York: Herder, 1969); G. Vermes, *Jesus the Jew* (New York: Macmillan, 1973); Heinemann, *Prayer*, p. 120. The significance for Jesus is his relationship to God in terms of the attribute of love. His prayer (Matthean version) begins with three eschatological petitions and ends with four existential petitions, a reversal of the middle section of daily Jewish prayer. This structure indicates that Jesus regarded the eschatological realization as imminent. The Lukan recension, according to its setting, indicates that it is a "prayer on the road," meant as a liturgical guide for disciples in mission.

24. For further exploration see the Targumic exempla in the works of M. McNamara.

25. See the work of Longenecker and B. Lindars, *New Testament Apologetic* (London: SCM, 1961).

26. For Paul see W. D. Davies, *Paul and Rabbinic Judaism* (New York: Harper and Row, 1948); for Jesus see A. Finkel, *A Sample of a Revised Commentary of Strack and Billerbeck: Matt. 5:17, 20* (St. Louis: Concordia, 1975).

27. The Sons of Light are mentioned in Luke 16:8 with regard to stewardship. As regards the Sabbath (Luke 14:5) and divorce (Mark 10:6-9) contrast Dam. Doc. 11:12 and compare 4:20, respectively.

28. On priests and defilement by a corpse see Babylonian Talmud Nazir 48b. On parental support see Babylonian Talmud Qiddushin 32a. Similar to Jesus, the Jamnian schools took the position that the Sabbath law can be revoked when human life is in jeopardy (Mekhilta to Exod. 31:13).

29. This is the view of W. D. Davies, *Torah in the Messianic Age*, JBL Monograph Series, Vol. 7 (Philadelphia: SBL, 1952). I. Abarbanel, *Yeshu'oth Meshiḥo* (Carlsruhe, 1828) had already explained the organic meaning of the texts collected by Davies. See the comments of P. Schäfer, *Zeitschrift für die neutestamentliche Wissenschaft* 65 (Berlin, 1974), 27-42.

30. See G. Vermes, *Scripture*, ch. 8. Consult P. Winter, *The Trial of Jesus* (Berlin: De Gruyter, 1961); J. Bowman, *The Gospel of Mark: The New Christian Jewish Passover Haggadah* (Leiden: Brill, 1965).

8

EDWIN M. YAMAUCHI

Concord, Conflict, and Community: Jewish and Evangelical Views of Scripture

Evangelical scholars have enjoyed a relative *concord* with Jewish scholars with respect to their mutual regard for the Old Testament. There is, however, inevitable *conflict* over the interpretation of the New Testament. There should, nevertheless, be a *community* of effort in preventing any interpretation of the New Testament which might serve as a basis for anti-Semitism.

I. Relative Concord With Respect to the Old Testament

Evangelical Old Testament scholars owe an immeasurable debt to Jewish scholarship. They have appreciated in particular the archaeological contributions of Nelson Glueck and his high regard for the historicity of the Old Testament.[1] Evangelicals have especially welcomed the critical studies of Jewish scholars who have rejected the dominant analytical dissection of the Old Testament as in the documentary hypothesis of the Pentateuch. They have appreciated Umberto Cassuto's *The Documentary Hypothesis* and M. H. Segal's *The Pentateuch*.[2] Evangelicals have defended the historicity of the Old Testament, and have espoused conservative views on questions of the date and the authorship of particular books.[3]

Evangelicals have been especially indebted to the noted Jewish Old Testament scholar, Cyrus H. Gordon. Professor Gordon first at Dropsie College and then at Brandeis University trained a generation of evangelical Old

154

Testament scholars.[4] His rejection of the documentary hypothesis has been congenial with their approach.[5]

There are differences, of course. Whereas Jewish scholars have accepted liberal views of Daniel as a "prophecy" composed after the event by an anonymous writer of the Maccabean period,[6] evangelicals take the presumed setting of Daniel in the neo-Babylonian and Persian epochs seriously,[7] and are also interested in the predictive aspects of Daniel.[8]

Whereas Jews continue to value the Old Testament together with subsequent rabbinical interpretations of it[9] as law or *halakot* to provide principles for behavior,[10] Christians have come to believe that the Torah as law was fulfilled in Jesus Christ and have laid stress instead upon the Old Testament as history of salvation. Whereas Jews have regarded practice as paramount, Christians have emphasized beliefs.[11]

Jewish Old Testament scholars from the Hebrew University, teaching at the evangelical Institute for Holy Land Studies in Jerusalem, have added immensely to the education of evangelical students. Would it be too bold to suggest a comparable exchange of scholars in the United States? That is, I would like to see Jewish Old Testament scholars lecturing in evangelical seminaries, and evangelical New Testament scholars teaching in such Jewish schools as Brandeis, Dropsie, Hebrew Union College and Yeshiva University.

II. Inevitable Conflict Over the New Testament

A. The Holocaust, Anti-Semitism, and the New Testament

The mass murder of six million Jews by the Nazis has forced Christians to examine the possible role of anti-Jewish statements in the New Testament as a contributing factor in the development of the most virulent and vicious form of anti-Semitism ever known. Eliezer Berkovits testifies:

> And indeed, the most scurrilous of all Nazi antisemitic publications, Streicher's *Der Stürmer*,

drew heavily on the Gospel passages about the Jews for support. As a young student in Berlin I was introduced to the New Testament by the showcases in which *Der Stürmer* was so widely displayed in the streets of the German capital.[12]

The reaction of Catholics and Protestants to the Nazi regime was mixed. The role of the Protestant churches ranged from the shameful chauvinism of the "German Christians" and the self-serving neutrality of many Lutheran and Baptist churches to the courageous opposition of Martin Niemoeller of the "Confessing Church."[13] Catholic bishops in Germany were unconscionably silent.[14] On the other hand, Catholics and Protestants risked their lives to harbor Jews in France and the Netherlands.[15] *The Hiding Place,* a movie produced under evangelical auspices, depicts with moving realism the true experiences of Corrie ten Boom and her family who were imprisoned by the Nazis for hiding Jews. Although the film tells only part of the story, it is a timely reminder to Americans in general and to evangelicals in particular, especially the younger generation, of the murderous Nazi hatred of Jews and of Christians.

The terrible agony of the holocaust has caused scholars to re-examine the New Testament and its relationship to anti-Semitism. A number of these scholars, such as Gregory Baum, Jules Isaac, H. J. Schoeps, and Paul Winter were directly and personally affected by Nazi executions.

The writings of Jules Isaac, in particular, have been very effective in influencing the Catholic Church to reconsider some of its traditional teachings about the Jews. Isaac was an eminent historian who became Inspector General of Education in France in 1936. While hiding from the Nazis he wrote a passionate and moving plea, *Jesus and Israel,* published in French in 1959 and translated into English in 1971.[16] There is no question but that his writings influenced the Second Vatican Council in 1965.[17]

B. *Liberal Revisionist Views of the New Testament*

Isaac's approach was effective because he refrained

from attacking the historicity of the New Testament itself, and from denouncing it as an anti-Semitic document. Understandably other Jews cannot read the New Testament so dispassionately:

> The tenor and tone of the New Testament are such that they put him immediately on the defensive. He reads what are no more and no less than direct or oblique attacks on Jews and on Judaism, for much of the New Testament was composed in a time of sharp conflict between Jews and Christians. As the Jewish reader identifies himself with his fellow Jews, he is apt to identify historical events, such as the Crusades, the Black Plague, the expulsion from Spain, Hitler, and the like, with sentiments to be found in the New Testament.[18]

Some Jewish scholars, joined by liberals such as James Parkes, have therefore suggested that those New Testament passages which they see as patently anti-Semitic, the products of an age which saw the progressive shifting of the blame for the crucifixion of Jesus from the Romans to the Jews, be repudiated by Christians.

Under the influence of Neo-Orthodoxy, which holds that the New Testament is not the Word of God but *contains* the Word of God, some liberal Catholics who are especially concerned with relations with Jews have also accepted the viewpoint that the gospels are more tendentious apologies than historical accounts.[19] According to Rosemary Ruether, "Further, it is now fairly well established that the New Testament account is an apologetic reworking of history to shift the blame from the Roman to the Jewish authorities."[20]

Inasmuch as a sizable minority of Christians seek support for their unchristian anti-Semitism in a particularistic orthodox understanding of the New Testament, a liberal revisionist interpretation of the New Testament might indeed reduce anti-Semitism. But Charles Glock and Rodney Stark, who are sociologists of religion, realize that such an approach is, to say the least, impractical:

> But a solution of this kind, which would attempt to derail the process by which religion fosters anti-Semitism by combating orthodoxy, is unacceptable and unrealistic. Those committed to traditional orthodoxy simply would not yield to any such appeals, nor would it be moral to ask them to do so. Who can ask a man to surrender what he considers to be the ground of his being?[21]

A more fundamental objection is that the modern critical approach to the New Testament is really not as "unbiased" as Samuel Sandmel, for one, supposes. Sandmel, who has been the leading Jewish scholar of the New Testament, says:

> My own bias will be evident in that I find myself operating within the suppositions of the liberals. The liberal Protestant scholarship is free, objective, and rigidly honest. In it, predisposition and prejudgment are reduced to the vanishing point, and reverence for the New Testament has seemed to evoke as full and open-minded a study and investigation as fallible man can undertake.[22]

He further acknowledges that his greatest debt is to his teacher at Yale, Erwin R. Goodenough.[23]

Goodenough was indeed the embodiment of the independent liberal scholar. But to maintain that his monumental and magisterial *Jewish Symbols in the Greco-Roman Period,* for example, is virtually free from "predisposition and prejudgment" is quite untenable.[24] To suggest that liberal New Testament scholars, such as Goodenough, operate without presuppositions or biases is so far off the mark that evangelicals may be excused for smiling at such an uncritical statement.[25]

Evangelicals are not unmindful and unappreciative of modern analytical approaches, such as form critical studies, especially as used by moderate scholars such as Joachim Jeremias and C. F. D. Moule.[26] On the other hand, some radical critics are disposed to use such tools not as a surgeon's scalpel, but as a blade to whittle away all substance from the gospels. Their subjective bias is quite evident in the manner in which they will steadfastly reject the testimony of the early New Testament documents while credulously accepting quite late apocryphal and secondary material. As I have shown elsewhere, Rudolf Bultmann, who hardly accepts any information about Jesus except that he existed, at the same time reconstructs a hypothetical pre-Christian Gnosticism from medieval Mandaean texts.[27]

Such a radical approach to the sources, leading in some cases to nihilistic results or to complete reversals of traditional views, is not the kind of methodology which prevails in the study of ancient history or in classical scholarship.[28] The Jewish scholar, Joseph Klausner, had more common sense in rejecting the extreme hypercriticism of some of the *Formgeschichtliche Schule*.[29] Klausner noted that the application of some of the principles of form critics would yield totally misleading results if they were applied to such writers as Theodor Herzl, Emile Zola, and Goethe.[30]

C. The New Testament Documents as Historical Sources

Accepting the most radical conclusions of liberal New Testament scholars, some Jewish writers have assumed late dates and in some cases non-Jewish authorship for the books of the New Testament. This conclusion undermines the authority of those books as historical sources.[31]

Sandmel, for example, maintains: "The Gospel According to Matthew, in my judgement, was composed not by a Jewish Christian, but by a Gentile."[32] His position is based upon Matthew's hostility to the synagogue and its Pharisaic leadership as manifested, for example, in Matthew 23.

On the other hand, the recent monograph on the subject by D. R. A. Hare concludes:

> Indeed, were it not for the persecution it would
> be difficult to avoid ascribing the First Gospel to
> a Gentile simply on the basis of its view of Israel.
> The bitterness of the persecution and the frus-

tration of a fruitless mission are sufficient, however, to account for so pessimistic a view of Israel on the part of a Jewish Christian author.[33]

The evangelical scholar, Richard Longenecker, notes: "The preponderance of critical opinion today favours Matthew as a Jewish-Christian Gospel written for Jewish Christians or for Jews."[34]

Sandmel would place the date of the third gospel in the early second century: "The Gospel of Luke comes from the Greek dispersion at some time between 100 and 140. . . . I would date it nearer 150 than 100."[35] Klausner, however, would accept a date after 70.[36] Evangelicals would argue for a date before 70, or at the latest between 75 and 85, which is the date favored by most scholars today.[37]

Sandmel lightly dismisses the Book of Acts as a historical source:

> In my own view, "Luke" was not a historian, but an artist. Acts is not a work of history, but rather a freely composed set of vignettes about the growth of the church. The dimness in which possible written or oral sources are discernible indicates that these were, at their best, no more than points of departure for Luke, and he did not hesitate to depart.[38]

Although such a negative view corresponds to that of the dominant German school of criticism, it does not do justice to the archaeological investigations of Sir William Ramsay, whose researches in Asia Minor caused him to reverse his initially skeptical view of the historical value of Acts derived from the Tübingen School of radical criticism.[39] Ancient historians and classical scholars such as A. T. Ehrhardt, G. A. Williamson, B. H. Armington, and A. N. Sherwin-White have been deeply impressed by the trustworthiness of Acts as a historical source.[40]

Jewish writers would maintain that the Gospel of John was composed not by a Jewish apostle but by a Gentile in the second century. According to Klausner, "The Fourth

Gospel is not a religio-historical but a religio-philosophical book. It was not composed until about the middle of the second Christian century, at a time when Christians were already distinct from Jews."[41] Sandmel maintains, "Modern scholarship does not accept the tradition of an eyewitness, or even the proposed compromise of an eyewitness and his secretary or redactor."[42]

The publication of the Dead Sea Scrolls from Qumran and the perception that their dualism is strikingly close to the Johannine dualism has forced a reappraisal of the alleged Hellenistic provenience of John. The Qumran evidence supports a date in the first century and a Palestinian Jewish provenience. W. F. Albright, the *doyen* of biblical archaeologists, maintains:

> All the concrete arguments for a late date for the Johannine literature have now been dissipated, and Bultmann's attempts to discern an earlier and later form of the Gospel have proved to be entirely misleading, as both of his supposed redactions have similar Jewish background. The date which I personally prefer is the late 70's or early 80's, i.e. not more than thirty or forty years after the composition of the earliest Pauline epistles.[43]

W. D. Davies likewise concludes:

> Few would not now concede that the Fourth Gospel is rooted both in Judaism and in Hellenism, and that to deny it an interest in the land of Israel on the ground of the Hellenistic mould of its thought would be unjustifiable. Recent study has revealed that however Hellenistic its spread, the Fourth Gospel had drawn upon sources of a Palestinian origin, which might be expected to preserve "primitive" tendencies.[44]

D. The Alleged Anti-Semitism of John's Gospel

No other book in the New Testament has been as troublesome to Jews as the fourth gospel. This has been true for several reasons. From the period of the early church through the medieval period and even in more recent times it has been used to support anti-Semitic views.[45] In Sandmel's words, "In its utility for later Jew-haters, the Fourth Gospel is pre-eminent among the New Testament writings."[46]

A further problem is presented by John's exalted view of Jesus, which is one of the most important bases for the Christian belief. As Sandmel notes, "For the modern Jew, however, the Fourth Gospel presents the problem that he can respond to a laudatory appraisal of Jesus only to the point at which no special measure or kind of divinity is imputed to him."[47] Hugh Schonfield goes so far as to denounce John's Jesus as "a posturing polemical figure with a streak of antisemitism" and "a pathological egoist" who claims to be the Son of God.[48]

All scholars note the sharp opposition against "the Jews" in John's gospel. This may be understood in the light of the relatively late date of the gospel, which conservatives as well as moderate scholars would place around A.D. 90.[49] The definitive rejection of Christianity by Judaism involving the expulsion of Jewish Christians from the synagogues is to be dated no later than A.D. 85 when the twelfth benediction was inserted into the *Shemoneh Esreh* or "Eighteen Benedictions," the prayer recited thrice daily by Jews. The twelfth benediction reads in part: "Let the Nazarenes and the Minim be destroyed in a moment. And let them be blotted out of the Book of Life and not be inscribed together with the righteous."[50] The breach was made even more complete by the Bar Kochba war of A.D. 132-35.[51]

J. L. Martyn's study suggests that much of the hostility against "the Jews" in the fourth gospel must be understood in the light of the mutual antagonism between the synagogue and the church after A.D. 85. His examination of John 9:22, 12:42, and 16:2a leads him to conclude:

> Thus the Fourth Gospel affords us a picture of a Jewish community which has been (recently?) shaken by the introduction of a newly formu-lated means for detecting those Jews who want to

> hold a dual allegiance to Moses and to Jesus as
> Messiah. . . . the Heretic Benediction is now
> employed in order formally and irretrievably to
> separate the church from the synagogue.[52]

In view of this historical situation a number of studies
have attempted to demonstrate that the Gospel of John is
not in itself anti-Semitic. Though the term *Jew* is used in
the gospel seventy times, only in half of those instances
does it designate the opponents of Jesus. There are some
passages which are indeed "pro-Jewish," such as John 4:9
where the Samaritan woman describes Jesus as a Jew, and
John 4:22 where Jesus affirms that salvation is of the
Jews.[53]

III. Jewish Views of Jesus

A. Mutual Hostility Between Jews and Christians

Though Christianity developed from Judaism, its teachings were soon seen to be in opposition to Judaism. In
Klausner's words, "Hence the strange sight:—Judaism
brought forth Christianity in its first form . . . but it thrust
aside its daughter when it saw that she would slay the
mother with a deadly kiss."[54] That this antagonism affected the composition of the New Testament writings is
not denied by evangelical scholars.[55] Though they would
deny that the New Testament books are in themselves
anti-Semitic, they certainly recognize that later church
fathers used the New Testament in their harsh anti-Jewish
polemic.[56] A key point is reached in A.D. 160 when for the
first time the church appropriates for itself the term *Israel*.[57]

There was, to be sure, a time when the Jews were in the
majority as compared to the infant Christian community.
Saul of Tarsus by his own confession persecuted members
of the Way to the death. Though Jewish persecution of
Christians has been denied by some Jewish scholars,[58]
there is certainly evidence for this in the New Testament
itself and in the writings of Justin Martyr, Origen, and

Eusebius.[59] Indeed it would be surprising if there had been no persecution.

Though they are not numerous we have important polemical passages against Jesus in the Talmud. In Babylonian Talmud Sanhedrin 107b (cf. Babylonian Talmud Sota 47a and Palestinian Talmud Hagiga 2.2) we read in part:

> One day he [Rabbi Joshua] was reciting the Shema when Jesus came before him. He intended to receive him and made a sign to him. He [Jesus] thinking that it was to repel him, went, put up a brick and worshipped it. . . . And a Master has said, "Jesus the Nazarene practiced magic and led Israel astray."

In Babylonian Talmud Sanhedrin 43a we read:

> It was taught: On the eve of the Passover Yeshu [ms. M: the Nazarene] was hanged. For forty days before the execution took place, a herald went forth and cried, "He is going forth to be stoned because he has practiced sorcery and enticed Israel to apostasy. Anyone who can say anything in his favor, let him come forward and plead on his behalf."[60]

As indicated in these passages the Talmud does not deny the miracles of Jesus but attributes them to magic. Jesus is identified in some sources as a student of Rabbi Joshua ben Perahya, who flourished around 100 B.C. and who was noted for his magic.[61] Indeed a few scholars have accepted this hostile characterization of Jesus as a magician as an accurate record.[62]

The Talmud also contains a number of Ben Pandera stories according to which Jesus was the son of the Roman mercenary Pandera, "who begot a child with Joseph's adulterous wife, Mary, during her menstrual period."[63] These calumnies were expanded by the ninth century into the notorious anti-Christian traditions of the *Toledoth Jeshu*.[64] They include such fanciful stories as Jesus and Judas fighting in mid-air, Jesus crossing the Sea of Galilee on a millstone, and the hanging of Jesus on a cabbage stalk. In spite of their late and legendary nature, some of the roots of the *Toledoth* may go back to the early periods of antagonism between the Jews and the Christians.[65]

B. *Modern Jewish Views of Jesus*

Recent Jewish scholarship repudiates, of course, the altogether distorted and polemical portrait of Jesus in the *Toledoth*. Attempts have been made to rehabilitate and to recover Jesus as a Jewish rabbi.[66] Perhaps the most noteworthy treatment is the classic work, *Jesus of Nazareth,* by Joseph Klausner. This was published in Hebrew in 1922, and translated into English in 1925.

Klausner as a Zionist emphasizes the "Jewish national side of Jesus' character."[67] In the days of Jesus the Jews harbored nationalist expectations. Klausner finds that the crucifixion of Jesus put an end to his claim as a political Messiah. "Thus Jesus became an ethical Messiah *only,* and not a political Messiah at all."[68]

The contrast between the Christian understanding of Jesus as Messiah or Christ, and the contemporary Jewish expectations of a political deliverer may be seen in the Targumic interpretation of Isaiah 53.[69] Note the phrases which I have italicized in the text as set forth by Samson Levey.

Masoretic Text	*The Targum*
53:1 Who will believe what we have heard, and the arm of the Lord to whom has it been revealed?	Who would have believed this, our good tidings, and the *powerful* arm of the *might* of the Lord, for whom is it now revealed?
53:3 He was despised and forsaken of men, a man of torments and acquainted with infirmity, and like one from whom one hides his face, he was despised and we esteemed him not.	Then he shall be *contemptuous of, and bring to an end, the glory of all the kingdoms, they* shall become weak and afflicted, lo, like a man in pain and accustomed to illness, and like us, when the

	Shekinah had departed from us, leaving *us* despised and without esteem.
53:5 And he was wounded by our transgressions, he was crushed by our iniquities; the chastisement of our peace was upon him, and with his stripes we were healed.	And *he shall rebuild the Temple, which was profaned because of our sins, and which was surrendered because of our iniquities;* through his instruction, his peace shall abound for us, and when we teach his words our sins shall be forgiven us.

As Levey concludes, "At the very least, this passage shows beyond a doubt that in Jewish Messianic thought of the Targum there is no room whatsoever for a suffering and dying Messiah."[70] He suggests that the Targum probably dates to the period of Bar Kochba's rise (A.D. 132-35).

Though most Jewish scholars believe that Jesus himself claimed to be the Messiah, Paul Winter in his radical criticism of the gospels has gone so far as to deny this. He affirms rather:

> In historical reality Jesus was a Pharisee. His teaching was Pharisaic teaching.[71]
> Jesus was a normal person—he was the norm of normality—and he neither identified nor equated himself with anyone except Jesus of Nazareth.[72]

Such a reduction of Jesus to an innocuous Pharisaic rabbi by citing parallels from Tannaitic Pharisaic sources[73] in order to discard everything that was distinctive about him will hardly explain the phenomenon of Jesus.

Evangelicals believe that both the New Testament[74] and nonbiblical sources bear testimony to a unique person who aroused opposition to his authoritative teachings.[75]

IV. The Trial of Jesus

A. Jewish Studies of the Trial of Jesus

Inasmuch as the unjust charge of "deicide" against the Jews down through the ages has been based upon the accounts of Jewish participation in the trial of Jesus leading to his crucifixion, it is understandable that Jewish scholars have been concerned to scrutinize carefully those particular passages. Even in the more ecumenical climate of recent times, sociological studies have shown a high correlation between an orthodox belief in Jewish guilt for the crucifixion and an anti-Semitic prejudice against Jews.[76] One Jewish scholar, Robert Gordis, has gone so far as to assert that "the traditional account in the New Testament . . . has helped create a stream of blood from Calvary to Treblinka."[77] Sandmel remarks, "The trial of Jesus is not really a historical problem, but a problem in apologetics."[78]

There is an enormous amount of Jewish writings on the subject of the trial of Jesus.[79] The general Jewish approach is to dismiss the accounts in the gospels as unhistorical. For example, Mantel maintains that "the Gospel stories of Jesus' defiance of Pharisaic law are not historical but evangelical."[80] Commenting upon *The Nazarene Gospel Restored*, a book written in 1953 by the Jewish writer Joshua Podro with Robert Graves, Shalom Ben-Chorin writes:

> The Podro-Graves book, like all Jewish apologetic presentations, emphasizes that the crucifixion was a purely Roman death penalty, that the process recorded in the gospel does not correspond to the court regulations of the Sanhedrin, etc. But this approach is almost universal in Jewish Jesus-scholarship, questioned only by Professor Zeitlin.[81]

The most radical approach is the novel theory of Haim Cohn, an Associate Justice of the Supreme Court of Israel. He suggests that far from seeking to condemn Jesus, the Sanhedrin was seeking to find men to testify in favor of Jesus and was attempting to persuade Jesus to plead not guilty before the Romans.[82]

B. Jesus as a Political Agitator

Relying in part on the Slavonic text of Josephus and on the *Toledoth Jeshu,* the Jewish scholar Robert Eisler in 1930 published a learned work, *Iēsous Basileus ou Basileusas,* in which he portrayed Jesus as a political revolutionary. Ben-Chorin comments:

> Eisler joins to significant scholarship an unbounded imagination, which has misled him into the most daring constructions with often very doubtful material and to a mistreatment and a violence not only of New Testament reports, but also of other historical documents.[83]

In recent years Eisler's ideas have been plagiarized and popularized in Joel Carmichael's book, *The Death of Jesus,* published in 1963.[84] This work received great publicity in Europe and was translated into French in 1964 and into German in 1965.[85]

A more scholarly attempt to set forth the thesis that Jesus was a political agitator, indeed a sympathizer with the Zealot movement, is found in the writings of the late S. G. F. Brandon, professor of comparative religion at the University of Manchester.[86] His work has been hailed by Jewish scholars.[87]

Many objections, however, have been raised against Brandon's theories.[88] His view that Jesus sympathized with the Zealot movement is quite questionable and even anachronistic. Jesus' disciple Simon may have been simply "the zealous one" rather than a Zealot as the term is used by Josephus of the specific faction which developed prior to the outbreak of the Jewish War of A.D. 66-73.[89] In any case, after the uprising of Judas of Galilee in A.D. 6, Josephus does not mention any uprising until the activity of Theudas in 44. The Sicarii first became active under Felix (52-60). Martin Hengel, the leading authority on the Zealots, has been quite critical of Brandon's work.[90]

Brandon's idea that Mark and the other gospels present a pacifist Christ for apologetic purposes has been severely criticized by D. R. Catchpole.[91] The Jewish historian Elias Bickerman remarks:

> Nor can I believe that Marc, writing after A.D. 70 [according to Brandon], wanted to demonstrate Jesus' independence of Jewish national life and to shift the blame of the Crucifixion from the Romans to the Jews. In the first place, Marc is no more "anti-Jewish" than the first Evangelist whose "anti-gentile" bias Brandon stresses. As a matter of fact, the Passion stories in all four Gospels clearly distinguish between the role of the Jews and that of the Romans.[92]

Most disturbing is Brandon's highly selective use of the gospel passages.[93] To sustain his thesis Brandon has to argue that the famous pericope on the payment of tribute (Mark 12:13-17) must originally have had Jesus denouncing the payment of tribute to Caesar! He repeatedly emphasizes the presence of Simon Zelotes but says little of the fact that another disciple of Jesus was a hated tax-collector for the Romans. M. de Jonge remarks: "Every single piece of evidence is selected and presented so as to support the author's main thesis. The author has constructed an impressive building, but as soon as one removes one brick the whole edifice goes to pieces."[94]

Brandon rejects the tradition that the early Christians adopted a pacifist rather than a Zealot position before the fall of Jerusalem, and fled to Pella in Transjordan south of the Sea of Galilee. Though the excavations at Pella by Robert H. Smith of Wooster College were halted by the 1967 war, his discovery of an early Christian sarcophagus lends some archaeological support to the tradition.[95] The literary tradition in Eusebius is quite sound, going back to Hegesippus (second century). Eusebius also mentions that Justin (second century) referred to the hostility between Bar Kochba and the Christians during "the recent war" of A.D. 132-35, presumably because they would not bear arms.[96]

C. The Role of Pontius Pilate

The gospels seem to portray Pilate as a vacillating, indecisive governor. As some non-Christian sources present quite a different portrait, Mantel maintains, "The idyllic

picture of Pilate presented in the Gospels is hardly reconcilable with the *unbiased* reports we have of his wickedness."[97] Philo, in particular, describes Pilate as "naturally
inflexible, a blend of self-will, relentless."

The apocryphal *Acts of Pilate* portray him as quite sympathetic to Jesus and antagonistic to the Jews in an exaggerated degree.[98] Although many scholars have dated
these *Acts* to the fourth century, F. Schedweiler believes
that they date to the second century.[99] Tertullian around
A.D. 200 spoke of Pilate as a "Christian in his conscience."
The Greek Orthodox Church canonized Pilate's wife, who
is given the name Procla, and the Ethiopian Church recognizes June 25 as "St. Pilate and St. Procla's Day."

Scholars such as Loisy, Goguel, Brandon, and Winter
believe that this tendency to present Pilate in a favorable
light began with the writing of the gospels themselves.
Klausner maintained: "The truth of the matter is that all
the stories of Pilate's opposition to the crucifixion of Jesus
are wholly unhistorical, emanating from the end of the
first Christian century, when large numbers of Gentiles
had embraced Christianity."[100] The reason for this distortion of the record was an apologetic one. The Christians
wished to transfer the responsibility from the Romans to
the Jews to curry favor with the Roman authorities.[101]

Though there are differences between the description
of Pilate in the gospels and in the accounts of Philo and
Josephus, this does not necessarily prove that the former is
false. For one thing, we cannot agree with Mantel that
Philo's account is "unbiased."

Paul L. Maier in an examination of the sources on Pilate
points out that of the descriptions of Pilate in the New
Testament, Josephus, and Philo, only Philo is frankly hostile. And even he describes Pilate's vacillation between the
twin pressures of the outraged Jews and the emperor
Tiberius in the incident of the golden shields dedicated at
Herod's palace.[102] Philo wrote after Caligula's death in
A.D. 41, and it was in his interest to portray to Claudius
the previous Roman administrations of Palestine in the
worst possible light.

Professor David Flusser of the Hebrew University also believes that the picture of Pilate in the gospels is not as discordant as most other Jewish scholars hold:

> I think that if one reads the two incidents carefully, especially the first one, and compares them with Pilate's reactions in the case of Jesus, one becomes aware of a consistency in the behaviour of this Roman governor of Judaea. We see the same typical mixture of cruelty and weakness. Pilate engaged in machinations because he was sure that he was very clever, but his weakness made him hesitate and finally, abandon his original project. This is evident both from the incident of the busts of the emperor and in the case of Barabbas where we see Pilate's hesitating behaviour toward the crowd. He began to argue with the demonstrators, but, finally, his cleverness abandoned him, he was overwhelmed by his natural weakness and submitted to the will of the multitude.[103]

A further factor to be considered concerns the date of the crucifixion of Jesus. If this is to be placed not in A.D. 30, as it usually is, but in 33 after the fall from power of Sejanus, the anti-Semitic praetorian prefect who was Pilate's patron, we would have a further explanation for Pilate's uncertain behavior. That the later date is to be preferred has been argued by a number of scholars.[104]

The argument that the gospels modified the guilt of Pilate to placate the Romans and avoid persecution is a specious one.[105] The pagan Romans would hardly be concerned with who was responsible for the crucifixion of Jesus. The very fact that Christians worshiped one who was crucified was scandalous enough. There is a crude graffito on the wall of a palace on the Palatine hill in Rome, dating from the end of the second century, that depicts a young man adoring a crucified man with the head of an ass.[106] Minucius Felix (third century) reports the sentiments of a pagan concerning the worship of one who was crucified: "And anyone who says that the objects of their worship are a man who suffered the death penalty for his crime, and the deadly wood of the cross, assigns them altars appropriate for incorrigibly wicked men, so that they actually worship what they deserve."[107]

D. The Jewish Right of Capital Punishment

In 1914 J. Juster published a learned work called *Les Juifs dans l'Empire Romain* in which he sought to prove that during the first century A.D. the Romans had allowed the Jewish Sanhedrin the right of capital punishment. Following Juster, the famous church historian, Hans Lietzmann, argued that if the Jews had the right of capital punishment, it would have been unnecessary for them to get Roman ratification as the gospels depict. Since Jesus was crucified in the Roman fashion and not stoned in the Jewish fashion the narratives of the gospels are unhistorical.

The erudite work of Paul Winter, *On the Trial of Jesus,* published in 1961, added to the arguments of Juster a radical form of criticism that pruned away as secondary adaptations such accounts as the investigation by Annas, the mockery of Jesus, and the examination by Herod Antipas.[108] Winter's main argument against the historicity of the accounts in the gospels is his conviction that the Jews *did* have the right of capital punishment until A.D. 70. The statement in John 18:31, which reports the Jews saying to Pilate, "It is not lawful for us to put anyone to death," is, according to Winter, false.[109]

To support his thesis Juster had adduced the following examples to demonstrate the authority of the Jews: (1) the warning inscription on the balustrade in the Temple (cf. Acts 21); (2) the death of Stephen (Acts 7); (3) the stoning of James, the brother of Jesus, in A.D. 62, recorded in Josephus and in Eusebius. The execution of James, the son of Zebedee, in A.D. 44 (Acts 12:1, 2) is not relevant here because at that time a Jewish client king, Herod Agrippa I, rather than a Roman governor was in charge.

A distinguished Roman historian, A. N. Sherwin-White, has examined the arguments of Juster, upon which

Lietzmann and Winter relied, and found them unconvincing. He shows that the examples adduced by Juster are but exceptions which prove the rule that the Jews did not have capital jurisdiction. (1) The temple warning is a special exception and applies to Gentiles. (2) The stoning of Stephen, which followed no formal sentencing, was an illegal lynching. His stoning may very well have taken place in the interim between Pilate's removal in A.D. 36 and the arrival of the next governor, Marullus, in A.D. 37, that is, during the interregnum of Marcellus (who was but a subordinate of the legate).[110]

(3) According to Sherwin-White, "The story of the execution of James in Josephus, as the text stands, explicitly disproves the thesis of Juster."[111] Josephus tells how Ananus the high priest seized the opportunity provided by the interim between the death of Festus in A.D. 62 and the arrival of Albinus to condemn James to death (*Antiquities* 20.9.1). Later other Jews told the new governor that the high priest had no authority to act in such a manner.

The most searching examination of all of the arguments used by Juster, Lietzmann, and Winter to reject John 18:31 has been conducted by Catchpole. His conclusion is as follows:

> The distinction asserted by Blinzler between the right to pass a sentence and the right to execute it turns out to be entirely justified. The conclusion which seems most in accord with the evidence is that the Sanhedrin could pass sentence but that the execution could not be in their hands but was restricted by and to the Romans.[112]

That is, just as John 18:31 asserts, the Jews did not have the right of capital punishment in the time of Jesus.

E. *Illegalities of the Sanhedrin Trial*

As further objections to the gospel accounts of the trial of Jesus, Jewish scholars and others have pointed to numerous discrepancies between the examination of Jesus before the high priest and the directions for trials set forth in the Mishnah Tractate Sanhedrin.[113] Convinced that no court could have so flagrantly disregarded its own rules, many writers have concluded that the accounts in the gospels are anti-Jewish inventions.

However, the Mishnah as we now have it is the compilation of oral traditions edited by Rabbi Judah ha-Nasi at the end of the second century. According to the Mishnah the Sanhedrin was all-powerful without the slightest hint of the ruling Roman power. The Mishnah also tells us nothing of the role of the rival Sadducees, who were the dominant group in the Sanhedrin before A.D. 70.[114]

Josef Blinzler has argued that before A.D. 70 the Sanhedrin followed a Sadducean code, and not the Pharisaic code as recorded in the Mishnah.[115] Josephus (*Antiquities* 13.10.6) reveals that the essential difference between the two groups was that the Sadducees were more severe in judgment and in punishment.[116]

The very fact that not a single one of the purely Pharisaic and notably humane regulations of the Mishnah was observed in the trial of Jesus, far from disproving the historicity of the trial of Jesus, proves only that the Sadducean rules were observed.[117] Blinzler concludes: "Thus the thesis that the Tractate Sanhedrin did not yet apply in Jewish penal law in the period before A.D. 70, which is so important for a correct assessment of the trial of Jesus, can be regarded as unshaken."[118]

F. The Issue of Blasphemy

According to Sanhedrin VII.5: " 'The blasphemer' is not culpable unless he pronounces the Name itself. . . ." Therefore, according to a number of Jewish scholars, the high priest's rending of his garments in Mark 14:63 could not have been a protest against a legally indictable instance of blasphemy.[119] Indeed, according to Winter, Jesus was theologically unexceptionable: he said and did nothing meriting prosecution by the Sanhedrin; he was not in any way different from the Pharisees and did not claim to be the Messiah.

But according to the gospels (John 5:18ff.; 8:57ff.; 10:30ff.) Jesus' statements equating himself with God the Father sounded so blasphemous to the Jews that on several occasions they picked up stones against him. Technically, this was not blasphemy according to the Mishnaic ordinance. In any case there is no record of anyone being tried under such a ruling.

According to the Jewish scholar, H. Schoeps:

> E. Stauffer has carefully investigated traces of the liturgical theophany formula *Ani (we) Hu* [literally, "I and He," but meaning, "I am He"] in Jewish writings. It seems to me to be proved that this lies behind the *egō eimi* statements, and that in the mouth of Jesus it implied that He predicated of Himself divine nature, while in the ears of the high priest it sounded, of course, like a horrible blasphemy.[120]

Similarly C. H. Dodd states:

> The evangelists, I conclude, John and the Synoptists alike, take the view that Jesus was charged with blasphemy because he spoke and acted in ways which implied that he stood in a special relation with God, so that his words carried divine authority and his actions were instinct with divine power. Unless this could be believed, the implied claim was an affront to the deepest religious sentiments of his people, a profanation of sanctities; and this, I suggest, is what the charge of "blasphemy" really stands for, rather than any definable statutory offence.[121]

G. The Degree of Jewish Participation

With respect to the sensitive question of the degree of official or unofficial Jewish participation in the trial of Jesus, extreme positions have sometimes been maintained. In medieval times both the distorted Christian traditions and the polemical Jewish *Toledoth Jeshu* agreed that the

Jews were fully involved. According to Bammel, "It is to be noted that none of the versions [of the *Toledoth*] is designed to exculpate the Jews; on the contrary, the Jewish accusation of Jesus is always prominent."[122]

In reaction against the excesses of anti-Semitic interpretations, some scholars have understandably denied any Jewish participation whatsoever. As Sandmel points out:

> Respecting deicide, the premodern Christian view held that we Jews, all of us, were guilty of the death of Jesus; for that reason our Jewish scholars went to what I regard as an extreme in denying that any Jews *at all* had anything *at all* to do with it. To my mind, unclear as are the historical facts, it would have been quite natural for some individual Jews to have been involved; indeed, it would be understandably human if that were the case.[123]

A number of Jewish scholars have proposed that the high priest and a political sanhedrin rather than the Great Sanhedrin were involved in trying Jesus. Solomon Zeitlin has suggested that "Jesus was tried by a state synedrion and not by a religious Sanhedrin."[124] Mantel has also maintained that Jesus was tried before the small or political sanhedrin rather than before the Great Sanhedrin.[125] Flusser suggests that Jesus was tried before a Temple committee of the chief priests, the elders, and the scribes.[126]

On the other hand, after a thorough examination of the various theories proposed by these Jewish scholars, Catchpole concludes with a reconstruction which closely follows the traditional gospel accounts:

> Jesus was taken after his arrest by Jewish officials to the house of Annas, where he was examined, tested and treated unofficially with some violence. The following morning he was conducted before a meeting of the Sanhedrin in its customary place on the Temple Mount, and his case passed to, and remained in the hands of, Pilate.[127]

V. The Resurrection and the Deity of Jesus Christ

A. The Resurrection of Jesus

An area where Jews and Christians have completely divergent views is the subject of the resurrection of Jesus. One ingenious attempt to explain away the Easter event is the best-selling book, *The Passover Plot*, by the Jewish writer, Hugh Schonfield. According to Schonfield, Jesus cleverly plotted with some of his disciples to partake of a drug in order to feign death. Though the plot went awry when Jesus was speared, the disciples were so confused by the appearance of an anonymous young man that they mistakenly believed that Jesus had risen.[128] Samuel Sandmel is not impressed:

> Schonfield's imaginative reconstruction is devoid of a scintilla of proof, and rests on dubious inferences from passages in the Gospels whose historical reliability he himself has antecedently rejected on page after page. In my view, the book should be dismissed as the mere curiosity it is.[129]

Sandmel himself as a liberal Reform Jew would prefer to substitute the concept of immortality for that of resurrection in the Jewish prayer book.[130] He therefore has the following advice for Christians:

> If I were a Christian, I think I would not be dismayed by the idea of resurrection. I think I would [find simple prose] that would say: Here is a message that has to do with man's potential perfection. . . . I would not let this array of values suffer because one element—in view of the present environment—has to be interpreted allegorically or be divested of its pristine meaning and given a different meaning.[131]

In contrast, evangelicals affirm their belief in the resurrection of Jesus Christ as the central event of history rather than a concept derived from myth or from subjective hallucinations.[132] They would argue that only the resurrection can satisfactorily explain how Jesus' skeptical brother James became a leader in the early church, how despondent Peter became a fearless preacher at Pentecost, and how a fanatical persecutor of Christians became Paul, the greatest missionary of the gospel.

B. The Deity of Jesus Christ

The Christian concept of the deity of Christ and of the Trinity is, of course, incomprehensible if not anathema to the Jewish view of monotheism. Klausner asks, "What is Jesus to the *Jewish nation* at the present day?" and answers, "To the Jewish nation he can be neither God nor the Son of God, in the sense conveyed by belief in the Trinity. Either conception is to the Jew not only impious and blasphemous, but incomprehensible."[133] Geza Vermes likewise maintains:

> Indeed, it is no exaggeration to contend that the identification of a contemporary historical figure with God would have been inconceivable to a first-century AD Palestinian Jew. It could certainly not have been expressed in public, in the presence of men conditioned by centuries of biblical monotheistic religion.[134]

The clear references in the New Testament to the divine nature of Jesus are often dismissed by Jewish writers as late Gentile interpolations.[135] J. Morgenstern even suggests ancient Canaanite antecedents for the Trinity:

> In John, however, we find the formulation of another doctrine of early Christianity which must have had its roots in the same soil of Canaanite mythology as the doctrine of the Virgin birth. This is the doctrine that God, the Father, and Jesus, the Son, are one. As we have seen, the doctrine that the annual crop is embodied in the divine son was basic to ancient Canaanite religion.[136]

In spite of its apparent plausibility the view which seeks to trace the doctrine of the deity of Christ to Gentile

converts runs counter to the evidence that the former
Pharisaic Jew, Paul, expressed this doctrine unequivocally.
As the Jewish scholar, H. J. Schoeps, points out:

> In Phil. 2:6 Paul speaks of an *isa einai theō* of
> Christ, which can only mean that "Christ was and
> is equal with God." In 2 Cor. 11:31 Paul relates
> the Jewish formula of benediction, the word
> *eulogētos* (blessed) . . . which applies to God, to
> Jesus Christ and no doubt feels no scruple in so
> doing.
>   The equation of the *Christos* with God Himself,
> which cancels the line of demarcation between
> the God of the Old Testament and the Messiah,
> leads logically to the fact that Paul transfers all
> the Old Testament statements about God to the
> exalted *Christos Iēsous*.[137]

We may agree with Jewish scholars that Jews at the time
of Jesus were not expecting a divine Messiah. But Jesus
and the early Christians interpreted a number of Old
Testament passages as indicating a Messiah who is one with
God in a unique sense (such as Ps. 2:7 cited in Acts 13:33;
Ps. 45:6 quoted in Hebrews 1:8; Ps. 110:1 quoted by Jesus
in Mark 12:35-37, etc.).[138]

The Hebrew text of Isaiah 9:5 reads: "For to us a child is
born, to us a son is given; and the government will be upon
his shoulder, and his name will be called Wonderful Counselor, Mighty God, Everlasting Father, Prince of Peace"
(RSV). The post-Christian Aramaic Targum sought to
eliminate the Christian use of this passage by paraphrasing
it as follows:

> A boy has been born unto us, a son has been
> given unto us, who has taken the Torah upon
> himself to guard it; and his name has been called
> *by* the One who gives wonderful counsel, the
> Mighty God, He who lives forever: "Messiah," in
> whose day peace shall abound for us (the italics
> are mine).[139]

It is, of course, the doctrine of the incarnation and the
deity of Christ which makes Christianity distinctive. As W.
D. Davies observes:

> But once Jesus is claimed to be God incarnate, and this is already the case in parts of the New Testament itself, then the Rubicon has been crossed and Christianity stands completely outside the conceivable confines of Judaism, the quintessence of which is expressed in the *Shema*. If Christianity be interpreted kerygmatically in terms of the Divinity of Jesus, the Christ, then we must speak of a new religion, not merely of a schismatic emergence.[140]

The historic orthodox faith in the deity of Christ is upheld by evangelicals, who have devoted many studies to the person and the work of Christ.[141]

VI. A Community of Effort Against Anti-Semitism

Evangelicals who regard the New Testament as a historical source for their orthodox faith have the gravest responsibility for joining others in combating anti-Jewish prejudice. Anti-Semitism is surely the antithesis of the teachings of Jesus. Evangelicals distinguish between regenerate "Christians" in the biblical sense of the word, whose lives have been transformed by a personal commitment to Jesus Christ, and cultural or nominal "Christians." But this distinction between the "invisible" church and the "visible" church should not blind evangelicals to the fact that they also are not immune to the prejudices latent in human nature and reinforced by culture and society. In fact, according to the analysis of Glock and Stark, the particularism of orthodoxy can contribute to the reinforcement of anti-Semitic prejudices.

Though they may have been the most serious offenders, it has not been just the Roman Catholic Church in medieval and modern Europe and the Orthodox Church in Russia which have been guilty of anti-Semitic words and actions.[142] Martin Luther turned from his initially hopeful view of the Jews and denounced them furiously:

> Let their synagogues be burnt for the Glory of our Lord and of Christendom, so that God might see that we will not tolerate right under

our noses a meeting house in which God is blasphemed. Let their houses be razed so that they may know that they are not lords in our land. Let their prayer books and talmuds be confiscated. Let Rabbis be forbidden to teach.[143]

Calvin was less hostile to the Jews.

Both Catholics and radical Protestant opponents accused him of being a "Judaizer" by virtue of his use of traditional Jewish commentaries on Scripture, his tendency to consider Jews as though on an equal footing with Christians, and his zeal for "the rigor of the Law." It must be recognized, nevertheless, that Jews were never indigenous or welcomed in countries where Calvinism flourished.[144]

During the Nazi regime many Protestants as well as Catholics remained passive or even collaborated. Not every evangelical acted as nobly and courageously as the ten Boom family. Reflecting upon a recent visit to Auschwitz, the evangelical historian, Dr. Richard V. Pierard of the Conference of Faith and History, had these observations:

What struck me most forcefully was the stark reality of sin. . . . Furthermore, I have long known that the Holocaust exposed like no other event in recent memory the anti-Semitism latent in professing Christians. . . . Thus, I had to face up to the harsh reality that the explanation for this catastrophe which most of us learned in our youth and unconsciously internalized—it is the fulfillment of Matthew 27:25, "His blood be on us and our children"—is really just a cheap rationalization. It enables us to evade any responsibility whatsoever for the injustice and mistreatment that the Jewish people have suffered since time immemorial. . . .
    Try as I may, it was impossible for me to suppress the feeling that, if nothing more than because of sins of omission, I and my fellow

> evangelicals must share in the guilt for this incredible tragedy. With tears in my eyes I could only cry out in my inner being, "Lord, have mercy on me and my brethren."[145]

Professor Pierard urges that Auschwitz should teach us to beware of "regarding one group of people as somewhat less human than another."

Though the Scriptures teach sacrificial love for all men, it is a sad fact that the Bible has been misused by bigoted Christians to reinforce their own prejudices against others. Southerners have quoted Genesis 9:25, the curse on Ham's son Canaan, to buttress their case for segregation.[146] Peter Berger has suggested that eleven o'clock to noon on Sunday is the most segregated hour in American life. The surveys by Glock and Stark indicate that 30 percent of the Protestants and 15 percent of the Catholics interviewed would prefer to have Negroes attend their own churches rather than white churches.[147] There is deep irony in the fact that some evangelical churches will send missionaries to Africa but will not welcome blacks to their services.

Deep-seated racial suspicions and fears were aroused by Japan's attack on Pearl Harbor on December 7, 1941. As a result of the public clamor stirred up by journalists such as Walter Lippmann, a government order was signed in 1942 relocating more than 100,000 Japanese from the West Coast to what were essentially concentration camps in desert areas. Two-thirds of those who were relocated were American citizens.[148] Though many churches, and the Quakers in particular, protested the injustice of the order and did what they could to alleviate the hardships that were suffered, anti-Japanese prejudice surfaced even in so-called gospel-preaching churches. Toru Matsumoto relates one case which reveals the gap between Christian profession and action:

> At another church in Denver where Mr. Susu-Mago took two Nisei (second-generation Japanese) girls, one a Buddhist interested in Christ, the pastor promised to have some of his young people call on them, but after a period of

weeks no one had been to see the girls. The Nisei minister investigated. He learned that the pastor had told his adult Bible class that "these Japs" were coming to the church only to find out what they could and that if they were admitted to church fellowship, they would soon take over. This man had preached on evangelism that morning, saying that after the war Germany and Japan must be won for Christ.[149]

There is quite clearly no necessary correlation between what a person may profess and how he actually behaves. According to Glock and Stark, "upon careful examination, it is apparent that vast numbers of Christians are able safely to compartmentalize their religious morality so that it will not intrude into their practical affairs."[150]

More searching analyses of the relationship between religion and prejudice do indicate that there is a difference between extrinsic (utilitarian) and intrinsic (devout) believers, for example, among the Southern Baptists.[151] Empirical studies indicate that it is largely the extrinsic believers who are prejudiced.[152]

One very important area where evangelicals can work against anti-Semitic prejudices is in the field of the Sunday school curriculum. At the very least, the Jewish background of Jesus and his disciples has often been eliminated; at the very worst, the Jews have simply become the villains. The Catholic scholar, Gregory Baum, notes:

> We have been unjust to the Jews in our thought. We have removed the Jews from the origins of Christianity; they have become for us simply its opponents. Jesus is no longer a Jew; he is simply man, universal, belonging to no people . . . . In our imagination Judas is more Jewish than Mary, Caiaphas more Jewish than Peter, the spiteful crowd more Jewish than the daughters of Jerusalem weeping for Christ.[153]

John Spong recollects:

> Strangely enough, the Jesus of my childhood was so radically cut away from his Hebrew roots that

> I hardly thought of him as a Jew. The only pictures I ever saw portrayed him as a northern European with long, flowing blond hair and soft blue eyes. . . . As I was taught the Christian story in Sunday school, Jews were consistently pictured as villains. We Christians obviously have been insensitive through the ages to the anti-Semitism that we have perpetuated in so innocent a weapon as our Sunday school material.[154]

According to the thesis of Glock and Stark theological orthodoxy and particularism tend to correlate with prejudices against outsiders in general, and against Jews in particular. In view of this, it is necessary for us to be on guard against unbiblical biases. Bernard Olson, who carefully studied Sunday school literature from different groups, reports that the evangelical Scripture Press materials, which he designates as "fundamentalist," have been written so that they are freer of prejudicial materials than are the "orthodox" Missouri Synod Lutheran lessons:

> The fundamentalists treat only the Jews in a slightly favorable manner. The conservatives depict adversely all other religious groups but their own.[155]
>
> Not only do fundamentalist educators manage to avoid a negative orientation in their over-all teachings, but they and the conservative ones speak about *all* racial, ethnic, and national groups with a positive impact.[156]
>
> One set of results shows that 48 per cent of fundamentalist lessons mentioning Jews are positive in impact . . . while more than one-third of the conservative lessons were positive.[157]

We conclude then that in spite of an inevitable conflict over basic doctrines, evangelicals with their high regard for the Old Testament as well as the New Testament must recognize the Jewish background of their roots,[158] and join their Jewish friends in a spirit of humility and compassion in a community of effort against the prejudices which are endemic to fallen men. They must be particularly vigilant against the specter of anti-Semitism which may be unconsciously fostered by a false or careless interpretation of New Testament passages.[159] Only then will they deserve a hearing for the gospel which they profess.

NOTES

1. For evangelical books on Old Testament archaeology see Merrill F. Unger, *Archaeology and the Old Testament,* revised third edition (Grand Rapids: Zondervan, 1956); R. K. Harrison, *The Archaeology of the Old Testament* (New York: Harper and Row, 1963); Edwin Yamauchi, *The Stones and the Scriptures* (Philadelphia: J. B. Lippincott, 1972).

2. Umberto Cassuto, *The Documentary Hypothesis* (Jerusalem: Magnes Press, 1961); M. H. Segal, *The Pentateuch* (Jerusalem: Magnes Press, 1967). For my review of Cassuto see *Journal of the American Oriental Society,* LXXXV (1965), 582-83.

3. For evangelical views on the Old Testament see Edward J. Young, *An Introduction to the Old Testament,* revised edition (Grand Rapids: Eerdmans, 1958); Samuel J. Schultz, *The Old Testament Speaks* (New York: Harper and Brothers, 1960); K. A. Kitchen, *Ancient Orient and Old Testament* (Chicago: Inter-Varsity Press, 1966); Gleason L. Archer, *A Survey of Old Testament Introduction* (Chicago: Moody Press, 1964); R. K. Harrison, *Introduction to the Old Testament* (Grand Rapids: Eerdmans, 1969); J. B. Payne, ed., *New Perspectives on the Old Testament* (Waco, TX: Word Books, 1970).

4. A very selective list of Professor Gordon's students would include Carl Armerding (Regent College), Harry Hoffner (University of Chicago), Walter Kaiser (Trinity Evangelical Divinity School), Meredith Kline (Gordon-Conwell Seminary), William S. LaSor (Fuller Seminary), Charles Pfeiffer (Central Michigan University), Anson Rainey (Tel Aviv University), Elmer Smick (Gordon-Conwell Seminary), Marvin Wilson (Gordon College), and G. Douglas Young (Institute of Holy Land Studies). The writer also had the privilege of studying under Professor Gordon at Brandeis.

5. Cyrus H. Gordon, "Higher Critics and Forbidden Fruit," *Christianity Today,* IV (Nov. 23, 1959), 131-34.

6. E. Bickerman, *Four Strange Books of the Bible* (New York: Schocken Books, 1967); David Flusser, "The Four Empires in the Fourth Sibyl and in the Book of Daniel," *Israel Oriental Studies,* II (1972), 148-75.

7. D. J. Wiseman, T. C. Mitchell, R. Joyce, W. J. Martin, and K. A. Kitchen, *Notes on Some Problems in the Book of Daniel* (London: Tyndale Press, 1965); Edwin Yamauchi, *Greece and Babylon* (Grand Rapids: Baker, 1967).

8. Edward J. Young, *The Prophecy of Daniel* (Grand Rapids: Eerdmans, 1949); John F. Walvoord, *Daniel, the Key to Prophetic Revelation* (Chicago: Moody Press, 1971).

9. Samuel Sandmel, *Two Living Traditions* (Detroit: Wayne State University Press, 1972), p. 99.

10. James Sanders, "Torah and Christ," *Interpretation,* XXIX (1975), 374.

11. Samuel Sandmel, *We Jews and You Christians* (Philadelphia: J. B. Lippincott, 1967), pp. 65, 70. Cf. W. D. Davies, *The Gospel and the Land* (Berkeley: University of California Press, 1974), p. 394.

12. Eliezer Berkovits, *Faith After the Holocaust* (New York: KTAV, 1973), pp. 22-23.

13. Donald D. Wall, "The Lutheran Response to the Hitler Regime in Germany," David T. Priestley, "The Baptist Response in Germany to the Third Reich," and Karl-Heinz Heller, "The Protestant Church in Nazi Germany," in *God and Caesar,* ed. Robert D. Linder (Longview, TX: The Conference on Faith and History, 1971), pp. 85-134.

14. Guenter Lewy, *The Catholic Church and Nazi Germany* (New York: McGraw Hill, 1964), p. 293.

15. E. H. Flannery, *The Anguish of the Jews* (New York: Macmillan, 1965), pp. 224-25.

16. Jules Isaac, *Jesus and Israel* (New York: Holt, Rinehart, and Winston, 1971); cf. *The Teaching of Contempt* (New York: Holt, Rinehart, and Winston, 1964).

17. Arthur Gilbert, *The Vatican Council and the Jews* (Cleveland: World, 1968); Claire H. Bishop, *How Catholics Look at Jews* (New York: Paulist Press, 1974).

18. Samuel Sandmel, *A Jewish Understanding of the New Testament* (Cincinnati: Hebrew Union College, 1956), p. 10.

19. Willehad Eckert et al., ed., *Antijudaismus im Neuen Testament?* (Munich: Chr. Kaiser, 1967), p. 8.

20. Rosemary Ruether, "Theological Anti-Semitism in the New Testament," *The Christian Century,* LXXXV (Feb. 14, 1968), 191; *Faith and Fratricide* (New York: Seabury Press, 1974), pp. 88ff. Cf. Gerard S. Sloyan, *Jesus on Trial* (Philadelphia: Fortress Press, 1973), pp. 132-34.

21. Charles Y. Glock and Rodney Stark, *Christian Beliefs and Anti-Semitism* (New York: Harper and Row, 1966), p. 209.

22. Sandmel, *A Jewish Understanding,* p. xvi.

23. Ibid., p. xviii.

24. Cf. Morton Smith, "Goodenough's *Jewish Symbols* in Retrospect," *Journal of Biblical Literature,* LXXXVI (1967), 53-68.

25. Professor Goodenough reacted against his own fundamentalist background and was quite cynical about conservative Christianity. He could not understand how his son, a physicist at MIT, could embrace an evangelical faith in Christ.

26. Cf. George E. Ladd, *The New Testament and Criticism* (Grand Rapids: Eerdmans, 1967); Richard N. Longenecker and Merrill C. Tenney, ed., *New Dimensions in New Testament Study* (Grand Rapids: Zondervan, 1974).

27. Edwin Yamauchi, *Gnostic Ethics and Mandaean Origins* (Cambridge: Harvard University Press, 1970); *Pre-Christian Gnosticism* (Grand Rapids: Eerdmans, 1973).

28. Edwin Yamauchi, *Composition and Corroboration in Classical and Biblical Studies* (Philadelphia: Presbyterian and Reformed, 1966); "Homer, History, and Archaeology," *Bulletin of the Near East Archaeological Society,* III (1973), 21-42; "The Archaeological Confirmation of Suspect Elements in the Classical and the Biblical Traditions," in *The Law and the Prophets,* ed. John Skilton et al. (Nutley, NJ: Presbyterian and Reformed, 1974), pp. 54-70.

29. Joseph Klausner, *From Jesus to Paul* (Boston: Beacon Press, 1961), p. 259.

30. Ibid., pp. 239-40.

31. For evangelical views on the dates and the authorship of the various New Testament documents see F. F. Bruce, *The New Testament Documents,* revised edition (London: The Inter-Varsity Fellowship, 1960); Donald Guthrie, *New Testament Introduction,* 3 vols. (Chicago: Inter-Varsity Press, 1961-65).

32. Sandmel, *A Jewish Understanding,* p. 167; cf. p. 162.

33. D. R. A. Hare, *The Theme of Jewish Persecution of Christians in the Gospel According to St. Matthew* (Cambridge: Cambridge University Press, 1967), p. 170; cf. "The Relationship between Jewish and Gentile Persecution of Christians," *Journal of Ecumenical Studies,* IV (1967), 446-56.

34. Richard N. Longenecker, *The Christology of Early Jewish Christianity* (Naperville, IL: Alec R. Allenson, 1970), p. 19, n. 44; cf. R. V. G. Tasker, *The Gospel According to St. Matthew* (Grand Rapids: Eerdmans, 1961).

35. Sandmel, *A Jewish Understanding,* pp. 190-91.

36. Klausner, *From Jesus to Paul,* p. 229.

37. Guthrie, *New Testament Introduction: The Gospel and Acts,* pp. 106-09; cf. E. E. Ellis, *The Gospel of Luke* (London: Thomas Nelson, 1966); I. Howard Marshall, *Luke: Historian and Theologian* (Grand Rapids: Zondervan, 1971).

38. Sandmel, *A Jewish Understanding,* p. 256.

39. W. Ward Gasque, *Sir William M. Ramsay* (Grand Rapids: Baker, 1966); *A History of the Criticism of the Acts of the Apostles* (Tübingen: Mohr [Paul Siebeck], 1974); Horton Harris, *The Tübingen School* (Oxford: Clarendon Press, 1975); F. F. Bruce, *The Acts of the Apostles,* revised edition (Grand Rapids: Eerdmans, 1952).

40. See Yamauchi, *The Stones and the Scriptures,* pp. 96-97.

41. Joseph Klausner, *Jesus of Nazareth,* revised edition (Boston: Beacon Press, 1964), p. 125.

42. Sandmel, *A Jewish Understanding,* p. 270.

43. W. F. Albright, *New Horizons in Biblical Research* (London: Oxford University Press, 1966), p. 46; cf. "Recent Discoveries in Palestine and the Gospel of John," in *The Background of the New Testament and Its Eschatology,* ed. W. D. Davies and D. Daube (Cambridge: Cambridge University Press, 1954), pp. 170f.; see also William S. LaSor, *The Dead Sea Scrolls and the New Testament* (Grand Rapids: Eerdmans, 1972), pp. 191-205.

44. Davies, *The Gospel and the Land,* pp. 288-89. See also J. H. Charlesworth, ed., *John and Qumran* (London: Geoffrey Chapman, 1972); E. Malatesta, *St. John's Gospel 1920-1965* (Rome: Pontifical Biblical Institute, 1967); Leon Morris, *Commentary on the Gospel of John* (Grand Rapids: Eerdmans, 1971).

45. It should be clearly noted that the use of John by anti-Semites is neither a necessary or sufficient reason to consider the fourth gospel as originally an anti-Semitic document, any more than the use of John and of Pauline writings by the Gnostics makes these documents Gnostic. See S. S. Smalley, "Diversity and Development in John," *New Testament Studies,* XVII (1971), 276-92; Elaine H. Pagels, *The Johannine Gospel in Gnostic Exegesis* (Nashville: Abingdon Press, 1973); *The Gnostic Paul* (Philadelphia: Fortress Press, 1975).

46. Sandmel, *A Jewish Understanding,* p. 269. Cf. Ernest L. Abel, *The Roots of Anti-Semitism* (Rutherford, NJ: Fairleigh Dickinson University Press, 1975), p. 137.

47. Sandmel, *A Jewish Understanding,* p. 283.

48. Hugh J. Schonfield, *The Passover Plot* (New York: Bernard Geiss, 1965), p. 99.

49. Guthrie, *The Gospels and Acts,* pp. 257-62; Morris, *Gospel of John,* pp. 30-35.

50. J. L. Martyn, *History and Theology in the Fourth Gospel* (New York: Harper and Row, 1968), p. 36; K. L. Carroll, "The Fourth Gospel and the Exclusion of Christians from the Synagogues," *Bulletin of the John Rylands Library,* XL (1957-58), 23; C. K. Barrett, *The Gospel of John and Judaism* (Philadelphia: Fortress Press, 1975), pp. 47, 69. Ben Zion Bokser, *Judaism and the Christian Predicament* (New York: Alfred A. Knopf, 1967), points out that in the modern Jewish prayer book "this prayer has been changed, replacing the term *minim,* 'sectarians,' with the term *rishah,* 'wickedness'" (p. 141).

51. Peter Richardson, *Israel in the Apostolic Church* (Cambridge: Cambridge University Press, 1969), p. 203.

52. Martyn, *The Fourth Gospel*, pp. 40-41. Cf. Erich Grässer, "Die Juden als Teufelssöhne in Johannes 8, 37-47," in Eckert, *Antijudaismus*, pp. 157-70.

53. Gregory Baum, *The Jews and the Gospel* (London: W. Newman, 1961); G. J. Cuming, "The Jews in the Fourth Gospel," *Expository Times*, LX (1948-49), 292; Robert T. Fortna, "Theological Use of Locale in the Fourth Gospel," *Anglican Theological Review*, supplemental series III (1974), 94; Erich Grässer, "Die Antijüdische Polemik im Johannesevangelium," *New Testament Studies*, X (1964-65), 85, 90; W. W. Sikes, "The Anti-Semitism of the Fourth Gospel," *Journal of Religion*, XXI (1941), 30.

54. Klausner, *Jesus of Nazareth*, p. 376.

55. Richardson, *Israel*, pp. 200-02; cf. Hare, *Jewish Persecution*, p. 168.

56. David Efroymson, "Jews and Judaism in Tertullian's Apologetic," *Philadelphia Seminar on Christian Origins*, XII, 2 (1974-75), 1-3; Flannery, *Anguish of the Jews*, passim; Ruether, *Faith and Fratricide*, ch. 3.

57. Richardson, *Israel*, p. 1.

58. E.g., Solomon Grayzel in *Torah and Gospel*, ed. Philip Scharper (New York: Sheed and Ward, 1966), p. 8.

59. See W. H. C. Frend, *Martyrdom and Persecution in the Early Church* (New York: New York University Press, 1967), pp. 146-47 and passim; cf. J. Duncan Derrett, "Cursing Jesus (I Cor. XII.3): The Jews as Religious 'Persecutors,'" *New Testament Studies*, XXI (1975), 548. Professor David M. Scholer of Gordon-Conwell Theological Seminary is writing a dissertation which deals with the topic of the Jewish persecution of Christians. The dissertation is being written under the direction of Professor Helmut Koester of Harvard. I am indebted to Professor Scholer for some of my references in this paper.

60. See R. Travers Herford, *Christianity in Talmud and Midrash* (London: William and Norgate, 1903).

61. Joshua ben Perahya occurs prominently in the Jewish Aramaic magic bowl texts of the sixth century A.D. Cf. J. Montgomery, *Aramaic Incantation Texts from Nippur* (Philadelphia: University Museum, 1913), pp. 225ff.; J. Neusner, "Archaeology and Babylonian Jewry," in *Near Eastern Archaeology in the Twentieth Century*, ed. J. A. Sanders (Garden City, NY: Doubleday & Co., 1970), pp. 334-41; Edwin Yamauchi, "Aramaic Magic Bowls," *Journal of the American Oriental Society*, LXXXV (1965), 511-23.

62. E.g., Morton Smith, *The Secret Gospel* (New York: Harper and Row, 1973). For a review, see Edwin Yamauchi, "A Secret Gospel of Jesus as 'Magus'?" *Christian Scholar's Review*, IV (1975), 238-51. Cf. John M. Hull, *Hellenistic Magic and the Synoptic Tradition* (London: SCM Press, 1974). The most radical extension of this thesis is the contention of John M. Allegro, *The Sacred Mushroom and the Cross* (Garden City, NY:

Doubleday and Co., 1970), that both Christianity and Judaism are but disguised magic and fertility cults centered on the hallucinogenic mushroom.

63. Cf. Joseph Bonsirven, *Textes Rabbiniques des Deux Premiers Siècles Chrétiens* (Rome: Pontifical Biblical Institute, 1955), nos. 677, 749, 1885, 2004.

64. William Horbury, "The Trial of Jesus in Jewish Tradition," in *The Trial of Jesus,* ed. Ernst Bammel (London: SCM Press, 1970), p. 106.

65. Ernst Bammel, "Christian Origins in Jewish Tradition," *New Testament Studies,* XIII (1967), 317-35.

66. Thomas Walker, *Jewish Views on Jesus* (London: Allen Unwin, 1931; New York: Arno Press, 1973 reprint); Shalom Ben-Chorin, "The Image of Jesus in Modern Judaism," *Journal of Ecumenical Studies,* XI (1974), 403.

67. Ben-Chorin, "Image of Jesus," p. 405.

68. Klausner, *From Jesus to Paul,* pp. 438-39. Cf. Sandmel, *A Jewish Understanding,* p. 33.

69. For an evangelical interpretation see Edward J. Young, *Isaiah Fifty-Three* (Grand Rapids: Eerdmans, 1952); for a Jewish exposition, see Harry M. Orlinsky, *The So-called "Suffering Servant" in Isaiah 53* (Cincinnati: Hebrew Union College Press, 1964). For the suffering Messiah in the works of Paul as understood by a Jewish scholar, see H. J. Schoeps, *Paul* (Philadelphia: Westminster Press, 1961), pp. 126-67.

70. Samson H. Levey, *The Messiah: An Aramaic Interpretation* (New York: Hebrew Union College—Jewish Institute of Religion, 1974), p. 67.

71. Paul Winter, *On the Trial of Jesus* (Berlin: Walter de Gruyter, 1961), p. 133.

72. Ibid., p. 148.

73. Cf. Morton Smith, *Tannaitic Parallels to the Gospels* (Society of Biblical Literature monograph, 1951); Asher Finkel, *The Pharisees and the Teacher of Nazareth* (Leiden: E. J. Brill, 1964); John Bowker, *Jesus and the Pharisees* (London: Cambridge University Press, 1973).

74. For evangelical studies on the person of Jesus, see Carl Henry, ed., *Jesus of Nazareth: Saviour and Lord* (Grand Rapids: Eerdmans, 1966); J. D. G. Dunn, "The Messianic Secret in Mark," *Tyndale Bulletin,* XXI (1970), 92-117; Longenecker, *Christology;* G. N. Stanton, *Jesus of Nazareth in New Testament Preaching* (Cambridge: Cambridge University Press, 1974); Edwin Yamauchi, *Jesus, Zoroaster, Buddha, Socrates, Muhammad* (Downers Grove, IL: Inter-Varsity Press, 1972).

75. Cf. F. F. Bruce, *Jesus and Christian Origins Outside the New Testament* (Grand Rapids: Eerdmans, 1974). See also Paul Winter, "Josephus on Jesus," *Journal of Historical Studies,* I (1968), 289-302; D. S. Wallace-Hadrill, "Eusebius of Caesarea and the *Testimonium Flavianum . . . ,*"

Journal of Ecclesiastical History, XXV (1974), 353-62; Shlomo Pines, *An Arabic Version of the Testimonium Flavianum and Its Implications* (Jerusalem: Israel Academy of Sciences and Humanities, 1971).

76. Glock and Stark, *Christian Beliefs,* p. 69.

77. In a review of Paul Winter, *On the Trial of Jesus,* in *Journal of Semitic Studies,* XXVII (1965), 187.

78. Samuel Sandmel, "The Trial of Jesus: Reservations," *Judaism,* XX (1971), 73.

79. The literature has been examined thoroughly and comprehensively by D. R. Catchpole, *The Trial of Jesus: A Study in the Gospels and Jewish Historiography from 1770 to the Present Day* (Leiden: E. J. Brill, 1971).

80. H. Mantel, *Studies in the History of the Sanhedrin* (Cambridge: Harvard University Press, 1961), pp. 280-81.

81. Ben-Chorin, "Image of Jesus," p. 409.

82. Haim H. Cohn, "Reflections on the Trial and Death of Jesus," *Israel Law Review,* II (1967), 332-79; *The Trial and Death of Jesus* (New York: Harper and Row, 1971); "Reflections on the Trial of Jesus," *Judaism,* XX (1971), 10-23.

83. Ben-Chorin, "Image of Jesus," p. 406.

84. Joel Carmichael, *The Death of Jesus* (New York: Macmillan, 1963; London: Victor Gollancz, 1963; Harmondsworth: Penguin Books, 1966 reprint).

85. Cf. *Der Spiegel,* XX (Jan. 31, 1966), 48-67.

86. S. G. F. Brandon, *The Fall of Jerusalem and the Christian Church* (London: S.P.C.K., 1951); *Jesus and the Zealots* (Manchester: Manchester University Press, 1967); *The Trial of Jesus of Nazareth* (New York: Stein and Day, 1968); "Jesus and the Zealots: Aftermath," *Bulletin of the John Rylands Library,* LIV (1971), 47-66; "The Trial of Jesus," *Judaism,* XX (1971), 43-48.

87. E.g., by Samuel Sandmel in *The Saturday Review,* LII (Jan. 4, 1969), 87-89. Cf. Cohn, *The Trial and Death of Jesus:* "I am content to be able to quote, and adopt, this analysis of a distinguished Christian theologian, Professor S. G. F. Brandon, who is not suspect of overstating his case" (p. 169).

88. For criticism of Brandon's theories, see Edwin Yamauchi, "Historical Notes on the Trial and Crucifixion of Jesus Christ," *Christianity Today,* XV (April 9, 1971), 6-11.

89. Marc Borg, "The Currency of the Term 'Zealot,' " *Journal of Theological Studies,* n.s. XXII (1971), 504-12; Morton Smith, "Zealots and Sicarii: Their Origins and Relation," *Harvard Theological Review,* LXIV (1971), 1-19.

90. See Martin Hengel's review of Brandon's *Jesus and the Zealots* in the *Journal of Semitic Studies*, XIV (1964), 231-40; cf. Hengel, *Was Jesus a Revolutionist?* (Philadelphia: Fortress Press, 1971); Oscar Cullmann, *Jesus and the Revolutionaries* (New York: Harper and Row, 1970).

91. Catchpole, *The Trial of Jesus*, pp. 120-26.

92. In a review of Brandon's *The Fall of Jerusalem and the Christian Church* in *Bibliotheca Orientalis*, X (1953), 37.

93. Cf. Davies, *The Gospel and the Land*, pp. 340-43; Walter Wink, "Jesus and the Zealots," *Union Seminary Quarterly Review*, XXV (1969), 37-54.

94. In a review of *Jesus and the Zealots* in *Vigiliae Christianae*, XXIII (1969), 229.

95. Robert H. Smith, "An Early Roman Sarcophagus of Palestine and Its School," *Palestine Exploration Quarterly*, CV (1973), 71-82; "A Sarcophagus from Pella: New Light on Earliest Christianity," *Archaeology*, XXVI (1973), 250-56.

96. Sidney Sowers, "The Circumstances and Recollection of the Pella Flight," *Theologische Zeitschrift*, XXVI, 5 (1970), 305-20; M. Simon, "La Migration à Pella," *Judéo-Christianisme* (Paris: Recherche de Science Religieuse, 1972), pp. 37-54.

97. Mantel, *The Sanhedrin*, p. 287 (the italics are mine).

98. M. R. James, *The Apocryphal New Testament* (Oxford: Clarendon Press, 1924), pp. 94-146. The *Acts of Pilate* is also known as *The Gospel of Nicodemus*. Cf. P. Winter, "A Letter from Pontius Pilate," *Novum Testamentum*, VII (1964), 37-43; Paul L. Maier, "The Fate of Pontius Pilate," *Hermes*, XCIX (1971), 362-71.

99. In E. Hennecke and W. Schneemelcher, *New Testament Apocrypha* (Philadelphia: Fortress Press, 1963), Vol. I, pp. 444ff.

100. Klausner, *Jesus of Nazareth*, p. 348.

101. Cohn, *The Trial and Death of Jesus*, pp. xv-xvi.

102. Paul L. Maier, "The Episode of the Golden Roman Shields at Jerusalem," *Harvard Theological Review*, LXII (1969), 109-21; "Pontius Pilate: The Judge Who Changed History," *Mankind*, II (Feb. 1970), 26-35.

103. David Flusser, "A Literary Approach to the Trial of Jesus," *Judaism*, XX (1971), 36; cf. Sloyan, *Jesus on Trial*, p. 131.

104. Paul L. Maier, "Sejanus, Pilate, and the Date of the Crucifixion," *Church History*, XXXVIII (1968), 3-13; Harold W. Hoehner, "The Year of Christ's Crucifixion," *Bibliotheca Sacra*, CXXXI (1974), 332-48; "The Significance of the Year of Our Lord's Crucifixion for New Testament Interpretation," in Longenecker and Tenney, *New Dimensions*, pp. 115-26; cf. Baum, *The Jews and the Gospel*, p. 73.

105. Cf. E. Bickerman's judgment (see note 92).

106. For Tertullian's comment on a similar depiction see *Apology* xvi.12 in *The Fathers of the Church* X, ed. R. Arbesmann, E. Dayl, and E. Quain (Washington, DC: The Catholic University of America Press, 1950), pp. 51-52.

107. Minucius Felix, *Octavianus,* p. 336.

108. The authenticity of this account is maintained by Harold W. Hoehner, "Why Did Pilate Hand Jesus over to Antipas?" in Bammel, *The Trial of Jesus,* pp. 84-90; Hoehner, *Herod Antipas* (Cambridge: Cambridge University Press, 1972).

109. Winter's thesis has been well received by other Jewish scholars— Isaac, *The Teaching of Contempt,* p. 140; Cohn, *The Trial and Death of Jesus,* p. 31. For a list of the numerous reviews, see the second edition of Winter's work, published in 1974.

110. Bo Reicke, *The New Testament Era* (Philadelphia: Fortress Press, 1968), p. 192.

111. A. N. Sherwin-White, *Roman Society and Roman Law in the New Testament* (Oxford: Clarendon Press, 1963), pp. 36-38; "The Trial of Jesus," in D. E. Nineham et al., *Historicity and Chronology in the New Testament* (London: S.P.C.K., 1965), pp. 97-116. For a critique see T. A. Burkill, "The Condemnation of Jesus," *Novum Testamentum,* XII (1970), 321-42.

112. Catchpole, *The Trial of Jesus,* pp. 238-54. The same conclusion is also reached by Ernst Bammel, "Die Blutgerichtsbarkeit in der Römischen Provinz Judäa vor dem Ersten Jüdischen Aufstand," *Journal of Jewish Studies,* XXV (1974), 48-49; and by Robert M. Grant, "The Trial of Jesus in the Light of History," *Judaism,* XX (1971), 41.

113. For a list of the alleged discrepancies, see Yamauchi, "Historical Notes."

114. H. Danby, "The Bearing of the Rabbinical Criminal Code on the Jewish Trial Narratives of the Gospels," *Journal of Theological Studies,* XXI (1919-20), 51-76.

115. Josef Blinzler, *The Trial of Jesus* (Westminster, MD: Newman Press, 1959); "The Trial of Jesus in the Light of History," *Judaism,* XX (1971), 49-55. Cf. J. Jeremias, *Jerusalem in the Time of Jesus* (Philadelphia: Fortress Press, 1969), p. 178.

116. Cf. Klausner, *Jesus of Nazareth,* p. 343.

117. Josef Blinzler, "Das Synedrium von Jerusalem und die Strafprozessordnung der Mischna," *Zeitschrift für die Neutestamentliche Wissenschaft,* III (1961), 60.

118. Josef Blinzler, "The Jewish Punishment of Stoning in the New Testament Period," in Bammel, *The Trial of Jesus,* p. 161. Cf. Catchpole, *The Trial of Jesus,* p. 260.

119. Cohn, *The Trial and Death of Jesus,* p. 129; Mantel, *The Sanhedrin,* pp. 268-75; Schonfield, *The Passover Plot,* p. 148.

120. Schoeps, *Paul,* p. 161.

121. C. H. Dodd, *More New Testament Studies* (Manchester: Manchester University Press, 1968), p. 99.

122. Bammel, "Christian Origins in Jewish Tradition," p. 328. According to Horbury, "The Trial of Jesus": "Many passages from Jewish texts would, if found in Christian sources, certainly be ascribed to anti-Jewish sentiment" (p. 115).

123. Sandmel, *We Jews and You Christians,* p. 133.

124. Solomon Zeitlin, *Who Crucified Jesus?* (New York: Bloch, 1964), p. xviii; the same view is adopted by Bokser, *Judaism,* p. 24.

125. Mantel, *The Sanhedrin,* pp. 92-93, 268, 286.

126. Flusser, "A Literary Approach," pp. 33-34. Cf. Franz E. Meyer, "Einige Bemerkungen zur Bedeutung des Terminus 'Synhedrion' in den Schriften des Neuen Testaments," *New Testament Studies,* XIV (1967-68), 545-51.

127. Catchpole, *The Trial of Jesus,* p. 271.

128. See Edwin Yamauchi, "Passover Plot or Easter Triumph?" *The Gordon Review,* X (1967), 150-60; this is reprinted in the *Journal of the American Scientific Affiliation,* XXI (1969), 27-32.

129. In *The Saturday Review* (Dec. 3, 1966), p. 43.

130. Sandmel, *We Jews and You Christians,* p. 78.

131. Samuel Sandmel in *Jesus and Man's Hope,* ed. D. Miller and D. Hadidian (Pittsburgh: Pittsburgh Theological Seminary, 1971), p. 324.

132. Daniel P. Fuller, *Easter Faith and History* (Grand Rapids: Eerdmans, 1965); Paul L. Maier, *First Easter* (New York: Harper and Row, 1973); Merrill C. Tenney, *The Reality of the Resurrection* (Chicago: Moody Press, 1972); Edwin Yamauchi, "Easter—Myth, Hallucination, or History?" *Christianity Today,* XVIII (March 15, 1974), 4-7; (March 29, 1974), 12-14, 16.

133. Klausner, *Jesus of Nazareth,* pp. 413-14.

134. Geza Vermes, *Jesus the Jew* (London: Collins, 1973), p. 212.

135. Cohn, *The Trial and Death of Jesus,* p. 126; Schonfield, *The Passover Plot,* pp. 99, 200; Vermes, *Jesus the Jew,* pp. 212-13.

136. J. Morgenstern, *Some Significant Antecedents of Christianity* (Leiden: E. J. Brill, 1966), p. 91; cf. p. 96.

137. Schoeps, *Paul,* pp. 152-53; cf. *The Jewish-Christian Argument* (New York: Holt, Rinehart, and Winston, 1963), p. 23.

138. E. Ellis, *Paul's Use of the Old Testament* (Grand Rapids: Eerdmans, 1957); F. F. Bruce, *New Testament Development of Old Testament Themes*

(Grand Rapids: Eerdmans, 1969); Richard Longenecker, *Biblical Exegesis in the Apostolic Period* (Grand Rapids: Eerdmans, 1975).

139. Levey, *The Messiah,* p. 45. It may be no coincidence that in twice quoting Isaiah 9, Schonfield omits the phrase, "Mighty God, Everlasting Father, Prince of Peace" *(The Passover Plot,* pp. 202, 223).

140. Davies, *The Gospel and the Land,* p. 402.

141. G. C. Berkouwer, *The Person of Christ* (Grand Rapids: Eerdmans, 1954); Walter Elwell, "The Deity of Christ in the Writings of Paul," in *Current Issues in Biblical and Patristic Interpretation,* ed. G. F. Hawthorne (Grand Rapids: Eerdmans, 1975), pp. 297-308; Donald Guthrie, *Jesus the Messiah* (Grand Rapids: Zondervan, 1972); Wilbur M. Smith, *The Supernaturalness of Christ* (Boston: W. A. Wilde, 1954). See also note 74.

142. See Jacob R. Marcus, *The Jew in the Medieval World* (Philadelphia: Jewish Publication Society, 1960); A. Roy Eckardt, *Your People, My People* (New York: Quadrangle, 1974).

143. Cited by Gilbert, *The Vatican Council,* p. 20; cf. Paul Opsahl and Marc Tanenbaum, ed., *Speaking of God Today: Jews and Lutherans in Conversation* (Philadelphia: Fortress, 1974), p. 94.

144. Gilbert, *The Vatican Council,* p. 21.

145. Richard V. Pierard, "Reflections on Auschwitz," *The Covenant Quarterly,* XXXIII (Feb. 1975), 43-44.

146. J. Buswell, *Slavery, Segregation and Scripture* (Grand Rapids: Eerdmans, 1964).

147. Glock and Stark, *Christian Beliefs,* p. 169.

148. Harry Kitano, *Japanese Americans* (Englewood Cliffs, NJ: Prentice-Hall, 1969), pp. 31-36.

149. Toru Matsumoto, *Beyond Prejudice: A Story of the Church and Japanese Americans* (New York: Friendship Press, 1946), p. 68.

150. Glock and Stark, *Christian Beliefs,* p. 169; cf. G. Lenski, *The Religious Factor,* revised edition (Garden City, NY: Doubleday & Co., 1963). For a tragic instance of the breakdown between ethical ideals and practical actions, see Arthur D. Morse, *While Six Million Died* (New York: Random House, 1967), p. 261.

151. J. Feagin, "Prejudice and Religious Types: A Focused Study of Southern Fundamentalists," *Journal of the Scientific Study of Religion,* IV (1964), 3-13.

152. G. Allport, "The Religious Context of Prejudice," *Journal of the Scientific Study of Religion,* V (1966), 447-57.

153. Baum, *The Jews and the Gospel,* p. 8.

154. John Spong and Jack Spiro, *Dialogue: In Search of Jewish/Christian Understanding* (New York: Seabury, 1975), p. 52.

155. Bernard E. Olson, *Faith and Prejudice* (New Haven, CT: Yale University Press, 1962), p. 26.

156. Ibid., p. 27.

157. Ibid., p. 45.

158. Edith Schaeffer, *Christianity Is Jewish* (Wheaton, IL: Tyndale House, 1975).

159. For a refutation of the charge that Jewish participation in the trial of Jesus is tantamount to the rejection of Jesus by the Jewish people, see J. Jocz, *A Theology of Election* (London: S.P.C.K., 1958), pp. 149-50.

9

ROGER NICOLE

The Attitude of Jesus Toward Scripture

One point on which it should be relatively easy to establish a contact between the evangelical community and some portions at least of the Jewish community is in the attitude toward the Scripture. Obviously, with respect to the scope of Scripture there is a substantial difference, since Christians emphasize the divine authority of the New Testament in addition to the Hebrew canon, but with respect to the Jewish Scriptures there is a common bond which should not be overlooked when an effort is made to establish closer contact.

The evangelical Christian will look to the attitude of Jesus and the apostles toward the Scriptures as it is recorded for us in the New Testament documents. The attitude of Jesus will be deemed especially significant since the evangelical Christian believes that he is God and therefore that he cannot have been in error, particularly with respect to matters that deeply affect faith and ethics. Now, it is fairly evident that Jesus was in very substantial agreement with the prevailing attitude of his Jewish contemporaries with reference to the authority of the Old Testament Scripture,[1] although his use of the Old Testament and his method of interpreting exhibit notable areas of difference.

When an attempt is made to ascertain Jesus' view on any subject, we are manifestly dependent upon the record available to us in the four gospels. Scholars have differed in their assessment of how factual such materials are. Evangelicals together with the overwhelming preponderance of Christians through the ages have been satisfied that the record may be taken at face value as expressive of fact. It is, therefore, the intention of this paper to make a very brief presentation in summary form of some data concerning Jesus' attitude toward the Hebrew Scriptures without stopping for an investigation as to whether or not some recorded sayings of Jesus are to be viewed as historical. For the purpose of this discussion anything that he is represented as saying in the four gospels will be accepted at face value.[2]

The record of the attitude of Jesus toward the Old Testament Scripture is clear. From the very start to the very end we find him in unqualified agreement with the Old Testament. In John 5:39 he says to the Jews, "You diligently study the Scriptures because you think that by them you possess eternal life."[3] He does not frown upon their attitude or object to their expectations but endorses fully their approach. He adds, "These are the Scriptures that testify about me."

In Matthew 5:17-20 Jesus emphasizes the principles of the kingdom of God and addresses himself to the expectation that as an inspired teacher he would introduce new material to cancel out the old order. He says, "Do not think that I have come to abolish the law or the prophets. I have not come to abolish them but to fulfill them. I tell you the truth; until heaven and earth disappear, not the smallest letter, not the least stroke of the pen, will by any means disappear from the law until everything is accomplished." This very emphatic statement acknowledges that even in its minutest details the Old Testament will be more lasting than heaven and earth. If Jesus thought that the Bible was merely the expression of the opinion of men, how could he expect it to outlast the handiwork of God? It is very plain in this passage that Jesus views the law and the prophets as the embodiment of divine truth. Therefore, to disregard the law is to court disaster. To practice it and teach it is the path to greatness (v. 19). This statement of Jesus is especially important since it appears at the beginning of the Sermon on the Mount, a most moving summary of the teaching of Jesus at the beginning of his brief career.

In Luke 16 we have the story of the rich man and Lazarus. Jesus represents the rich man as asking to have a warning sent to his brothers lest they should follow him in his misery. But Abraham responds, "They have Moses and the prophets. Let them listen to them" (v. 29). Undoubtedly, the intent of the rich man was to excuse himself, suggesting that he never had a chance, because he was not sufficiently warned. This explains the sharp answer of Abraham to the seemingly rather unselfish request made of him. It also explains why the rich man persists, saying, "No, father Abraham, but if someone from the dead goes to them, they will repent" (v. 30). This statement is tantamount to saying, "Moses and the prophets are an inadequate warning. A person who disregards them may yet not be culpable. What we need is a miraculous messenger from heaven." But Abraham cuts this short by saying, "If they do not listen to Moses and the prophets, they will not be convinced even if someone rises from the dead" (v. 31). This constitutes a very impressive witness to the sufficiency of Old Testament Scripture.

In John 10 Jesus is locked in argument with some of his Jewish antagonists. They have rightly understood his claim to deity and they have already picked up stones to punish him for this blasphemy. Jesus answered them, "Is it not written in your law, 'I have said ye are gods'? If he called them gods to whom the Word of God came—and the Scripture cannot be broken—what about the one whom the Father set apart as his very own and sent into the world? Why then do you accuse me of blasphemy because I said, 'I am God's son'?" (John 10:34-36). It is not relevant to the present inquiry to discuss here the nature of the argument of Jesus. I would judge that he is arguing a fortiori that, since the Old Testament on occasion used the word *Elohim* to refer to human beings vested by God's appointment with the divine prerogative of judgeship, a glib charge of blasphemy should not be pressed against him without a careful examination of his credentials. What is of special concern for us here is the emphatic affirmation, "the Scripture cannot be broken," which underlines the significance of his whole argument from Scripture. We furthermore note that here Jesus was not hesitant to base his justification on one word, found once in one psalm written by Asaph, a secondary author in the Book of Psalms. This reflects the tremendous confidence which Jesus had in the irrefragable authority of even very minute details of the Old Testament record.

The use of the term *law* in connection with a passage from the Psalms is not a case of mistaken reference, but must be construed as an implied recognition that the whole Old Testament Scripture, even the Psalms, has a legal and binding authority. This is consistent with the usage of the term in other teachings of Jesus (John 15:25) as well as in other passages in the New Testament.

Even after his resurrection Jesus is represented as maintaining the same view of Scripture. In Luke 24 he does not tell the apostles that he misled them in placing excessive confidence in the Old Testament, but he confirms what he taught them in the days of his flesh, "This is what I told you while I was still with you. Everything must be fulfilled that is written about me in the law of Moses, the prophets, and the Psalms" (v. 44). Surely the disciples would have been ready to accept on his own authority the message of one who had just risen from the dead. But Jesus is interested in perpetuating precisely what he taught them before his death. A similar lesson can be derived from Jesus' approach to the disciples on the way to Emmaus (vv. 25-27).

Jesus made frequent and extensive use of the Old Testament throughout his career. His recorded words occupy some 1870 verses in the gospels. Of this number at least 180 include either a direct quotation of or a very clear allusion to specific portions of the Old Testament. This is to say that almost 10 percent of the recorded words of Jesus are very directly related to Old Testament Scriptures. Jesus used the Scripture with his opponents and with his friends, with human beings and with Satan, even in his prayers! He makes reference to it to answer questions, to establish his teaching, to confute his opponents, to comfort his friends. There is scarcely any type of situation in which the Scripture is not invoked in order to provide the divine answer. In the way in which he introduces these quotations, Jesus makes clear his high opinion of the authority of Scripture. In fact, he ascribes to God himself statements which are not directly attributed to God in the Old Testament but which are simply an element in the narrative. For instance, in Matthew 19:4, 5 he quotes a statement of the Genesis historian as the utterance of the Creator himself.

In contrast to the orthodox Jews of his time Jesus did not accept as authoritative the tradition of the Jews. In Matthew 15 and Mark 7 we have a very clear expression of Jesus' attitude on this point. He takes the scribes and the Pharisees to task for nullifying "the Word of God by your tradition that you have handed down" (Mark 7:13). Thus, it is apparent that Jesus' acceptance of Old Testament Scripture does not represent a mere accommodation to prevailing views, for then, surely, he would also have accommodated himself to the prevailing acceptance of tradition as authoritative. Jesus draws a sharp distinction between the "commands of God" and human prescription. In discussing this issue Jesus made it very plain that he did not hesitate to set aside human traditions in order to emphasize the authority of the Word of God. This is evident also in the way in which Jesus handled the observance of the Sabbath. In this matter he adopted a collision course with many of the Jewish scholars by repudiating the traditional elaboration. At no point, however, did Jesus violate the laws of the Sabbath as contained in the Old Testament.

It is sometimes thought that in Matthew 5:21-48 we have a series of statements by Jesus which invalidate the authority of the Old Testament law. Nothing could be further from the truth! If this passage is considered carefully, it will be apparent that Jesus reinforces the Old Testament law, showing that its full bearing goes beyond what some superficial interpreters might have thought at first. Thus the commandment "not to murder" demands not merely abstaining from the willful taking of life, but implies that God also frowns on the attitudes which, when carried to their fullest limit, lead to murder—pride, anger, jealousy, contempt (Matt. 5:21-26).

Similarly, it is not enough to abstain from physical adultery in order to please God, for God desires a heart and thoughts that are oriented to purity rather than to prurient interests.

The treatment of divorce in this passage (Matt. 5:31, 32) is amplified in Matthew 19:3-11. The Old Testament law was meant to curb irresponsible arbitrariness on the part of the male spouse. It demanded that a divorce be sealed by a written text to be delivered to the wife. This would have the effect of slowing up the process (since many people could not write), of introducing the possibility of arbitration, and of providing a cooling-off period during which momentary bitterness might be dissipated. Obviously, a settlement with respect to the dowry would have to be reached also. All these elements militated against divorce and prevented the males from making unilateral arbitrary decisions which would be very damaging to the women and which in many cases might leave them in a quandary concerning the final intentions of their husbands. Jesus goes beyond these limits to emphasize that the original design of marriage is to unite one man and one woman for life. The marriage is to last until the death of one of the partners. This truth he grounds on an appeal to Scripture (Gen. 2:24).

With respect to swearing, the same principle obviously applies. Jesus is not satisfied with those who tell the truth only when they are under oath, but he wants his disciples to be truthful at all times (Matt. 5:33-37).

It is often thought that in Matthew 5:38-42 Jesus repudiates the principle of retaliation which was enjoined in the Old Testament law—"An eye for an eye and a tooth for a tooth" (Exod. 21:24; Lev. 24:20; Deut. 19:21). This Old Testament principle was meant more as a guideline for judges than as a pattern for individual vengeance, although some people had used it in the latter direction. Even in this case, however, the statement confines vengeance within the range of the ill originally inflicted. The tendency of man is to do harm beyond what he has experienced in order to punish his enemies. These enemies in turn have new reasons for desiring to retaliate and a spiraling vendetta starts in which people seek an eye for a tooth, a life for an eye, and several lives for a life. Now the Old Testament law established a limit—"no more harm can be inflicted than was suffered." Jesus carries this principle one step further; he shows that it is the vindictive spirit, not merely the size of the vengeance, that is heinous to God. The passage in Matthew therefore is not in opposition to the law, but carries through its intent.

The final example appears at first to confront us with a flat contradiction, for the commandment, "Love your neighbor and hate your enemy," is set in contrast with Jesus' command, "Love your enemies" (Matt. 5:44). It is noteworthy, however, that the commandment, "Hate your enemies," does not appear in Scripture. That was a distortion of the meaning of the injunction, "Love your neighbor as yourself" (Lev. 19:18), where the neighbor was interpreted to mean only a fellow Jew. Jesus shows here that the intent of God goes beyond one particular race of men and that love is enjoined for all human beings. Thus, even in this example Jesus does not repudiate the law but he illumines in a very challenging way the full meaning of the Old Testament commandment.

Throughout this pericope (Matt. 5:21-48), by giving this spiritual interpretation of the law of Moses, Jesus has indicated his conviction that it was not Moses, a man, who was the author of the law but God himself. The law must be interpreted in the light of God's purposes. This is a very significant endorsement of the divine authority of the Old Testament. What appeared at first a difficulty turns out to be a significant confirmation of the major trend of Jesus' teaching on this subject.

When the divine authority and inspiration of the Old

Testament are recognized, there is a close bond that is established between those who share that view. Far from having distrust and hatred in their hearts toward Jewish people, evangelical Christians should receive with immense gratitude from them "the oracles of God" (Rom. 3:2), a gift so great that it is second only to the gift of him whom we call our Lord, even Jesus, our Messiah.

NOTES

1. We are aware that the term *Old Testament* is a Christian expression. It is not being used here as a means to flout the Jewish approach to Scripture. Rather, it is intended to express, in a term understandable to all, reference to the Hebrew canon of thirty-nine books. We dare to hope that this nomenclature will not be deemed offensive by anyone.

2. If someone is inclined to deny the historicity of any statement of Jesus, he would have to face the necessity of giving an answer to two questions:

   (1) If we assume that some representations of the gospels are not factual, what reliable evidence do we possess concerning the life and preaching of Jesus?

   (2) Since the statements falsely ascribed to Jesus would presumably not represent his views, on what ground would the gospel writers be emboldened to place gratuitously in his mouth statements that should have been known to be contrary to his view? This procedure would appear not only stupid but fundamentally dishonest, and this is a heavy charge to level against the writers of the gospels.

3. If the verb is construed as an imperative, "study diligently," the inference presented here would be even stronger.

BIBLIOGRAPHY

Anderson, J. N. D. "Christ and the Scriptures." *The Word of God and Fundamentalism.* London: Church Book Room, 1961, pp. 46-59.

Branscomb, B. H. *Jesus and the Law of Moses.* New York: Richard Smith, 1930.

Brown, Hugh D. *Critics or Christ?* London: Partridge, 1905, pp. 121-54.

Burrell, David James. *The Teachings of Jesus Concerning the Scriptures.* New York: American Tract Society, 1904.

Dijk, Klaas. *Itet Prophetische Woord.* Amsterdam: de Standaard, 1931, pp. 183-221.

France, R. T. *Jesus and the Old Testament. His Application of Old Testament Passages to Himself and His Mission.* London: Tyndale Press, 1971.

Gaussen, Louis. *Théopneustie.* Second edition. Paris: Delay, 1842, pp. 132-52.

Gilbert, George Holley. *Jesus and His Bible.* New York: Macmillan, 1926.

Grant, W. M. *The Bible of Jesus.* London: Hodder and Stoughton, 1927.

Kaehler, Martin. *Jesus und das Alte Testament.* Leipzig: Deichert, 1896 (also in *Dogmatische Zeitfragen,* I, 111-75).

Kuyper, Abraham. *Encyclopedia of Sacred Theology.* Translated by J. H. de Vries. New York: Scribner, 1898, pp. 429-41.

Ladd, George T. *The Doctrine of Sacred Scripture.* New York: Scribner, 1883. I, 27-74.

Leathes, Stanley. *Christ and the Bible.* London: Partridge, 1885.

Lightner, Robert P. *The Saviour and the Scriptures.* Philadelphia: Presbyterian and Reformed, 1966.

Mc'Intosh, Hugh. *Is Christ Infallible and the Bible True?* Third edition. Edinburgh: Clark, 1902, pp. 171-216.

Marcel, P. Ch. "Our Lord's Use of Scripture." *Revelation and the Bible.* Edited by Carl F. H. Henry. Grand Rapids: Baker, 1958, pp. 121-34.

Mirtow, Paula. *Jesus and the Religion of the Old Testament.* London: S.P.C.K., 1957.

Saphir, Adolph. *Christ and the Scriptures.* New edition. London: Morgan & Scott, n.d., pp. 8-26.

Wenham, John W. *Christ and the Bible.* London: Tyndale Press, 1972.

_____ . *Our Lord's View of the Old Testament.* London: Tyndale Press, 1953.

10

BERNARD MARTIN

Scriptural Authority, Scriptural Interpretation, and Jewish — Christian Relations

I am reluctant to inject a discordant note into this apparently harmonious and congenial assemblage, in which most of my Jewish colleagues seem to join our Christian brethren in affirming that Scripture is literally inspired by God (the Jews, of course, affirming this only of the so-called Old Testament). Honesty, however, compels me to assert that I do not share that view of the Bible, and—what is far more important—that most contemporary Jews, even those who consider themselves "religious," do not either. There are, to be sure, a good many Jews who do believe in the verbatim revelation by God of the Torah, or Pentateuch, at Mount Sinai, but for the majority of Jews living today a direct or second-hand acquaintance with the teachings of biblical criticism have made this belief problematic and, indeed, quite untenable.

The Jewish-born philosopher Benedict Spinoza (1632-1677) is generally considered the father of the higher criticism, which deals with such problems as the authorship, date of writing, literary style, and particular theological and doctrinal tendencies of the various components of which the Bible is presumed to be constituted. It is true that in his *Theologico-Political Treatise* (published anonymously in 1670) Spinoza noted many internal contradictions in the Bible and specifically called in question the rabbinic claim that the whole of the Pentateuch, except for the last eight verses, was written by Moses at the direct dictation of God; and it is true that Spinoza further suggested that Ezra was actually the compiler of the Torah and of the historical books of the Bible. In point of fact, however, something of the critical spirit had occasionally emerged, at least in hesitant and tentative fashion, among both Christian and Jewish scholars hundreds of years earlier. For instance, the great Spanish-Jewish Bible exegete and poet Abraham Ibn Ezra (1089-1164) mentions, although he himself rejects, the idea that the passage beginning at Genesis 36:31 was written during the time of King Jehoshaphat, and comments on the puzzling phrase "and the Canaanite was then in the land" at the end of Genesis 12:6: "He who is wise will be silent."

Personally I would suggest that, in a very important sense, the truly central figure in the general development of biblical criticism was a Jew who lived more than nineteen hundred years ago, Philo of Alexandria. It was Philo who made the most massive and intensive of efforts to reconcile Athens and Jerusalem, Greek philosophy and biblical revelation. It was Philo who brought to the zenith of perfection the method of allegorical interpretation of the Bible, and who inspired (though frequently indirectly, and without their being aware of the fact) the efforts of so many Christian and Jewish scholastic theologians during the course of more than a millennium and a half to harmonize Plato and Scripture and, in the process, often disastrously to distort the image of the biblical deity, to transform the living "God of Abraham, Isaac, and Jacob" into the abstract, impassive, eternally unchanging "God of the philosophers."

But the historical reality is that Philo himself was completely forgotten among Jews (only in the sixteenth century did the pioneering and brilliant Italian-Jewish scholar Azariah dei Rossi [c. 1511-1578] rediscover the fact that the Alexandrian philosopher was a Jew); Ibn Ezra's counsel about the wisdom of silence in regard to enigmatic and embarrassing passages and expressions in the Bible was generally heeded; and Spinoza was excommunicated by the Jewish community of Amsterdam and regarded as a blasphemous heretic by Jews and Christians alike.

It was only in the nineteenth century, under the cumulative impact of the work of Jean Astruc, de Wette, and Graf and Wellhausen (who formulated the documentary theory in its classical shape), that biblical criticism and the consequent rejection of the unity and the divinely revealed character of the Torah began to penetrate significantly into the Jewish world. Some of the most prominent Reform rabbis of Germany, led by Abraham Geiger (1810-1874), the major theoretician of the Reform movement, accepted the conclusions of the then regnant biblical criticism. These conclusions were taught throughout the entire term of existence of the Hochschule für die Wissenschaft des Judentums, established in Berlin in 1870 and, until its destruction in 1942 by the Nazis, the chief seat of liberal Jewish scholarship in Europe. They even found their way into the Conservative Breslau Rabbinical Seminary (founded in 1854). Even the most eminent member of the faculty, the great historian Heinrich Graetz (1817-1891), while still approaching the Pentateuch in orthodox fashion, occasionally adopted quite radical positions in regard to the prophets and the Hagiographa, affirming, for instance, the existence of two Hoseas and no fewer than three Zechariahs!

Isaac Mayer Wise (1819-1900), the founder and leader for the initial twenty-five years of its existence of the first liberal rabbinical seminary in America, the Hebrew Union College (established in Cincinnati in 1875), appears to have had little use for biblical criticism, although it must be said—in all honesty—that the general theological confusion and ambiguity so obviously manifest in virtually all of his religious writings are apparent in this area also. However, his successor as president of the Hebrew Union College, Kaufmann Kohler (1843-1926), was a consistently radical adherent of this mode of Bible study and added to the faculty some equally consistent exponents of it. The tradition was continued by Kohler's successor Julian Morgenstern (1881-1977) and, to a somewhat lesser degree, by the latter's successor Nelson Glueck (1900-1971). The Conservative Jewish Theological Seminary in New York City, founded in 1886, has also had, and continues to have, representatives of biblical criticism—both higher and lower—on its faculty. Thus, for several generations, practically all of the non-Orthodox rabbis of America and Europe have been exposed to the methodology and conclusions of the critical-historical study of the Bible, and the inevitable consequence has been a general inability to accept, in any literal sense, the divinely revealed character of Scripture.

The attitude of these rabbis has naturally percolated down into the minds of the laymen (I use this term in full awareness of the fact that Judaism theoretically recognizes no distinction between clergy and laity) whom they teach and to whom they preach. These men and women, like their spiritual mentors, simply do not, in general, regard the Bible as the Word of God, and it is not, therefore, the ultimate authority for either their faith or their actions. They may admire certain passages in it for their religious sublimity or moral grandeur, but they do not consider it as revealed in its entirety or as providing the final norms for belief and conduct.

Some non-Orthodox rabbis and laymen—and it is non-Orthodox Jews who constitute the majority of Jews living today—do, to be sure, speak of certain elements of Scripture as "divinely inspired," and a few may even apply the term *revealed* to these elements. But what is acknowledged as "divinely revealed" or "divinely inspired" is simply that which conforms to their reason and moral sense. Hence, human capacities—reason and moral sense, or moral experience—and not Scripture itself, are the ultimate authority for their religious belief and practice. This, I submit, is an undeniable fact.

Yet, there are signs that the claim of classical Judaism —that the Torah, and indeed the Bible as a whole, are, in a significant sense, the product of divine revelation—has been taken with increasing seriousness in recent years by many liberal Jews (under this term I mean to include those who, in America, identify themselves as either Reform or Conservative Jews). More than a few have managed, at least to some extent, to liberate themselves from the dogmas of the higher criticism.

On a personal note, I can testify that the process of liberation is by no means an easy one. I was well indoctrinated in these dogmas a quarter of a century ago at the Hebrew Union College by Julian Morgenstern, Sheldon H. Blank, and the late Julius Lewy, a truly great Assyriologist—all scholars and men for whom I continue to cherish a very profound respect. It took me years of independent reflection after I left their tutelage, as well as the rigorous training in logic and scientific method required to obtain a doctorate in a university department of philosophy, to realize how little of the truly scientific there is in what Morgenstern especially liked to call "Biblical science"; how weakly grounded in substantive evidence were many of the ingenious and finespun hypotheses of Julius Wellhausen and his intellectual heirs; what tremendous "scholarly" arrogance is implicit in Paul Haupt's *Polychrome Bible;* how frequently the critics have succumbed to that vice which Samuel Sandmel has aptly called "parallelomania" and which has led them on the basis of one or two identical or even similar-sounding words or phrases, to ascribe an entire psalm to a Ugaritic or Babylonian origin (for an example of this method carried *ad absurdum,* see Father Dahood's work on the Psalms in the *Anchor Bible Commentary* series); how much there is, in view of the critics' tendency to deny as much of the originality of the Old Testament as possible and to present it as massively derivative from earlier Near Eastern prototypes, in Solomon Schechter's characterization of the higher criticism as the "higher anti-Semitism."

I do not wish to suggest that in rejecting the cruder dogmas of biblical criticism (and it is *these* that I have cast off; some of its more thoughtful insights and well-grounded conclusions I readily accept) I have taken the leap of faith to a simple belief in the conception of Scripture as literally and unambivalently revealed by God. I am afraid I am too much of a rationalist by temperament and too much the product of my education and intellectual nurture for that to have happened. I cannot believe that the biblical mandate to burn witches and the order to the ancient Israelites to kill all male prisoners of war were really divine commands. Indeed, I would have to regard a God who issues such commands as demonic—certainly not an object to whom worship is properly directed.

But I do believe wholeheartedly in divine revelation, and I have come increasingly to regard the Bible as the *product* of revelation—as well as of human comprehension and miscomprehension of it (e.g., foolish and fallible men believed in witches and thought that God wished to have them burned).

By divine revelation I mean nothing more or less than God's self-disclosure. And that God has disclosed himself, and continues to disclose himself and his love—of that I have no doubt. In the history of Israel, or the Jewish people, the crucial experience of God's self-revelation took place at Mount Sinai, resulting in the covenant between God and Israel. For me the covenant is an indisputable historical fact; otherwise, the whole history of Israel—and especially its survival to the present day—is an insoluble enigma.

It was, I believe, in response to God's self-disclosure that various prophets, sages, and chroniclers in ancient Israel wrote the Bible. Thus, in my view, the Bible is the work of men. But, insofar as it is the direct response to God's revelation, it is also divine. Martin Buber, I think, put the matter well when he characterized the Bible as the record of a thousand-year "dialogue between God and Israel."

In the Bible God speaks to Israel, and Israel responds. Its response is sometimes halting, sometimes even radically misguided. It took a long time before the classical Hebrew prophets of the eighth to the sixth centuries B.C.E. arrived at what I regard as the central religious truth of the Bible—that God is essential Moral Will and that his fundamental demand of men is justice and righteousness. Earlier and later Israelites were often mistaken and ascribed to God unworthy qualities and unseemly acts, but there were those who responded to him by writing into the Bible sentences, paragraphs, and chapters that are truly God's Word.

On what basis do I make this distinction? I admit it readily—on the basis of my God-given reason and moral sense.

One final comment on the question of scriptural authority and Jewish-Christian relations. Proponents of a liberal and critical view of the Bible certainly have no monopoly on making significant contributions to the improvement of relations between the adherents of the two faiths. But a literal view of verbatim inspiration may be—and has been—a major stumbling block thereto. To cite one of many possible examples, the Roman Catholic Church's document *Nostra Aetate* adopted twelve years ago at Vatican II did not, contrary to widespread opinion, clearly and unequivocally absolve either the Jews living in Jerusalem in the year 29 C.E. or all other Jews throughout the ages of the charge of deicide which has brought so much death and destruction to the Jewish people. The Catholic Church could not, in principle, do so—despite the massive historical evidence to the effect that the Romans were primarily responsible for the execution of Jesus—simply because it clings to the dogma of the divinely revealed character of the *ipsissima verba* of the gospels.

To sum up what I have been saying: There is undoubtedly a certain grandeur and nobility in the view that the Bible is clearly and unambiguously the Word of God, and biblical criticism has certainly been guilty of much folly and dogmatism. But, I am convinced, we come closer to the truth when we see that the Bible is a human response to the divine self-disclosure and therefore both divine and human, and that faith illuminated by reason and critical evaluation is preferable to blind reliance on authority.

PART 5

Response to Moral Crises and Social Ferment

11

MARC H. TANENBAUM

Jews and Social Responsibility

In his first comprehensive work on psychoanalytic theory, Dr. Erich Fromm explains that he started with the study of aggression and destructiveness because, aside from being one of the fundamental theoretic problems in psychoanalysis, "the wave of destruction engulfing the world makes it also one of the most practically relevant ones."[1]

Noting that the preoccupation of professionals and the general public alike with the nature and causes of aggression is rather recent—dating in fact only to the middle of the 1960s—Dr. Fromm asserts that "one probable reason for this change was the fact that the level of violence and the fear of war had passed a certain threshold throughout the world."

As noted in a 1973 study of "Violence, Non-Violence and Struggle for Social Justice" prepared for the World Council of Churches, "violence today has become demonic in its hold on human life. In the life of some nations and among many severely oppressed peoples, it seems more like an addiction than like rational behavior."

Amnesty International, reporting on its world-wide study of the use of torture by individuals and governments, came to the conclusion, "torture can exist in any society," and indeed "the practice of torture is becoming internationalized." Although there are exceptions, torture has been *standard* administrative practice in more than thirty countries and has occurred in more than sixty.

Writing from the perspective of an economic historian in post-Vietnam, post-Watergate America, Robert L. Heilbroner writes pessimistically of the "malaise of civilization." He states:

> There is a feeling that great troubles and changes loom for the future of civilization as we know it. Our age is one of profound turmoil, a time of deep change, and there is a widespread feeling that the world is coming apart at the seams.
>
> We have gone through "a drubbing of history," and a barrage of confidence-shaking events has filled us with a sense of unease and foreboding during the past decade or so. No doubt foremost among these has been the experience of the Vietnam War, an experience that has undermined every aspect of American life—our belief in our own invincible power, our trust in government, our estimate of our private level of morality.
>
> But the Vietnam War was only one among many such confidence-shaking events. The explosion of violence in street crime, race riots, bombings, bizarre airplane hijackings, shocking assassinations have made a mockery of the TV image of middle class American gentility and brought home with terrible impact the recognition of a barbarism hidden behind the superficial amenities of life.
>
> We switch on the evening TV and learn what's going to hit us next on the head—a hijacking, a murder, a rape, or some other daily terror. These things profoundly affect our outlook.[2]

An eighteen-month study released by the Subcommittee on Juvenile Delinquency of the United States Senate Judiciary Committee noted that the destruction of school property in 757 school districts costs $500 million a year—the amount spent on textbooks. Further, more than 100 murders are committed in schools each year and at least 70,000 assaults on teachers.

The president of the National Education Association told the Senate subcommittee that the student violence is a symptom of violence in society generally. He declared that students "see that violence is a fundamental way of life in our society."

Time magazine reports, "One study claims that the average American youth can be expected to watch 11,000 TV murders by the time he or she is 14." In the same special cover story on crime (June 30, 1975), it is asserted:

> By any measurement, crime has become an ominous national problem [in the United States]. Since 1961 the rate for all serious crimes has more than doubled. From 1973 to 1974 it jumped 17%—the largest increase in 44 years that national statistics have been collected.
>
> Violent crime has had an even sharper increase. In the past 14 years, the rate of robberies has increased 255%, forcible rape 143%, aggravated assault 153% and murder 106%. Preliminary reports to the FBI in 1974 show that the rate for violent crimes as well as property crimes like burglary is still sharply on the rise. Says a Chicago cop, "You just can't paint the picture too bad."

Social analysts report that since Hitler and the founding of the United Nations, more persons have been killed by massacre than by the traditional wars that have kept the world on edge. As Nathan Glazer has documented in his essay, "The Universalization of Ethnicity," "an epidemic" of conflicts is taking place literally on every continent of the world, conflicts in which race, religion, region, and nationality are involved, frequently resulting in practices of torture, mass aggression, and genocide.[3]

Africa

While most of the new nations of Africa have constitutional provisions that are designed to protect individuals and groups, torture has become a common tool for governments and for continuing tribal warfare. There have been large-scale religious-ethnic conflicts in Nigeria, Uganda, Sudan, and Burundi.

For example, Burundi has a population of 3.2 million,

of which the Hutu community constitutes 84 percent, but the government is in the hands of the Tutsi minority. When, in 1972, the Hutu unsuccessfully tried to displace the government, there followed massacres of Hutus estimated to number between 90,000 and 250,000. The United States sent relief supplies, and tried to get the United Nations and the Organization of African Unity to intervene to stop the killing. But the American ambassador, Thomas P. Melady (see his book, *Burundi: The Tragic Years*) grieved that more could not be done.[4] "Selective outrage" appears to dominate the United Nations and the massacre of black people in Africa cannot get the time of day before this international forum of human rights.

In the African Republic of Chad, President Ngarta Tombalbaye announced in August 1973 a "cultural revolution" or policy of "Chaditude" to divest the four million inhabitants of the influence of French colonialism. There has been a revival of the ancient tribal custom of Yondo, which imposes floggings, facial searings, and trials such as crawling naked through a nest of termites. It is reported that in July 1974 a thousand officials were sent to Yondo camps, many of whom did not return; those who did return behave as though they were divorced from their past and their families and friends. The 52 percent of the people who make up a Muslim majority, and the 5 percent Christians both oppose the Yondo rites. It has been reported that more than 130 native Protestant pastors and lay church leaders have been assassinated since November 1973. President Tombalbaye was assassinated recently, and the military junta that succeeded him has promised a new and honorable course.

Since its independence in 1962, Uganda has been regarded as the African state where human rights are violated most frequently. Tribal conflicts prevail. Prime Minister Obote ousted the president in 1966 and was himself ousted in 1971 by the military under General Idi Amin whose oppressive rule has done little to reduce tribal conflicts. Massacres and mutilations have been added to the older practices of torture.

On August 5, 1972, Amin launched one of the greatest acts of racism of this decade—the brutalization of Asians. By November 1972, he had expelled 50,000 Asians in circumstances of mass suffering and cruelty. Ambassador Melady reports that Amin is responsible for the massacre of 80,000 black Christians during the last four years. On July 2, 1975, sixteen Catholic priests were expelled from Uganda by Amin's government.

During November 1972, Amin hosted a state dinner for King Faisal of Saudi Arabia. The late "Protector of Islam" unleashed a bitter attack on the Jews of the world, and copies of the discredited *Protocols of the Elders of Zion* were distributed to each of the dinner guests as "mementos" of the occasion.

In Zambia, also, tribal conflicts continue along with an effort to institute a one-party system of government.

Congo-Zaire expelled all Nigerian traders after confiscating their assets. Many were kept for a year in detention, suffering torture and even death.

In the Sudan, the Arabic-speaking group in the north, who are Muslim, massacred an estimated one million blacks in the south, who were either Christian or pagan. The issue of wholesale slaughter was never allowed to surface for examination before any tribunal or commission of the United Nations.

Despite some recent gestures toward reconciliation, a highly threatening situation exists in Rhodesia and in South Africa, where white minorities persist in oppressive rule over the region. There is reason for genuine anxiety over the possibility that there will be severe bloodshed of both whites and blacks unless a solution more acceptable than apartheid can be found. The practice of racism and persecution by whites against blacks has managed to obtain the sustained interest of and action by the United Nations and the Organization of African Unity.

Asia

The situation in Asia has not been better. The events in

China call for an independent study of that nation alone. Suffice it to note for our purposes, before the Communists took over in 1949, 90 percent of the Chinese people practiced a mixture of Buddhism, Taoism, and Confucianism, while 1 percent were (at one time at least) nominally Christian. The Western missionaries came under repeated attack from various regimes, but the decisive blows were dealt by the Communists. After they took over in 1949, they seized most religious property as part of their land reform program. The foreign missions lost large holdings. Buddhist temples were gradually closed and pressure was applied to eliminate family ancestral shrines. The traditional religions of China—whose central focus is on the family rather than on service to the state—have gradually yielded to the cult of Mao.

Even though freedom of religion is specifically guaranteed in the Chinese Constitution, and the government maintains a bureau of religious affairs, religion is officially "discouraged." All that remains of the Catholic Church in China are 5,000 worshipers and ten cathedral priests in Peking. Protestantism, too, has all but disappeared, except for a Protestant church in Peking which conducts Sunday services for a congregation which is entirely foreign.

The military activities of Communist China against the people of Tibet in the 1950s deprived them of life and land, and drove their spiritual leader, the Dalai Lama, from their midst. Not far away, about 200,000 East Pakistanis were massacred by their own Muslim brothers. As a result, the sufferings in Bangladesh continue unabated. Some ten million refugees fled into India during the violent birth of Bangladesh as it broke away from Pakistan in 1971. Nearly a quarter million more, stranded in hostile territory, were shuttled by jet between West Pakistan and Bangladesh. Millions of lives were lost in Vietnam and in Cambodia, and the massacres are far from concluded. It is despairing to contemplate the fact that so much of the once productive lands and people of Southeast Asia has been destroyed by weapons produced in the "friendly"

United States, as well as in Communist countries which are ostensibly engaged in détente.

In Asia, the ordinary hazards of torture and massacre due to ethnic and religious differences and political conflicts tend to be overwhelmed by the severer pressures of poverty and overpopulation. As noted in the report of Amnesty International:

> In societies where the problems of malnutrition, disease and illiteracy have not yet been solved, torture and the denial of human rights may stand out with less clarity than in more economically developed areas; in most Asian countries, these problems are further compounded by population pressures, and in some by deep ideological division. . . .
>
> The situation [in Indonesia] is aggravated by a low popular level of legal awareness which means that many victims are deterred from describing their treatment not only through fear, but also through ignorance of the fact that they have basic rights which are being violated. Conversely, in the case of Indochina, the availability of evidence is determined not only by the gravity of the situation but also by the international character of the conflict.[5]

Several hundred thousand Communists were massacred in Indochina in the absence of any effective international protests. The World Council of Churches was compelled to cancel its 1975 General Assembly in Jakarta for fear of reprisals from Muslim fanatics.

In India, along with keen sensitivity to human rights, there has developed "an increasingly rigorous program of counter-insurgency" that has jailed many thousands of suspected Marxist-Leninists. This is in reaction to "selective assassinations of landlords, policemen and other 'agents of the state machinery' which began in the West Bengal countryside in 1967 and shifted to Calcutta in 1970" (p. 143). However, conditions in India appear almost beyond outside help as long as there are continuing growth of her population; general backwardness in technology, agriculture, and education; little initiative for self-help; and poor use of the resources of the nation. The great wealth of the land is limited to an elitist fraction whose concern for the nation as a whole appears to leave much to be desired. Although the caste system has been outlawed, its influence persists in the life of the people. Disease and malnutrition keep the life expectancy low, a condition that encourages bearing more children to assure care of the aged. The moves that Indira Gandhi took to silence the opposition raised grave concern about the future of democracy in this country.

Europe

In the European sphere, although conditions in Communist countries have improved substantially since the Stalin era, the use of torture and other modes of physical violence against the human person have been far from eliminated. In the Soviet Union in particular, the practice continues of forcibly committing to psychiatric hospitals individuals who are declared by government officials to be dissenters or who wish to exercise the "right to leave" as vouchsafed to them by the United Nations. The reciprocal bombings of civilians by Catholic and Protestant extremists in Ireland depress religious people everywhere.

Middle East

Massacre and torture gripped innocent civilians of both the Greek and Turkish communities on Cyprus. The plight of hundreds of thousands of refugees on Cyprus cried out for some of the attention and amelioration that seemed to be reserved exclusively for Palestinian Arabs. Muslim Kurds also suffered at the hands of their coreligionists in Iraq and Turkey. The complex problems of the Middle East, compounded as they are by the problems of the legitimate right of self-determination for the Jewish people of Israel and for the Palestinian Arabs, are bedeviled by a repetitive cycle of terrorism by the Palestine Liberation Organization and the ensuing Israeli reprisals in self-defense to prevent further massacres of innocent children as at Ma'alot, Nahariya, and elsewhere.

Latin America

In Latin America, where with a few exceptions governments tend to be dictatorships, police brutality and harsh prison treatments remain a traditional and largely accepted part of the social structure. Torture continues in Chile and is still widely used in Brazil despite pledges by the government to halt the barbaric practices. According to a report compiled by Brazilian Roman Catholics and by victims and their attorneys, over the past nine years thousands have been subjected to beatings, electric shocks, and other torments at the hands of the military security forces. The story as it applies to some of the Indian tribes of Brazil appears to add still larger dimensions to the tragedies and national problems. The story varies only in degree in the other nations of South and Central America.

North America

In the United States, while the policies are certainly intended to promote civil liberties, peace, and prosperity in the world, the revelations of Watergate and the Senate hearings regarding the planned assassinations by the Central Intelligence Agency and the invasion of privacy by the Federal Bureau of Investigation and the Internal Revenue Service with their data banks and compilations of "enemy lists" left millions of Americans feeling increasingly insecure about their constitutional democracy. Denial of rights and equal opportunities to many blacks, American Indians, and Latin-speaking people is very much part of the "unfinished agenda" of the American people.

The mood of pessimism, even despair, that has emerged over the human prospect in the face of these assaults against human life is further compounded by several universal problems that show no signs of going away in the foreseeable future.

First, there is the problem of world hunger and overpopulation. There are, despite the recent heroic efforts to provide massive food supplies, some four hundred million people in Asia, Africa, and Latin America who are starving or suffering from severe malnutrition. Despite its great wealth, in the United States some fourteen million people still are the victims of poverty and millions still go to bed hungry every night. It is estimated that several million people in the developing countries will die from hunger during the coming year.

The world's present economic condition, Robert Heilbroner writes, resembles an immense train in which a few passengers, mainly in the advanced capitalist countries, ride in first-class coaches, in conditions of comfort unimaginable to the enormously greater numbers crammed into the cattle cars that make up the bulk of the train's carriages!

Second, there are the arms race and the proliferation of nuclear weapons. In 1973, $240 billion were spent to train, equip, and maintain armed forces. The international trade in nonnuclear arms now tops $18 billion annually—up from a mere $300 million in 1952. In 1974, after processing nearly 14,000 export license applications from private firms, the Office of Munitions Control approved sales to 136 countries totaling $8.3 billion—representing 46 percent of total world sales.

The Soviet Union is second in international arms sales—$39 billion since 1950, $5.5 billion in 1974. The Middle East is the biggest customer of both the United States and Russia—first Iran, then Israel, next Saudi Arabia ($756 million). Russia's latest arms deal with Libya will further increase the Soviet stake in the Middle East arms game, which is characterized by cheap credit and cut-rate prices. France is third with a sale of $3 billion to eighty nations, and Britain follows with $1.5 billion.

In 1973, Third World nations imported $7.7 billion worth of arms, with Iran in the past two years spending $7.6 billion in the United States alone. (Pentagon officials joke that the Persian Gulf will sink under all the arms that it is buying.)

Impoverished India has spent $3 billion in the Soviet Union for arms in the past three years. Pakistan, scrimping to find $250 million for a new fertilizer factory, spends at least that much on weapons annually.

The arms trade can scarcely advance peace. In each of the sixty military conflicts since the end of World War II, imported weapons were used almost exclusively, and those arms have brought not only violence and destruction but death to more than ten million people (according to the MIT Center for International Studies).

Third, the advent of nuclear weapons with their potential for "irreparable" damage, as contrasted with the much more restricted and more easily repaired damage of most conventional wars, has created a whole new technology of war for the coming decades. Unleashing the warheads now possessed by the United States and by the Soviets could bring fatalities ranging from 50,000,000 to 135,000,000 people in the United States alone. Moreover, many small or relatively poor nations, even though they possess no fully developed industrial base or highly skilled labor force, can gain possession of nuclear weapons—witness China and India. Today there are 426 nuclear power plants in thirty-nine nations, a number of which could produce atomic bombs as well as electricity. Poor nations can be expected to obtain nuclear weapons as a by-product of the atomic power plants that many of them are now building or contemplating, and it is quite conceivable that some may use these as instruments of blackmail to force the developed world to undertake a massive transfer of wealth to the poverty-stricken world.

What are the implications of these facts for Christians and Jews today? What relation do these developments have to the Nazi holocaust?

It is evident that we live in an age of violence and of terror. There is not a continent on the globe that is not despoiled by terror and violence, by barbarism, by a growing callousness to human suffering, and by pain and threat to human existence. At the center of the human crisis today is the fundamental depreciation of the meaning and value of human life. In theological terms, the biblical affirmation that each human life is created in the sacred image of God and is therefore of ultimate worth and preciousness is being battered from every side.

It is my conviction that this erosion in the belief of the sanctity of human life is one of the decisive black legacies bequeathed by Nazi Germany to mankind. By and large, with rare exception, the overwhelming majority of citizens and dominant institutions of the Western world have avoided confronting the magnitude of evil incarnate in the Nazi holocaust, and have therefore failed to learn how to cope with forces and structures of dehumanization that are being multiplied in many parts of the globe.

The Nazi campaign of genocide against the Jewish people was unique and in many ways unprecedented. Yet the Nazi trauma must not be seen as "a Jewish obsession," for the fateful meaning of that holocaust is of ultimate importance to the future capacity of mankind to understand itself and to acquire the resources to cope with the challenges to its survival.

As Lucy Dawidowicz has written in her recent study, *The War Against the Jews, 1933-1945*, the uniqueness of the Nazi holocaust against the Jewish people lay in the fact that

> the final solution of the Jewish Question was not just another anti-Semitic undertaking, but a metahistorical program devised with an eschatological perspective. It was part of a salvational ideology that envisaged the attainment of heaven by bringing hell on earth.[6]

André Malraux called it, *"le retour de Satan."*

To attain the goal of a heavenly hell on earth, the Nazi war killed over thirty-five million people, more than half of them civilians. The human cost of the 2,191 days of war surpassed the losses of any previous war in the history of the world.

The slaughter of six million Jewish men, women, and children—two out of every three European Jews—was the most massive destruction and disastrous catastrophe in Jewish history. Though one-third of the Jews survived, though Judaism and the Jewish people outlived the Third

Reich, the Germans succeeded in destroying irrevocably the life and culture of East European Jewry. Even the destruction of the Second Temple, the greatest Jewish national trauma, did not place the physical survival of Jews in such jeopardy as did the Nazi holocaust. (In 70 C.E. only about one-quarter of the Jews lived in Palestine, the rest were scattered throughout the diaspora. In 1939, two-thirds of the Jews lived in Europe; three-quarters of them—one-half of world Jewry—were in Eastern Europe.)

Never before in modern history, Dawidowicz writes, has one people made the killing of another the fulfillment of an ideology, in the pursuit of which the means were identical with the ends. The German state, deciding that the Jews should not live, arrogated to itself the judgment as to whether a whole people had the right to existence, a judgment that no person and no state have the right to make. The German dictatorship involved and engaged the entire bureaucratic and functional apparatus of the German state and the Nazi movement and employed the best available technological means.

And in that reality lodges the universal implication for the whole of mankind. The "final solution" destroyed East European Jews. In doing so, it subverted fundamental principles and every system of law that has governed, however imperfectly, human society for millennia.

A hitherto unbreachable moral and political barrier in the history of Western civilization was successfully overcome by the Germans in World War II, and henceforth the extermination of millions of citizens or subject peoples will forever be one of the capabilities and temptations of government. In a period in which a faltering economic system has condemned millions of able-bodied workers to redundance, in a time in which global overpopulation contends with scarcity of food supplies and other shrinking resources, the prospect of disposing of surplus population becomes a temptation more likely to be enhanced than diminished. Witness the calm, objective manner in which *triage* is discussed today in learned circles.

All this is to say that Auschwitz has enlarged our conception of the state's capacity to do violence. The Nazi period serves as a warning of what we may become if we are faced with a political crisis of overwhelming proportions.

Usually, progress in death-dealing capacity in the twentieth century has been reckoned in terms of technological advances in weaponry. Too little attention has been given to the "advances" in social organization that made it possible to cross residual moral barriers and massacre millions. To understand these advances it is necessary to consider the role of bureaucracy in modern political and social organization. Writing in 1916, the great German sociologist, Max Weber, said:

> When fully developed, bureaucracy stands under the principle of *sine ira ac studio* [without scorn or bias]. Its specific nature develops the more perfectly the more bureaucracy is dehumanized, the more completely it succeeds in eliminating from official business love, hatred and purely personal and irrational elements which escape calculation. This is the specific nature of bureaucracy, and it is appraised as its specific virtue.[7]

Both the Nazi and the non-Nazi bureaucrats insisted that anti-Jewish measures were to be taken in a disciplined, systematic, and methodical manner—as in the manufacture of a Leica or a Mercedes.

Max Weber's writings on bureaucracy were part of a larger attempt to understand the social structure and value of modern civilization. According to Weber, modern bureaucracy can be understood as a structural and organizational expression of related processes of *secularization, disenchantment of the world,* and *rationalization.*

The secularization process involves the liberation of ever wider areas of human activity from religious domination. The disenchantment of the world occurs when "there are no mysterious forces that come into play, but rather . . . one can, in principle, master all things by calculation." Rationalization involves "the methodical attainment of a definitely given and practical end by means of an increasingly precise calculation of adequate means."[8]

In the disenchantment of the natural and political orders, the domain of the sacred was increasingly relegated to the heavenly sphere. A beginning was made toward that secularization of consciousness which finally culminates in the most extreme form of secular disenchantment—the dehumanized, rationalized forms of modern political and social organization, including bureaucratically administered death camps.

In the biblical world all human activity stands under the judgment of a righteous deity. In the modern world, the supramundane deity has disappeared for all practical purposes—persons are alone in the world, free to pursue any end they choose, including mass murder, "by means of an increasingly precise calculation of adequate means."

Nevertheless, before the "dehumanized" attitude of bureaucracy in which "love, hatred and purely personal and irrational elements" are eliminated in one's dealing with his fellows could be acquired, the disenchantment process had to become culturally predominant; God and the world had to be so radically disjoined that it became possible to treat both the political and natural orders with uncompromisingly dispassionate objectivity. This occurred with the triumph of certain traditions of Protestantism and their insistence upon the radical transcendence of God.

Their triumph opened the path in the twentieth century to such radical secularization of consciousness that the question of eliminating "surplus people" lost all religious and moral significance and became a question only of bureaucratic problem-solving.

Contrary to popular opinion, as Richard Rubenstein has noted, the Nazi holocaust was not carried out by a group of irresponsible criminals on the fringes of society who somehow forced the German people to pursue a policy of ethnic hatred that was wholly at odds with the great traditions of Western civilization. Indeed, we are far more likely to understand the extermination of Europe's Jews if we regard it as the expression of some of the profound tendencies of twentieth-century Western civilization.

In an earlier age, most men and women genuinely stood in awe of the judgment of divinity, of a natural and God-ordained law binding upon all persons and nations; but is this any longer true, especially for the decision-making elites? Does not the history of the Nazi holocaust and the fate of its perpetrators demonstrate that there are absolutely no limits to the degradation and assault technicians of violence can inflict upon men and women who lack the power of effective resistance? (Reflect here on why Israelis—especially those who survived the holocaust—insist upon safe, genuinely secure borders and conditions of guaranteed nonbelligerency, and why they will not [indeed cannot afford to] rely on rhetorical flourishes of Arab leaders vaguely assuring peace and co-existence, particularly when these speeches are broadcast to the Western world but withheld from domestic Arab populations. What trust can any open-eyed Israeli or anyone else put in such assurances of public relations while all the Arab actions move in the opposite direction of rendering Israel impotent by trying to reduce it to pariah status through elimination from UNESCO, the WHO, the ILO, and quite possibly from the UN itself?)

It is true that a few miserable Nazi camp guards were incarcerated after World War II, but the government and corporate bureaucrats who planned the entire operation and really made it possible returned very quickly to places of dignity and honor in German society. If there is a law that is devoid of all penalty when it is violated, does it have any functional significance in terms of human behavior? Is not a law that carries no penalty functionally equivalent to no law at all? Even if it can be demonstrated to "exist" can it not be safely ignored? We are sadly forced to conclude that we live in a world that is functionally godless and increasingly lawless.

The process of secularization thus ends where it began. In the beginning it involved the demystification and limitation of a sovereign's power. In the end the secular state has dethroned all mystifications of power save its own. The state thus becomes the only true god on earth. It is possessed of the ultimate power of divinity, the power to decide who shall live and who shall die. No cold-blooded contemporary need worry like David about a modern Nathan the prophet proclaiming the ultimacy of God's law. This does not mean that the sovereign is above limits; he or she can be limited but only by the laws of persons acting in concert, at best a tenuous guarantee of a humane society.

Bleak as are the prospects for countering these forces of dehumanization in the world, "we need not complete the task," as Rabbi Tarphon admonished, "but neither are we free to desist therefrom." In concert, if we are to learn from the Nazi holocaust and not be doomed to allow its repetition, we must attempt at the very least the following:

First, Christians and Jews must help engender a national and international attitude of scorn and contempt for those who use violence or who advocate the use of violence. We must work to deromanticize all appeals to use violence and terrorism as means of liberation or of institutional oppression, since from a moral standpoint, no ends can justify such antihuman means.

Second, Christians and Jews must work to curtail the resort to inflammatory propaganda, especially from international forums which have psychological impact on an international scale. As Gordon Allport of Harvard University demonstrated in his monumental study, *The Nature of Prejudice,* there is an inevitable progression "from verbal aggression to violence, from rumor to riot, from gossip to genocide."[9]

Third, Christians and Jews must work toward educational development and communication among peoples to reduce the abrasive effects of "differences." Differences, as we have learned in the pluralistic experience of America, can be a source of enrichment rather than a threat.

Fourth, Christians and Jews should engage in a massive effort to establish on a global basis a "new humanism" that seeks to restore the biblical value of the infinite worth and preciousness of each human life. We must also engage in an urgent and sustained intellectual and educational effort to elaborate a theology and ideology of pluralism which presuppose the right of each religious, racial, and ethnic group to define itself in its own terms and to be accepted unconditionally under that definition. Christians and Jews have a decisive contribution to make to the building of the ideological foundations without which a stable world community cannot come into being.

Fifth, Christians and Jews should work toward making the economy of each nation as self-sufficient and stable as possible in the sense of not perpetually requiring relief support. Inextricably linked with such an effort is the control of the arms race on an international scale, gun control in America, and a rational reordering of priorities that allows for adequate defense and yet at the same time reallocates some of the billions wasted on arms to the crying needs of the hungry, the diseased, and the homeless.

And finally, Christians and Jews should work for the completion of the judicial instrumentalities called for by Article 6 of the Genocide Convention in the form of an international penal tribunal for trying those who are accused of genocide attempts anywhere in the world.

"The salvation of mankind," Alexander Solzhenitsyn reminds us, "will depend on everyone becoming concerned about the welfare of everybody everywhere."

NOTES

1. Erich Fromm, *The Anatomy of Human Destructiveness* (New York: Holt, Rinehart & Winston, 1973), p. 18.

2. Robert L. Heilbroner, *An Inquiry into the Human Prospect* (New York: Norton & Co., 1973), p. 24.

3. Nathan Glazer, "The Universalization of Ethnicity," *Encounter* (February 1975), 8.

4. Thomas P. Melady, *Burundi: The Tragic Years* (Maryknoll, NY: Orbis Books, 1974), p. 4.

5. Amnesty International, *Report on Torture* (London: Gerald Duckworth and Co., Ltd., 1973), pp. 138-39.

6. Lucy S. Dawidowicz, *The War Against the Jews, 1933-1945* (New York: Holt, Rinehart & Winston, 1975), p. 153.

7. Max Weber, *Essays in Sociology* (New York: Oxford University Press, 1958), p. 195.

8. Ibid.

9. Gordon W. Allport, *The Nature of Prejudice* (New York: Doubleday, 1958), p. 57.

12

PAUL E. TOMS

Evangelical Christians and Social Responsibility

James Stewart suggests very clearly to us where Christian action and responsibility lie.

> For after all, where is the Lord Jesus surely to be found today? Where is what a sacramental theology would call, "the real presence of Christ"? No doubt in word and sacrament and worship, in all the ordinances of the faith, here in this church, yonder in your own room when you kneel to pray. Yes, but also and most certainly in the flesh and blood of every needy soul throughout God's earth today. This, if only we had eyes to see and heart to understand, is where Christ the King comes forth to meet us. Did he not tell us this himself? "I was hungry, and you gave me no meat; sick and in prison, and you visited me not. Then shall they answer him, Lord, when saw we thee hungry or sick or in prison, and did not minister to thee? Then shall he answer them, inasmuch as you did it not to one of the least of these, you did it not to me."
> Here is the real presence: Every homeless refugee, every hungry child, every racially segregated soul from whom a western culture stands conditionally and patronizingly aloof; and to come nearer home—that troublesome neighbor, that handicapped sufferer, that poor bungler who has made a wretched mess of his life, that woman who carries a hidden tragedy in her heart, that paganized youth who will tell you he

233

has no use for your religion or for your God. This is the real presence; and if we are not prepared to see and serve him there, in his needy brethren, all our expressions of love of God are worthless and our religious professions frivolous.[1]

I chose this rather long quotation for its directness and its biblical understanding of concern for the so-called social issues. Professor William Barclay points out that the ancient world was inordinately obsessed with concern for genealogies and the tracings of family lineages.[2] Alexander the Great had created for himself a completely artificial pedigree that went back to the Greek gods. People seemed to spend tremendous amounts of time working on romantic and fictitious tales concerning the foundations of cities and families.

Paul wrote to young Timothy at Ephesus: "Command certain men not to teach false doctrines any longer, nor to devote themselves to myths and endless genealogies. These promote controversy rather than God's work" (I Tim. 1:3, 4, NIV). Here is a biblical challenge not to sit around working on imaginary things when there are so many real problems in the world. Recently a friend told of this experience. A little girl and her father went to lunch together at an outdoor sandwich shop. They sat at a table enjoying the pleasant weather and throwing little pieces of bread to the birds. Suddenly a man, tattered, disheveled, and with a furtive look, picked up some of the crumbs and greedily stuffed them in his mouth. In astonishment, the little girl watched this scene and upon reflection turned to her father and said, "Let's take care of the man; God will take care of the birds." Perhaps one of the dangers with which we all are constantly faced is that of giving ourselves to the feeding of the pigeons when the real issues of life go unattended.

My task is to review a bit of the evangelical perspective as it relates to social action. I need only briefly remind you that I do not speak for all evangelicals. And though I have the happy privilege at the moment of being President of the National Association of Evangelicals, I would not purport to be speaking officially for that organization. We are very individualistic. We do not always give the impression that we are united in our efforts. We carefully guard our understanding of the "priesthood of every believer," and this often leads to individual efforts and interpretations. The extremely significant Lausanne Congress on World Evangelization produced a highly important document with clear and helpful statements, in my opinion, on a wide-ranging area of concerns, including social responsibilities. However, not *all* evangelicals would necessarily sign that document, some feeling it did not go far enough, and others feeling it went too far. Thus, my words are only widely representative of the general position of the evangelicals with whom I am acquainted. It will be necessary for you to sift through some of this material to find some basic principles and concerns declared and illustrated.

Biblical Principles

A friend of mine told me some time ago that in conversation with a Christian believer from Latin America, he was asked, "How is it that your creeds never seem to reflect justice when our observation is that so much emphasis is given to justice in Scripture?" We must face up to this question. Indeed, our creeds are vitally important to us. It is essential and necessary that we continue to study the Scripture carefully in order that we may be able to declare with precision and confidence a biblical groundwork of our faith.

We as evangelicals speak often of the need for presenting the gospel so that the winning of souls may be evident. Some of us have been challenged by the words of a Christian from the Third World who suggested that we are to come to the task of winning *people* to faith in Jesus Christ. Perhaps you have heard of the old farmer in the Midwest who was visited annually by members of the local church in order to attempt to get him to come to the yearly revival meeting held in their congregation. One year, the old man responded to the invitation by saying, "I wish you cared as much for me as you seem to care for my soul."

For some there seems to have been a recent broadening of the understanding that evangelism involves the whole man. Dr. George Peters, Professor of Missions at Dallas Theological Seminary, in an address I heard recently, spoke of the *whole* man, and pointed out that this kind of an understanding involves training and discipling of the individual. This opens up new vistas for social activities and involvement.

God surely is concerned with the whole person. The Old Testament speaks of this concern in dramatic and challenging language. For example, "He hath shewed thee, O man, what is good; and what doth the Lord require of thee, but to do justly, and to love mercy, and to walk humbly with thy God?" (Mic. 6:8). We might also note Amos 5:10-12, 21-24:

> They hate him that rebuketh in the gate, and they abhor him that speaketh uprightly. Forasmuch therefore as your treading is upon the poor, and ye take from him burdens of wheat; ye have built houses of hewn stone, but ye shall not dwell in them; ye have planted pleasant vineyards, but ye shall not drink wine of them. For I know your manifold transgressions and your mighty sins: they afflict the just, they take a bribe, and they turn aside the poor in the gate from their right. . . . I hate, I despise your feast days, and I will not smell in your solemn assemblies. Though you offer me burnt offerings and your meat offerings, I will not accept them: neither will I regard the peace offerings of your fat beasts. Take thou away from me the noise of thy songs; for I will not hear the melody of thy viols. But let judgment run down as waters, and righteousness as a mighty stream.

Isaiah 1:10-17 and 58:1-10 strike a similar chord. The Scriptures clearly point out that man is a social being, his very nature ties him in with his fellow man. His essence indicates that he is a total being. Human nature cannot be divided into spiritual and physical areas; we are one person. God, through his law, through his prophets, calls for a sense of obligation to the whole man. Man indeed is his brother's keeper.

Injustice, oppression, evil, and unrighteousness are all roundly condemned in the Old Testament. Men are charged with responsibility toward the disenfranchised, the poor, the maltreated, the widow and the orphan. It is impossible for us to find in the Old Testament a bifurcation of social justice and spirituality. With strength and authority the Old Testament calls for righteousness before God, evidenced by an obedience to his law and a right relationship with and concern for one's neighbor.

Turning to the New Testament, we read: "For even the Son of man came not to be ministered unto, but to minister, and to give his life a ransom for many" (Mark 10:45). The Scripture points out that Jesus fed the hungry, he healed, he restored, he had a basic concern for the material needs of people. To be sure, he did suggest very clearly that a man's life consists not in the abundance of the things that he possesses; but he was concerned for those who had no abundance. Certainly one of the most telling illustrations of our responsibility lies in the story of the Good Samaritan. We are challenged in the Scripture to love God, and our neighbor (Matt. 22:37-39). In the epistles we read: "He that loveth his brother abideth in the light, and there is none occasion of stumbling in him" (I John 2:10), and "My little children, let us not love in word, neither in tongue; but in deed and truth" (I John 3:18). The apostle James makes a similar suggestion:

> What doth it profit, my brethren, though a man say he hath faith, and have not works? Can faith save him? If a brother or sister be naked, and destitute of daily food, and one of you say unto them, Depart in peace, be ye warmed and filled; notwithstanding ye give them not those things which are needful to the body; what doth it profit? Even so faith, if it hath not works, is dead, being alone. Yea, a man may say, Thou hast

faith, and I have works: shew me thy faith without thy works, and I will shew thee my faith by my works. (James 2:14-18)

An extraordinary passage is found in the Book of Titus: "Not by works of righteousness which we have done, but according to his mercy ... he saved us, by washing of regeneration, and renewing of the Holy Ghost. This is a faithful saying, and these things I will that thou affirm constantly, that they which have believed in God might be careful to maintain good works. These things are good and profitable unto men" (Titus 3:5, 8). Evangelism calls for faith in Jesus Christ based upon his atonement. But the next emphasis is that once this has been acknowledged, the sky is the limit as to the amount of good works in which the evangelical should be involved.

In Acts 20:27, we see the emphasis upon the whole will of God. We are challenged to preach the whole counsel of God and this includes the kingship of Christ and the recognition that all of life is his. And in Romans 11:36—12:2 we read: "For of him, and through him, and to him, are all things: to whom be glory forever. Amen. I beseech you therefore, brethren, by the mercies of God, that ye present your bodies a living sacrifice, holy, acceptable unto God, which is your reasonable service. And be not conformed to this world: but be ye transformed by the renewing of your mind, that ye may prove what is that good, and acceptable, and perfect, will of God." Again we see that *all* of life belongs to him. God owns everything. We are to acknowledge him as Lord of all. Both the psalmist and the writer of the Book of Hebrews emphasize this: "Thou madest him to have dominion over the works of thy hands; thou hast put all things under his feet: all sheep and oxen, yea, and the beasts of the field; the fowl of the air, and the fish of the sea, and whatsoever passeth through the paths of the seas" (Ps. 8:6-8). "Thou hast put all things in subjection under his feet. For in that he put all in subjection under him, he left nothing that is not put under him. But now we see not yet all things put under him" (Heb. 2:8). According to the Scripture, we will be held accountable. "But I say unto you, that every idle word that men shall speak, they shall give account thereof in the day of judgment" (Matt. 12:36). "Therefore is the kingdom of heaven likened unto a certain king, which would take account of his servants" (Matt. 18:23). "But he that knew not, and did commit things worthy of stripes, shall be beaten with few stripes. For unto whomsoever much is given, of him shall be much required: and to whom men have committed much, of him they will ask the more" (Luke 12:48). "So then everyone of us shall give account of himself to God" (Rom. 14:12). "For we must all appear before the judgment seat of Christ; that everyone may receive the things done in his body, according to that he hath done, whether it be good or bad" (II Cor. 5:10). The good news of God in Jesus Christ extends to all areas of life—politics, the community, the family, and personal behavior. For the evangelical Christian there is no difference between the secular and the sacred; all of life is sacred and must be treated as such.

The Implications and Interaction

Dr. Horace L. Fenton, Jr., the General Director of the Latin America Mission, told me recently that he was charged with an assignment similar to mine, except that his assignment took place ten years ago! He suggested that at that time it was almost impossible for him to find literature, even brief articles that were speaking to this point from an evangelical perspective. This is no longer true. Today a tremendous corpus of literature is available; I hope you have read some of it and will continue to profit by additional study. I list a few of these books at the end of this paper. For the moment, I can only review and suggest some general areas and trust that this will be sufficient to point up the availability of material for additional study.

One of the more recent volumes is *The Great Reversal* by Dr. David O. Moberg. He points out, "There was a time when evangelicals had a balanced position that gave proper attention to both evangelism and social concern, but a great reversal early in this century led to a lopsided emphasis upon evangelism and omission of most aspects of social involvement."[3] Moberg borrows the term *great reversal* from historian Timothy L. Smith. Both of these men have attempted to document this idea in great detail. We can say here only that historically evangelicals have indeed been deeply involved in attention to social evils. Missions, employment bureaus, orphanages, and agencies to meet the needs of the poor are illustrations of this concern.

It has been suggested that one of the reasons (and many reasons have been offered) for the apparent neglect of social concerns in more recent times has been the "concentration by evangelicals on other legitimate issues."[4] Carl F. H. Henry suggests that the neglect of the good news of salvation for sinners by advocates of the social gospel imposed upon conservatives the staggering burden of biblical evangelism and missions throughout the world.[5] There have been stronger suggestions along this line, sometimes laced with stronger language! Evangelicals have been berated for indeed being conformed to this world in defiance of Romans 12:2. They have "made it," and will not allow anything to threaten that; their catchword is, "Come weal or woe, my status is quo."

Religious News Service reported a few weeks ago the celebration of the twenty-fifth anniversary of the National Council of Churches. The report stated that a prevalent theme of that anniversary was the closing of the gap between Christians who stress social action and those emphasizing personal evangelism.

William P. Thompson, stated clerk of the United Presbyterian Church, and also the president of the National Council for the next three years, told a press conference that he sees the convergence of interests in the council. He noted that many who have stressed social action are expressing a growing concern for spiritual life, worship, and personal evangelism. Thompson also suggested that he sees new evidence that "conservative evangelicals" are realizing that personal evangelism without social initiatives forms an "incomplete gospel."

The picture is not all bleak. In spite of impediments, in spite of thinking that perhaps has led people to believe that conversion automatically ends all problems, and in spite of various gradations of understanding and activity, there indeed is renewed concern for the sharing of the gospel with the *whole* man.

A recent article by Dr. Ronald J. Sider, Dean of Messiah College (Philadelphia), in the *International Review of Mission,* has given to us a very careful treatment and review of our subject. This article is well worth reading. He very carefully points out that evangelism and social action are *not* one and the same. Dr. Sider leads up to this by reviewing what he understands to be several conflicting viewpoints on the purpose and the mission of the church. He suggests that these viewpoints range all the way from the notion that the *only* mission of the church is to save souls, to the extreme that the basic mission of the church is to understand that "evangelism is politics, because salvation is social justice." Dr. Sider, in my opinion, rightfully asserts that "there is no New Testament justification for talking about 'evangelizing political structures.' "[6] He concludes: "According to the New Testament, then, evangelism involves the announcement (through word and deed) of the good news that there is forgiveness of sins through the cross; that the Holy Spirit will regenerate twisted personalities; that Jesus is Lord; and that people today can join Jesus' new community where all social and economic relationships are being made new."[7]

Many evangelicals would agree that though our task of evangelism is not to be *confused* with the task of social action, both are vitally important parts of the responsibility of the church in the world today.

We are charged with the responsibility of preaching the gospel to the ends of the earth. It is our mission to proclaim the good news of redemption and new life and the truth of salvation as it is outlined for us in Scripture. This is not to say, however, that we have no responsibility in other directions. In a preface to a study guide to his book,

Knowing God, Dr. James I. Packer suggests that he would like to add a new dimension to his expressions in that volume. He says, "In addressing my readers as individuals, trying as best I can to single them out and search their hearts before God, I fail to show that it is only as one gives oneself in human relationships, in the home, in friendships, with neighbors, as members of Christian groups and teams—in relationships that sometimes go right and sometimes wrong, as all our relationships do—that experimental knowledge of God becomes real and deep."[8] This is in keeping with Moberg's statement: "To be true to God's will, the Christian must stretch out in love to bind up the bleeding wounds of humanity and to prevent future suffering."[9] We might add the words of Brady Tyson:

> No one (among the household of faith, at least) doubts that the church can and will survive new "dark ages," should they come: But this does not mean that the church is absolved of the responsibility to proclaim not only against existing injustice and evil, but also to warn against impending disasters, in the tradition of the great Old Testament prophets. It is perhaps not the time of the apocalypse, but the loss of political freedom by millions, and the muffling of those voices concerned with injustice and struggle against hunger, illiteracy and disease by a super-power détente must surely be the concern of the church.[10]

Evangelicals are actively engaged in a great variety of meaningful ministries that do indeed try faithfully to minister to the *whole* man. In keeping with the biblical perspective, the widows and orphans are of great concern to the evangelical. The preservation of the family structure with all of the tensions placed upon it by modern society is of high priority to an evangelical. People have needs that cause them to hurt and we consider our task only partly fulfilled unless we do all that we can to attempt to speak to those hurts. Thus, we try to be involved in not only feeding the starving, but helping people learn to read, encouraging them to improve their skills, suggesting ways and means by which they can better cope with some of the basic problems of life. We have special ministries for those who are addicted to drugs; we maintain "hot lines" for potential suicides in order that they may speak with someone who cares; we try to minister to the runaway, the disenchanted, the rejected and the rebellious. We are trying to assist people in their educational processes. Sometimes we are able to pay their rent, sometimes we are able to provide counsel and direction in terms of decisions that must be made.

A time of awakening has begun, particularly in the post-World War II years. As far back as 1947, Carl Henry was calling for the application of the whole gospel to all the spheres of man's welfare. Since the formation of the National Association of Evangelicals, those committed to this position have endeavored to apply the gospel to every phase of life, stressing humanitarian efforts as continued evidence of faith and the expression of the will of God. Bruce Shelley, in a brief review of evangelicalism in America, said, "While the evangelical ministry of World Relief and social concern is not all that NAE leaders envision, it is nevertheless a significant service to the suffering masses of our shattered world."[11]

Evangelicals are actively engaged in varying ministries. These ministries include adoption agencies, programs for unmarried parents, foster care, family counseling, family life education, tutoring, and assistance in meeting other demands of our society.

We are concerned with the place of Christians in government, the obtaining of justice by minority groups, the feeding of the hungry and starving, and the meeting of physical needs. We give attention to the hurts and problems people have, especially those problems that are inadequately handled by government agencies.

Evangelicals operate hospitals, clinics, health centers, schools, feeding stations, and clothing depots. We do this because it is right, moral, and biblical. These projects often afford opportunities for witness to our faith, but we feel a responsibility to engage in them for their own sake as well. A few months ago, while traveling in upper Ethiopia, I landed in a small plane in the midst of a desert that looked more like a moonscape scene, with shimmering heat waves, with mud and sand everywhere, and with water unsafe to drink. The chief of a tiny village had gathered his people around to express appreciation to representative Christians for feeding his starving tribesmen. He then suggested that because concern had been shown in this fashion, he was willing to allow the introduction of the Bible and its teaching. However, this was a plus factor; evangelical missionaries had been happy to help feed the village with no promise of eventually being allowed to preach the gospel in return.

Christian compassion has always resulted in a helping hand, the binding up of wounds, and the giving of a new sense of help and hope.

We agree with the remarks of Francis Schaeffer: "All men bear the image of God. They have value, not because they are redeemed but because they are God's creation in God's image."[12] Schaeffer contends that Christians "are not to love their believing brothers to the exclusion of their non-believing fellow men" (cf. Matt. 5:43-48; Luke 6:32-36).[13]

In a recent book by Stanley Mooneyham we are reminded that today is a good time for us to recall the words of Pope Paul VI, "If you want peace, work for justice. . . ."[14] We desire to be true descendants of the evangelical social reformers who clearly demonstrated their faith in social action. Our Lord was active in the context of life: eating, drinking, working, socializing, commenting on government, work, and responsibility. We try to recognize the reality of the two dimensions of the world in which we live, that is, we try to fulfill our *vertical* responsibility as well as our *horizontal* responsibility. The apostle Peter speaks of this in I Peter 2:17 when he suggests that among other things we are to fear God *and* honor the king. We do have a responsibility to God and we are determined that by his grace we shall fulfill that responsibility. However, we recognize that part of that responsibility is best fulfilled in interpersonal relationships and compassionate ministry. I remember reading of a missionary nurse who was binding up the wounds of terrible and repulsive diseases. A visitor from overseas, watching this for a few moments, finally said, "I would not do that for $10,000." The lady responded, "Neither would I." Only genuine compassion and love can overcome natural resistance and repugnance to difficult and demanding situations.

I will conclude with a quotation called to my attention by Dr. Vernon C. Grounds, in his little pamphlet called *Evangelicalism and Social Responsibility.*[15] He quotes from the autobiography of Bertrand Russell:

> Three passions, simple but overwhelmingly strong, have governed my life: The longing for love, the search for knowledge, and unbearable pity for the suffering of mankind. These passions, like great winds, have blown me hither and thither, in a wayward course, over a deep ocean of anguish, reaching to the very verge of despair.
>
> Love and knowledge, so far as they were possible, led upward toward the heavens. But always pity brought me back to earth. Echoes of cries of pain reverberate in my heart. Children in famine, victims tortured by oppressors, helpless old people, a hated burden to their sons, and a whole world of loneliness, poverty and pain make a mockery of what human life should be. I long to alleviate the evil, but I cannot, and I too suffer.[16]

Christian compassion surely can do no less. I rejoice in the growing evidence of a deep concern that is calling forth sacrificial service and a genuine compassion to minister as best we can to human needs.

Let me repeat two of the Scripture texts cited earlier; this time I will quote the New English Bible: "Suppose a brother or a sister is in rags with not enough food for the day, and one of you says, 'Good luck to you, keep yourselves warm, and have plenty to eat,' but does nothing to supply their bodily needs, what is the good of that? So with faith; if it does not lead to action, it is in itself a lifeless thing" (James 2:15-17). "If a man has enough to live on, and yet when he sees his brother in need shuts up his heart against him, how can it be said that the divine love dwells in him? My children, love must not be a matter of words or talk; it must be genuine and show itself in action. This is how we may know that we belong to the realm of truth" (I John 3:17-19).

NOTES

1. James Stewart, *The Wind of the Spirit* (New York: Abingdon, 1968), pp. 156-57.

2. William Barclay, *Timothy, Titus and Philemon* (Philadelphia: Westminster Press, 1960), pp. 29-30.

3. David O. Moberg, *The Great Reversal* (Philadelphia-New York: Lippencott, 1972), p. 35.

4. Ibid., pp. 25-26.

5. Carl F. H. Henry, *Contemporary Religious Issues,* ed. Donald E. Harstock (Belmont, CA: Wadsworth Publishing Co., 1968).

6. Ronald J. Sider, "Evangelism, Salvation and Social Justice," *International Review of Mission,* Vol. 64, July 1975, p. 251.

7. Ibid.

8. *Evangelical News Letter,* ed. William J. Peterson (Philadelphia: Evangelical Foundation, Inc.), Vol. 3, No. 1, November 7, 1975, p. 2.

9. Moberg, *The Great Reversal,* p. 23.

10. Brady Tyson, "The Mission of the Church in Contemporary Brazil: The Case of a Church in a Land of Poverty and Repression," *Missiology,* Vol. III, No. 3, July 1975, pp. 290-91.

11. Bruce Shelley, *Evangelicalism in America* (Grand Rapids: Eerdmans, 1967), p. 108.

12. Francis Schaeffer, *The Church at the End of the Twentieth Century* (Downers Grove, IL: Inter-Varsity Press, 1970), p. 134.

13. Ibid., p. 135.

14. Stanley Mooneyham, *What Do You Say to a Hungry World?* (Waco, TX: Word Books, 1975).

15. Vernon C. Grounds, *Evangelicalism and Social Responsibility* (Scottdale, PA: Herald Press, 1969).

16. Bertrand Russell, *Autobiography of Bertrand Russell* (Boston: Little, Brown and Co., 1967), pp. 3-4.

ADDITIONAL REFERENCES

Henry, Paul B., *Politics for Evangelicals* (Valley Forge, PA: Judson Press, 1974).

Wells, David F., and John D. Woodbridge, ed., *The Evangelicals* (New York: Abingdon, 1975).

Wirt, Sherwood, *Social Conscience of the Evangelical* (New York: Harper and Row, 1968).

13

VERNON C. GROUNDS

Evangelical Views of Today's Moral Crisis

I call myself an evangelical. I know quite precisely what I mean when I use that designation. Yet I am aware that evangelicalism is one of those countless religious concepts which different people define differently—and the difference is often radical. So let me begin with Kenneth Kantzer's itemization of those central beliefs confessed by American Christians who avow themselves to be evangelicals. These essentials, resting on the assumption of the infallible authority of the Bible, may be arranged in the following more or less logical order:

(1) The eternal preexistence of the Son as the second person of the one God; (2) the incarnation of God the Son in man as the divine-human person—two natures in one person; (3) the virgin birth, the means by which God the Son entered into the human race and, without ceasing to be fully God, became also fully man; (4) the sinless life of Christ while sharing the life and experiences of alien men apart from sin; (5) the supernatural miracles of Christ as acts of his compassion and signs of his divine nature; (6) Christ's authoritative teaching as Lord of the church; (7) the substitutionary atonement in which God did all that was needed to redeem man from sin and its consequences; (8) the bodily resurrection of Christ as the consummation of his redemptive work and the sign and seal of its validity; (9) the ascension and heavenly mission of the living Lord; (10) the bodily second coming

of Christ at the end of the age; (11) the final righteous judgment of all mankind and the eternal kingdom of God; (12) the eternal punishment of the impenitent and disbelieving wicked of this world.[1]

For the sake of orientation, let me also cite Sydney E. Ahlstrom's rather tendentious explanation of evangelicalism. "The word evangelical," he writes, "refers to those Protestants who"

> (1) repudiate Roman Catholic polity, liturgics, piety, and doctrine, and at least used to regard the Roman Catholic Church as the Anti-Christ;
> (2) insist upon verbal inerrancy of the received biblical text, tend to interpret revelation in strict propositional terms, and question the value of historico-critical studies of biblical religion;
> (3) regard the doctrine of *sola scriptura* as having very serious import for the devotional life of every Christian;
> (4) emphasize the experiential dimensions of being or becoming a Christian and hence tend to diminish the significance of the sacraments, a sacerdotal clergy, authoritative hierarchical structures, and doctrinal complexities;
> (5) understand the ethical teachings of the Bible in a precisionistic or legalistic manner and oppose utilitarian or situational approaches;
> (6) resist the extension of fellowship or even the name of Christian to persons and churches that do not share these convictions.[2]

Assuming the substantial correctness of these two analyses, I now address myself to the task of sketching the spectrum of evangelical views on the moral crisis in our society. I doubt, you see, that it is possible to identify any one perspective as *the* evangelical view. Since a wide range of opinions comes under the capacious umbrella of evangelicalism (as, I suspect, is likewise true of Judaism), my procedure must be that of selecting dominant patterns of interpretation and reaction without putting my personal imprimatur on any one of them as being quintessentially evangelical.

I

Regarding one thing, there is, I think, a near unanimity within the ranks of evangelicalism. Our society is floundering today in a moral crisis of unprecedented virulence and pervasiveness. Evangelicals of every school, I am sure, agree with the diagnosis of our own country made by J. Herbert Fill, former Mental Health Commissioner of New York City.

> Ten years ago national and local surveys found approximately 80 per cent of the adult population suffering from some form of mental disturbance. Since then, admissions to psychiatric hospitals have increased annually, with our country's adolescents making up the fastest-growing segment of the inmate population. And new methods such as community psychiatry have been devised to treat the burgeoning numbers of patients outside hospitals. Depressive conditions, from the subtle agonies of passive discontent to the cold gloom of suicidal despair, have now reached epidemic proportions. And everywhere we turn are the horrors of the rapidly rising mental disturbances labeled antisocial personality disorders: defacement, vandalism, shoplifting, fraud, theft, robbery, mugging, assault, rape, torture, kidnapping, hijacking, murder, and mass assassination.[3]

One evangelical who concurs with this type of diagnosis is T. B. Maston, professor of Christian ethics at Southwestern Baptist Theological Seminary in Fort Worth, Texas. In his 1957 text on social issues he wrote at length about "The World in Crisis," arguing that "the real reasons for the crisis are spiritual." Among the forces destroying our planet, he singled out, first of all, a cancerlike inner decay, charging that secularism is at once a symptom and proof of the moral rot which is permeating and undermining Western civilization. As other causes of our planetary sickness, he focused on the dethronement of God and the loss of faith in the once accepted assumptions of the Christian religion.[4]

More recently, concurrence with this diagnosis was voiced by Harold Lindsell, editor of *Christianity Today*. In a major address at the International Congress on World Evangelization held in Lausanne, Switzerland, during July 1974, he spoke on "The Suicide of Man," elaborating the thesis that our world seems bent on self-destruction. Man, Lindsell asserted, is committing suicide ecologically, scientifically, morally, sociologically, intellectually, and even theistically—theistically since "God is denigrated by a homocentrism which places man at the center of life." Because my concern is primarily with the moral aspects of the crisis, let me quote Lindsell's thumbnail sketch of how man is committing suicide ethically.

> Within two-and-a-half blocks of my office in Washington there are more pornographic outlets than you are likely to find in any other major city around the world. Yes, indeed we have pornography. We have sexual freedom. We have fornication, adultery, homosexuality, wife-swapping, rape, sodomy, incest, pandering, prostitution, voyeurism. You name it. We've got it. The movies and legitimate theater are sex-oriented. They concentrate on the abnormal and the illegitimate under the guise of freedom of expression. A new morality that is immorality under an undefined and contentless concept of love abounds around the world. Every man, every woman, is doing what is right in his own eyes.[5]

Appraisals like those of Maston and Lindsell could be multiplied almost endlessly, but to no profit. My point, I take it, has been sufficiently italicized. Evangelicals, virtually without exception, are convinced that humanity is morally sick, so sick that apart from divine grace, despair of recovery is well warranted.

II

Evangelicals, again virtually without exception, are convinced, moreover, that our present crisis has been caused by factors such as Maston mentioned—inner decay, the dethronement of God, and the loss of faith in the once accepted assumptions of the Christian religion. Fervently they endorse D. Elton Trueblood's often-quoted verdict that "ours is a cut-flower civilization," threatened with death because it is being severed from its "sustaining roots."[6] Those roots are not merely some vague religious notions: they are the doctrines of Christianity. Trueblood leaves no doubt concerning this. In his extremely popular 1944 book, *The Predicament of Modern Man,* he flatly states that it is the erosion of Christianity which has brought on our alarming moral malady.

> Regardless of the personal position he takes, it is not possible for a thoughtful person to view lightly the apparent crumbling of the Christian pattern. Whether for good or ill, such a development is momentous. If Western man, who has long been the dominant man on the planet, should now lose those ultimate convictions which have been partly regulative for at least fifteen centuries, the change would be enormous. Temporarily, at least, the change has already occurred, and this change has been more crucial than any battle or other external event. *It is the chief event that has occurred.*[7]

But what, one is impelled to ask, has been responsible for this direly erosive process? A legion of causative culprits falls under evangelical indictment, everything from Cartesian rationalism on down through Skinner's neobehaviorism. Yet all of these in one form or another are really manifestations of that human pride which initially disclosed itself in the Garden of Eden and which continues to reveal itself in man's arrogant refusal to submit his mind and will to the Word of God.

One of the most sophisticated and applauded diagnosticians of twentieth-century darkness and despair is Francis A. Schaeffer whose book, *The God Who Is There,* has been a best-seller among evangelicals. He holds that the nihilistic mood and ethical bankruptcy of our time can be traced back to man's sinful misuse of his God-given intelligence. Not very long ago, up until, say, 1890 in Europe and 1935 in the United States (these are the dates Schaeffer rather specifically assigns), even non-Christians acted on Christian presuppositions. And what were those presuppositions?

> The basic one was that there really are such things as absolutes. They accepted the possibility of an absolute in the area of Being (or knowledge), and in the area of morals. Therefore, because they accepted the possibility of absolutes, though men might disagree as to what these were, nevertheless they could reason together on the classical basis of antithesis. So if anything was true, the opposite was false. In morality, if one thing was right, its opposite was wrong. This little formula, "If you have A, it is not non-A," is the first move in classical logic. If you understand the extent to which this no longer holds sway, you will understand our present situation.
>
> Absolutes imply antithesis. The non-Christian went on romantically operating on this basis without a sufficient base for doing so. Thus it was still possible to discuss what was right and wrong, what was true and false. One could tell a non-Christian to "be a good girl," and, while she might not have followed your advice, at least she would have understood what you were talking about. To say the same thing to a truly modern girl today would be to make a "nonsense" statement. The blank look you might receive would not mean that your standards had been rejected but that your message was meaningless.
>
> The shift has been tremendous. Thirty or more years ago you could have said such things as "This is true" or "This is right," and you would have been on everybody's wavelength. People may or may not have thought out their beliefs consistently, but everyone would have been talking to each other as though the idea of antithesis was correct.[8]

Schaeffer contends that during the last half-century or so a

momentous change has taken place, culminating in irrationalism, relativism, mysticism, pessimism, and im-
moralism. And all of this originated with G. W. F. Hegel,
who replaced Christian antithesis with philosophical
synthesis—which meant, needless to remark, a farewell to
absolutes. But suppose I defer to Schaeffer in rehearsing
this tragic faux pas—this sinful act of *hubris*—in our intellectual history.

> Imagine that Hegel was sitting one day in the
> local tavern, surrounded by his friends, convers-
> ing on the philosophical issues of the day. Sud-
> denly he put down his mug of beer on the table
> and said, "I have a new idea. From now on let us
> think in this way; instead of thinking in terms of
> cause and effect, what we really have is a thesis,
> and opposite is an antithesis, and the answer to
> their relationship is not in the horizontal move-
> ment of cause and effect, but the answer is al-
> ways synthesis." Now suppose also that a hard-
> headed German business man had been stand-
> ing by and had overheard his remark. He might
> have thought, "How abstruse and impractical!"
> But he could not have been further from the
> truth. Because whether Hegel himself or those
> listening understood it to be the case, when
> Hegel propounded this idea he changed the
> world.
>   It has never been the same since. If one un-
> derstands the development of philosophy, or
> morals, or political thought from that day to this,
> one knows that Hegel and synthesis have won.[9]

Hence modern thought and contemporary history, disastrously influenced by Hegel, illustrate Paul's teaching in
his letter to the Romans:

> Because, when they knew God, they glorified
> him not as God, neither were thankful, but be-
> came vain in their imaginations, and their foolish
> heart was darkened.
>   Professing themselves to be wise they became
> fools.
>   And even as they did not like to retain God in

their knowledge, God gave them over to a reprobate mind, to do those things which are not
seemly,
    Being filled with all unrighteousness, fornica-
tion, wickedness, covetousness, maliciousness;
full of envy, murder, strife, deceit, malignity;
whisperers,
    Backbiters, haters of God, insolent, proud,
boasters, inventors of evil things, disobedient to
parents;
    Without understanding, covenant breakers,
without natural affections, implacable, unmerci-
ful;
    Who, knowing the judgment of God, that they
who commit such things are worthy of death, not
only do the same but have pleasure in them that
do them. (Rom. 1:21, 22, 28-32, Scofield Reference Bible)

The moral decay of our period, in other words, is a
consequence of man's egocentric refusal to think God's
thoughts after him, obediently following the truth disclosed in divine revelation. Sin-warped thinking has led
inevitably to the kind of behavioral debacle which has been
growing steadily worse since 1914. Our all-encompassing
crisis is, therefore, God's judgment on man's attempt to go
it alone, deciding for himself what is true even if he decides that absolute truth is an illusion.

III

The moral decay and social distress of our twentieth
century are regarded ambivalently by a sizable segment of
American evangelicals. They sincerely deplore the worse
than ominous trends in our society which adumbrate—
unless God somehow intervenes—the emergence of a barbarism akin to Naziism that will reduce technopolis to
necropolis. They deplore these trends, and yet they are
pessimistically thankful to observe their development. For
many evangelicals are premillenarians. In the jargon of
our theological "in-group" many are premillennial dispensationalists who believe in a pretribulation rapture. Ex-

pressed with utmost concision, this view of eschatology holds that world conditions will, by prophetic necessity, become steadily more and more evil, corrupt, and inhumane, climaxing in a seven-year period of global travail; but before that time of intolerable tribulation begins, all believers in the gospel, who by definition belong to the true church, will be supernaturally removed from our earth into the presence of the Savior. So pretribulational premillenarians, to use that technical term, eagerly scan the international horizon for indications that the Lord's return may be imminent. Historical movements and political events—for example, the very fact of moral crisis—are interpreted as possible harbingers of the onrushing end with, bear in mind, the anticipated rapture of the church as its joyful prelude.

Billy Graham, for one, in his book, *World Aflame,* says what adherents of this eschatological position affirm.

> The world is on a moral binge such as was not known even in the days of Rome. We have at our fingertips every pleasure that man is capable of enjoying, and man has abused every gift God ever gave him, including sex, until he no longer finds joy and satisfaction in them. *Time* magazine reported recently on a "Festival of Free Expression" in a Paris youth center where young men and women performed before audiences immoral acts of such depravity that they cannot be recounted here. This is man, doing what he wants to do. This is human nature, without God, expressing itself. And it is a sign of the end.[10]

Hal Lindsey, for another, affirms this same position. His immensely popular study of prophecy, *The Late Great Planet Earth,* sets forth the convictions and expectations of, I dare guess, at least several million Americans who subscribe to pretribulational premillenarianism. Here is a typical passage which indicates his view of today's moral crisis.

> It doesn't take a "religious" person to discern the fact that what is happening is setting the world in the proper frame for a dictator. We see anarchy

growing in every country. We see established standards of morality thrown aside for a hedonistic brand which is attractively labeled the "New Morality." We see the super-weapons and the threats of atheistic leaders in world powers who would not hesitate to use those weapons if they would further their drive for conquest."[11]

The dictator alluded to is the predicted Antichrist whom Lindsey stigmatizes as the future Führer. Furthermore, since the signs of the times are the Christian's source of encouragement in a deteriorating planetary situation, Lindsey suggests to his fellow believers that they be on the alert for certain significant tendencies.

Look for the present sociological problems such as crime, riots, lack of employment, poverty, illiteracy, mental illness, illegitimacy, etc., to increase as the population explosion begins to multiply geometrically in the late '70s.
Look for the beginning of the widest spread famines in the history of the world.
Look for drug addiction to further permeate the U.S. and other free-world countries. Drug addicts will run for high political offices and win through support of the young adults.
Look for drugs and forms of religion to be merged together. There will be a great general increase of belief in extrasensory phenomena, which will not be related to the true God, but to Satan.[12]

Rather than being despondent as the planetary situation deteriorates, Christians, Lindsey exhorts, should rejoice at the imminency of the blessed hope.

As we see the circumstances which are coming on the world, this hope gets more blessed all the time. This is the reason we are optimistic about the future. This is the reason that in spite of the headlines, in spite of crisis after crisis in America and throughout the world, in spite of the dark days which will strike terror in the hearts of many, every Christian has the right to be optimistic![13]

Ambivalence, then, characterizes evangelicals like Lindsey and Graham as they consider our moral crisis. On the one hand, they rightly and vehemently deplore it; yet, on the other hand, they view it as a legitimate incentive to optimism. And not only an incentive to optimism: they also view it as a powerful incentive to evangelism. In Lindsey's words:

> Far from being pessimistic and dropping out of life, we should be rejoicing in the knowledge that Christ may return any moment for us. This should spur us on to share the good news of salvation in Christ with as many as possible. The Holy Spirit is working upon men in a dramatic way and He will lead you to people who are ready or who will be shortly if you trust Him.[14]

I ought to add that Lindsey apparently ignores social issues. I have failed, at any rate, to notice a single reference to such concerns in *The Late Great Planet Earth*. Graham, though, devotes an entire chapter of *World Aflame* to the "Social Involvement of the New Man." My own observation, let me add further, is that the premillennialism which dominates American evangelicalism seems, as a rule, to breed social indifference and pessimism. Quite understandably, if we are merely passengers at the airport awaiting the arrival of a delayed plane, it is rather pointless to bother upholstering the benches we impatiently occupy.

One additional comment, I feel, is in order since the purpose of our conference is to strengthen relationships between Jews and evangelicals. Premillenarians as a group are ardent Zionists; they interpret the re-establishment of the Jewish state in Palestine as an incontestable fulfillment of prophecy. So permit me to quote Lindsey's opinion on this matter, an opinion which today is the mainstream of American premillennialism:

> The one event which many Bible students in the past overlooked was this paramount prophetic sign: Israel had to be a nation again in the land of its forefathers.

Israel a nation—a dream for so many years, made a reality on 14 May 1948 when David Ben-Gurion read the Declaration of Independence announcing the establishment of a Jewish nation to be known as the State of Israel.

In 1949, Prime Minister Ben-Gurion said that Israel's policy "consists of bringing all Jews to Israel . . . we are still at the beginning."[15]

To substantiate the validity of his interpretation Lindsey quotes from an 1864 commentary by Dr. John Cumming:

How comes it to pass that as a nation they have been dispersed over every land, yet insulated, separated, and alone amid the nations? The predictions of their restoration are in words as definite only not yet fulfilled. As a nation they were cut off and dispersed, and it is *as a nation that they shall be gathered and restored.*

But one closing act in this great dramatic history of an extraordinary people is yet wanting to complete the whole. Their restoration is predicted and demanded. Who will stretch out his hand to move the scene and call forth the actors?[16]

Thus whatever criticisms one may properly level against dispensationalists like Lindsey, they are, nonetheless, the warmest friends and supporters of Israel anywhere, and their understanding of prophecy inspires a zealous concern for the re-established Jewish homeland.

IV

Not all evangelicals, however, take the view of our moral crisis which I have been hastily sketching. Some evangelicals join Carl Henry in his censure of dispensational premillennialism.

In its extreme forms it . . . evaporates the present-day relevance of much of the ethics of Jesus. Eschatology is invoked to postpone the significance of the Sermon and other segments of New Testament moral teaching to a later

Kingdom age. Dispensationalism erects a cleavage in biblical ethics in the interest of debatable eschatological theory. Dispensationalism holds that Christ's Kingdom has been postponed until the end of the Church age, and that the Kingdom-ethics will become dramatically relevant again only in the future eschatological era. . . . New Testament theology will not sustain this radical repudiation of any present form of the Kingdom of heaven.[17]

Many evangelicals endorse Henry's reading of prophecy and its impingement on ethics. He sets forth, they believe, a more balanced concept of New Testament eschatology.

In the Gospels the eschatological sanction for repentance and the new life is filled with urgency from the fact that the eschatological age is depicted as somehow already under way with the first advent of Christ. The eschatological period, while it looks for ultimate consummation at the end of the age of grace, gets under way with the proclamation of John the Baptist. It finds its center, and even its hidden climax, in the life, death, and resurrection of the historical Jesus. The Day of the Lord begins with the incarnation and atonement of Christ, and reaches its finale with his anticipated return. The Christian lives no longer merely in the age of Old Testament promise, but in the New Testament era of growing fulfillment. This suggests the element of truth in the statement that what the Jewish apocalyptist saw was "the *advent* of the Kingdom, but not the Kingdom itself." In his personal teaching Jesus gave the Christian community the content of the Kingdom in its present phase, although its full revelation must wait for the transcendent consummation of all things. "The 'Age to Come' had broken through into this present age," writes Sydney Cave, "and its redemptive powers were already in part realized."[18]

Because the powers of the coming age are already at work in the present age, some evangelicals regard our moral crisis as a challenge from God no less than a judgment by God. As they see it, we must not surrender to social apathy and defeatism. Instead we must, under the enablement of the Holy Spirit, battle evil, struggle for justice, pursue peace, and at the same time aggressively carry on evangelism. This is the policy advocated by Dr. Earle E. Cairns, chairman of the department of social sciences at Wheaton College. The conclusion of his helpful survey, *The Christian in Society,* is virtually an appeal:

> The modern Christian is to walk humbly before God, but he is also to deal justly and to love mercy (Mic. 6:8). We should not forget also that we were saved "unto good works" (Eph. 2:10) as well as to witness. Paul urged that those who believed should be "careful to maintain good works" (Titus 3:8). This keynote appears again and again in the New Testament. While we should be sure our social theory is genuinely biblical and Christian, we should when enlightened as to our responsibility—which enlightening is the task of the pastor—proceed to act as Christian citizens for the glory of God and for the good of men so as to "occupy" faithfully until our Lord's return (I Thess. 1:3; cf. 9, 10). Is our faith sufficient and our love deep enough to bring us to the point of action while we hopefully await His imminent return? Christ can transform in history as well as beyond history. Revival should, as it has in the past, result in service to society as well as the salvation of souls.[19]

Note a significant emphasis: "Christ can transform in history as well as beyond history." Maston has a similar emphasis. If personal and institutional Christianity is revitalized, he asserts, our entire civilization may in turn be revitalized. Unapologetically he voices his optimism, an optimism that centers in the gospel.

> Does the cross have any relevance for modern world issues? Can the ethic of the cross be applied to family problems, to racial tensions, to economic and political conflicts? The answer to these questions is definitely Yes. The church's message to the world is that there is no final

solution for the problems of human relations outside the ethic of the cross. The only assurance of the use of Christian methods to achieve desirable Christian ends is the application of the spirit of the cross. Really, the cross is *the* Christian method of social change. . . . We shall never achieve a perfect social order in this world, but we should move as far and as rapidly as possible toward the Christian ideal for the world.[20]

Maston, in short, cherishes the hope of world transformation. He consequently admonishes his fellow believers to work tirelessly for a closer and closer approximation of New Testament social and moral ideals even though the full realization of those ideals, he acknowledges, will be achieved only in the age to come.

Maston's hope and confidence are by no means uncommon among evangelicals today. A younger generation is arising which fuses a vibrant piety with social passion, interpreting the present crisis as an opportunity to demonstrate the effectiveness of the Holy Spirit as a transforming agent of unpredictable power. Across the years they listen approvingly to the prophetic words of Sir Richard Livingston.

If you allow the spiritual basis of a civilization to perish, you first change, and finally destroy it. Christianity and Hellenism are the spiritual bases of our civilization. They are far less powerful today than fifty years ago. Therefore, we are losing that spiritual basis, and our civilization is changing and on the way to destruction, unless we can reverse the process.[21]

And these younger evangelicals are giving themselves to the task of reversing that process.

V

Before ending this inadequate presentation, may I take the liberty of expressing my own viewpoint as an evangelical who is also a premillenarian? Obviously I am now addressing my own faith community. I perceive no prophetic necessity for the irreversible collapse of civilization in the years which lie immediately ahead. Instead, we may hope for an indeterminable delay of divine judgment, an era of peace, a time of spiritual renewal, an epoch of order and freedom and creativity. The Christian attitude, I suggest, is like that of a physician who knows that eventually his patient must die. All the skill doctors and surgeons possess cannot prevent the inevitable end of life. But does that inevitability discourage the physician when illness strikes? Does it reduce him to unethical apathy? By no means! He utilizes all of his abilities and resources not only to prevent that particular illness from becoming fatal, but also to restore health and vitality for how long a time only God knows. So the premillenarian—indeed the biblicist, no matter what his eschatological brand name—ought to view no particular world crisis as helpless. The Christian's God-assigned duty is not only to evangelize, but to pray and work for freedom, justice, and peace, doing everything he can within the limits of his opportunity and discernment to secure optimal conditions for a more successful extension of the gospel. This is the obligation which he is to discharge in faith, the obligation Paul lays down in I Timothy 2:1-4:

> I exhort therefore, that, first of all, supplications, prayers, intercessions, and giving of thanks, be made for all men; for kings, and for all that are in authority; that we may lead a quiet and peaceable life in all godliness and honesty. For this is good and acceptable in the sight of God our Saviour; Who will have all men to be saved, and to come unto the knowledge of the truth.

"A quiet and peaceable life," a situation of economic and political security which will promote freedom, justice, and evangelism—for these things we must pray and for these things we must work in the confidence that we are doing the will of God.

Of one thing we may be sure. God does not delight in wrath; he delights in peace. For what does Paul teach us in I Corinthians 14:33? "For God is not the author of confusion, but of peace, as in all churches of the saints." And what does Jesus teach us in Matthew 5:9? "Blessed are the peacemakers; for they shall be called the children of God."

Also, God delights in human repentance, as Ezekiel 33:11 indicates: "Say unto them, as I live, saith the Lord God, I have no pleasure in the death of the wicked; but that the wicked turn from his way and live; turn ye, turn ye from your evil ways; for why will ye die, O house of Israel?" According to Isaiah 28:21, the outpouring of wrath is the strange work of holy love, and therefore God delays wrath as long as possible (II Peter 3:9), striving by his goodness to bring men to a contrite faith (Rom. 2:4) which will pave the way for the outpouring of grace instead of wrath.

Our duty, then, is plain. But let a contemporary poet, T. S. Eliot, lay the burden of it upon our souls afresh.

> The only hope or else despair
> Lies in the choice of pyre or pyre —
> To be redeemed from fire by fire.
> We can live, only suspire,
> Consumed by either fire or fire.[22]

To say the same thing prosaically, we have a choice on the one hand of apocalyptic fire, the fire of atomic incineration, the fire of divine wrath; on the other hand, the fire which flamed in the hearts of the disciples at Pentecost.

> Bring us low in prayer before Thee,
> And with love our souls inspire,
> Till we claim by faith the promise
> Of the Holy Ghost and fire.

And if we choose the fire of the Holy Spirit, we can become God's instruments, as John Wesley was in the eighteenth century, for an evangelical renaissance which may profoundly modify history even in the twilight of the twentieth century.

NOTES

1. Kenneth Kantzer, "Unity and Diversity in Evangelical Faith," *The Evangelicals,* ed. David F. Wells and John D. Woodbridge (New York: Abingdon Press, 1975), pp. 53-54.

2. Sydney E. Ahlstrom, "From Puritanism to Evangelicalism: A Critical Perspective," *The Evangelicals,* ed. Wells and Woodbridge, pp. 270-71.

3. J. Herbert Fill, *The Mental Breakdown of a Nation* (New York: New Viewpoints, 1974), p. 4.

4. T. B. Maston, *Christianity and World Issues* (New York: The Macmillan Company, 1957), pp. 305-11.

5. Harold Lindsell, "The Suicide of Man," *Let the Earth Hear His Voice,* ed. J. D. Douglas (Minneapolis: World Wide Publications, 1975), pp. 422-24.

6. D. Elton Trueblood, *The Predicament of Modern Man* (New York: Harper & Brothers, 1944), pp. 59-60.

7. Ibid., p. 22.

8. Francis A. Schaeffer, *The God Who Is There* (Downers Grove, IL: Inter-Varsity Press, 1968), p. 14.

9. Ibid., p. 20.

10. Billy Graham, *World Aflame* (Garden City, NY: Doubleday & Company, Inc., 1965), p. 218.

11. Hal Lindsey, *The Late Great Planet Earth* (Grand Rapids: Zondervan, 1970), p. 102.

12. Ibid., p. 185.

13. Ibid., p. 138.

14. Ibid., p. 187.

15. Ibid., p. 43.

16. Ibid., p. 49.

17. Carl F. H. Henry, *Christian Personal Ethics* (Grand Rapids: Eerdmans, 1957), pp. 550-51.

18. Ibid., p. 561.

19. Earle E. Cairns, *The Christian in Society* (Chicago: Moody Press, 1973), p. 175.

20. Maston, *Christianity and World Issues,* pp. 338-39.

21. Quoted in Trueblood, *Predicament,* pp. 19-20.

22. T. S. Eliot, "Little Gidding," *The Complete Poems and Plays, 1909-1950* (New York: Harcourt, Brace and Company, 1958), p. 144.

14

EMANUEL RACKMAN

A Jewish View of the Present Moral Crisis

My theme is "A Jewish View of the Present Moral Crisis." It is not *the* Jewish view. I do not speak for all Jews—perhaps not even for all orthodox Jews. Among Jews there are those whose position is consistent with the most evangelical view as described by Dr. Grounds. And there are also Jews who are committed to the most extreme form of humanism.

Permit me to state what I hold.

First, for me ethics are not autonomous. I am committed to absolutes and their transcendent Source who revealed his will and holds me accountable for its fulfillment. I am well aware of the fact that, in the name of these absolutes, religionists have often acted immorally while using God's name. I am troubled that this should have happened. However, I also know that more people were killed in this century alone because of ideologies that are secularist in character and relativist in their ethics than were killed in all the religious wars of the past few millennia.

Second, I know that because I am finite I do not always correctly fathom the Infinite's will. Therefore, I am cautious and judicious. With reason and experience, with the study of history and its literature, and in many other ways, I engage God in a continuing partnership to discover for each situation what he would want me to do. Man alone is not the measure of all things. But man, under God, may approximate the right course to follow.

Yet, without commitment to the transcendent I fear

what will happen to our concern for humanity, for the future, even for the preservation of nature. What is more, humanity's lack of commitment to moral values today adversely affects the physical and emotional security of no people on earth as much as it adversely affects the survival of the Jewish people.

The Jewish people in their loneliness cannot truly depend even on the commitment to moral values of organized Christendom and Islam and thus the moral crisis is exacerbated when religion itself does not appear to be a force for morality. Alas, organized religions have become as opportunistic as political states.

Certainly political institutions—national and international—have contributed to the low state of morality in our day. We are reconciled to the wholly amoral character of politics and economics and rarely raise objections to it. Machiavelli has prevailed! The morality of the United Nations is the morality of its most barbarous members. And from the point of view of Jewish theology this is the true sin of Sodom—the United Nations has made the immoral lawful!

In such a crisis we Jews also have our premillenarians who hold that when all is so bad the advent of the Messiah is imminent. But most of us feel that our penitence will bring him more readily than will our tolerating further deterioration of the world's moral climate.

Our present moral crisis is encapsulated in Genesis 20:11, as Abraham exclaims, "For I said that there is no fear of God in this place." Abraham feared to be where there was no fear of God.

Jews today are wont to tell of a rabbi who in the middle of a trip in a horse-drawn coach told the driver to stop. He wanted to leave the coach and walk the rest of the way. He noticed that the driver had passed a church without paying it proper respect, so the rabbi feared to ride with him any longer. One who does not fear God is not to be trusted with human life.

And Jews today are afraid to be where the fear of God does not exist, where organized religion is hardly ever vocal, even when life is in danger—not only the lives of Jews but even the lives of Christians as in Lebanon. Because organized religion has vested interests in many parts of the world it too yields to blackmail. Further, the United Nations and all of its agencies are naught but forums for the propagation of hate and falsehood with the voice of conscience muted.

Thus it is not only the immorality of individuals, the individual adulterer or homosexual or thief, that depresses us now. It is rather the immorality of our group life—our states, our institutions, our United Nations, our organized religions. And this is my first thesis: the immoral is now the accepted norm of our behavior; the immoral is virtually lawful!

One of the greatest philosophers of Judaism made this point when he compared the sins of Sodom with the more heinous sins described at the end of the Book of Judges. There one finds one of the most heinous acts committed in universal history. Yet the Lord in that case did not destroy as he did the inhabitants of Sodom. Why? Says Isaac Armaah, what was described in the Book of Judges was known to be immoral and unlawful and one could hope for righteous people to punish the unlawful and establish the moral. But Sodom's sin was that the immoral was lawful. Then, what hope could there be for the vindication of the right? The judges themselves were the evil ones!

In our day too the evil ones have not only political and economic clout but the tribunals of the world are theirs as well. How can Jews not fear?

But how did we reach this point? This brings me to my second thesis. We subverted morality when the focus of law became the rights of man rather than the duties of man. In Judaism the focus is always on the duty rather than the right. Indeed, students of jurisprudence know that right and duty are correlatives—one has no right unless someone else is under a duty; and no one has a duty unless someone else enjoys a right. Nonetheless what is important is which of the two correlatives gets more of the attention. In modern society—in which God plays so minor a role—the emphasis is on the right—our rights against our government, our rights against our parents, our teachers, our employers. In a theocentric society one thinks less of one's rights against the Sovereign and more of one's duties to him—and our duties to parents, teachers, and employers.

That is why we hear so much today about women's rights with respect to their bodies, and not their duties to the lives they bear; we hear about the human right to die rather than our duty to make even the aged and infirm happy; we hear about the right to live in the "here and now" rather than the duty to our posterity in a distant future.

In biblical Hebrew we have no word for "right" but the word for "duty" or "commandment" is everywhere. And if we would reverse the trend and give moral fiber to our society, we must make the notion of duty, rather than the notion of right, dominant in our thought and speech.

My third thesis is that we have lost sight of the Judaic notion that law and ethics, or law and morality, are inseparable. Often we speak of the gap between the moral and the legal but by that we ought to mean only that the law chooses not to use its sanctions to enforce the highest standard of behavior and leaves something to the exercise of free will by society's constituents. It should never be taken to mean—as so many modern jurists want us to believe—that the law ought to be neutral with regard to morality. I may feel that a legal system would do well not to punish homosexuals and even protect them against the denial of some basic human rights. However, I cannot subscribe to the view that legislators should give support to the position that deviant sexual behavior is an acceptable option available to everyone. The law should not make possible the marriage of two males or two females. Nor should the law repeal statutes which express disapproval of the immoral even though such statutes are never acted upon. It was the great American philosopher Morris Raphael Cohen who said that criminal laws serve many purposes. They are designed to deter the commission of crimes, to prevent criminals from sinning again, to reform them, and also to punish them. But in addition, their mere presence on the statute books indicates the reprobate character of the behavior they disapprove and thus the law at least describes what is the approved morality. Today we too often seek to change law to sanction the immoral and make it moral.

In Judaism we do not speak of law. We speak of Halakah—the way to go, the road to take, the course to follow. And Halakah integrates law and morality—the rules for which there are legal sanctions and the rules with regard to which everyone is on his honor and accountable only to God.

And because Judaism is so preoccupied with the Halakah, my fourth thesis is that the education of our young should be principally in the Halakah. We need more legal education in our present world—not in law schools alone, but from the cradle to the grave. What is right and what is wrong ought to be the principal theme of the educational process instead of what is and what is not self-fulfilling. By making the latter the focus of all our educational striving we have reared generations of self-centered, irresponsible citizens. As in the case of rights and duties I do not seek the elimination of either of two polar aspirations. The highest form of morality is that which is a response to divine will because the individual finds the greatest self-fulfillment in that response. But what we have nurtured in education heretofore is not that type of self-fulfillment and we are therefore reaping the harvest that is ours because of the seed we sowed.

Jewish education was always legal education. Not even the stories of Genesis were as important as the legislation of Exodus and Leviticus. The modern world should ponder the Jewish experience for guidance. There is much that can be learned from it.

And for the same reason we in the modern world should give more encouragement to those groups who want to withdraw from our immoral society and create moral societies of their own. There are many such moves in the

United States by both Jews and Christians. Instead of forcing integration and acculturation on such groups we should even support their separatist preferences. Perhaps these groups will provide the models for the reintroduction of a broader-scaled morality into our national and international institutions.

Alas, our youth presently do not even have models at home—and certainly not highly publicized martyrs—for ethical correctness. In our day such martyrs would be ridiculed as fools. Yet we must remember that unless we fulfill moral values at the smallest unit of social and political organization—in the family—we are not going to fulfill them in higher echelons of government. For this we ought to penetrate the home and make parents moral persons in the eyes of their children—parents whose children do not see them "fix" traffic tickets, or hear them speak indecently of other folk, or try to evade taxes. Parenthetically one might say that the media today not only glorify violence, but make heroes of men and women whose search for sexual gratification even prompts them to abandon their responsibilities to their own progeny. It is a fact that in media programming no thought whatever is given to what the impact of the program will be on the moral values of the young viewer!

What is sad about this phenomenon is that the media and their advertisers would be responsive to the demand of even a minority of Americans who expressed their disapproval. In this connection even a minority has clout. The sponsors of programs do not want to lose customers and would be respectful of the wishes of an articulate group of the committed. Yet religious people are generally silent. They feel that they cannot reverse the trend. They are as inert in the face of the moral crisis as they were in the face of Hitler's holocaust.

Furthermore, we could encourage corporations to boast about the morality of their business management as they do about the excellence of their products. There are ways to promote such a program in American life. Very recently my own rabbinic group, which plays a very important role in the endorsement of kosher products, announced that hereafter it will be concerned with more than compliance with the dietary laws of Judaism. We will withdraw endorsement of a program if there are complaints about the manner in which the manufacturer conducts his business affairs. This is a beginning, and more, of course, would be accomplished if organized religion decided to use its clout against companies whose enterprises employ questionable morality. All of this can be done without involving government in the business of legislating morality.

Yet my last point calls for government to do something too. When the government supports a position which religious people deem immoral we have a right to expect that the government will at least make it known that it is supporting what in the eyes of many is foul. Our government allowed human beings to smoke, a habit which may shorten life, and is therefore immoral. The government compensates for its tolerance of smoking by insisting that the view of the Surgeon General be made known. Presently our government is making abortions easily available to everyone. In a way I cannot object because it is only proper to make available to the poor the opportunities which have always been available to the rich. But government has gone much further. It has practically eliminated any misgivings a person might have had in years past about destroying human life. Even if mothers do ultimately decide whether their fetuses will live or die, should not the government do something to make the pregnant woman who seeks the abortion aware that the relief she is seeking is immoral? The truth is that the law assumes what in the opinion of most of us is an immoral stance and thereby gives the stamp of morality to abortion. It is doing for abortions what Russia does for atheism. Atheism in Russia enjoys government support. Religion there receives no government support whatever and thus by sheer neglect religion has second-class status. In the United States the government supports the views of those against the right to life. The opposition must fend for itself without the billions of dollars available to the practitioners of abortions. The least that government should be forced to do is to inform pregnant women who want their fetuses removed that even if the Surgeon General may not deem their decision dangerous to physical health, they may experience mental anguish and feelings of guilt which should make them think twice about their intention. Or at the very least, the government should refer these women to agencies which can help them make their decision after due consideration of all the pros and cons.

I simply cannot reconcile myself to the notion that nothing can be done about our present moral crisis. In fact, I feel that combating this crisis should be the goal of our ecumenical movement. On most moral issues we are agreed while on almost all theological issues we are divided. If so, why not find a way to work together to reverse the gradual descent of our country into a gutter, perhaps, alas, even to another flood?

PART 6

Religious Pluralism

15

G. DOUGLAS YOUNG

Concepts of Religious Pluralism and Areas of Conflict in Israel

We surely have religious pluralism in Israel. The conflicts, however, are not between the various major religious groups and the minorities, but rather the conflicts exist within Christendom; they are not between Jews and Muslims or between Jews and the various branches of the Christian church. Within Christendom the areas of conflict center around theological differences, the relation of the churches to the *status quo,* and their attitudes towards the state of Israel (especially those Christians who live east of the line that used to divide Israel and the section of Mandate Palestine that was a part of Jordan from 1948 to 1967).

The word *conflict* has a very belligerent sound that does not truly represent the actual situation in Israel. As we all know, there have been and are actual conflicts, but in general, isolation of the groups from each other is more prevalent than conflict.

The religious communities of Israel include the several forms of Judaism, Arab Muslims, non-Arab Muslims such as Circassians, Arab Christians in many branches (Roman Catholic, Orthodox and Protestant), non-Arab Christians (also in many branches both indigenous and especially from outside of Israel), Druse, and others.

The majority of the population is, quite naturally, Jewish, and traditional or Orthodox in its expression. Conservative Judaism has its own traditions and a school in

Jerusalem; Reform Judaism is most active through the Hebrew Union College, the Leo Baeck School, and synagogues that reflect its tradition. Its constituency is still relatively small numerically. The Jewish Reconstructionist Movement is represented by Dr. Mordechai Kaplan, now living in Israel, and by some of his disciples. It is, however, a very small part of the whole. There is a large segment of the population that is not interested in religion in any of the accepted forms. This is, of course, a problem common to all nations and societies. Such people hold to the right to be religiously unaffiliated.

There are several problems within this Jewish pluralism. I refer to the problems of western Reform Judaism in a society where the majority is of eastern origin and certainly traditional in their Judaism. There are problems highlighted by Israeli "Black Panthers" who advocate equal opportunities for the oriental or eastern Jews in relation to the western Jewish population. Problems exist between the orthodox segment of the populace and those who are secularly oriented. But I do not believe that most Christians are especially interested in these internal Jewish problems.

What is important is the Jewish attitude towards the Muslims, the Circassians, the Druse and the Christians. Let me note a few illustrations from my personal observation. The Circassians are for the first time able to study their own language (in place of the Arabic which they have adopted) with textbooks published by the government of Israel (these textbooks, by the way, were prepared by evangelical Christians who began their work at our Institute of Holy Land Studies). Within the pluralism of Israel, the Druse, Arabic-speaking but with their own non-Muslim religion, and some other smaller groups have no particular problems as far as religious differences are concerned. While the non-Arab Muslims are small in number, represented by only a few villages, the Arab Muslims number some 400,000 within Israel itself and another million in the areas administered by Israel since 1967, that is, the West Bank and the Gaza Strip. In recorded history there have been times of religious conflict between Muslims and Jews and between Muslims and Christians also, but these conflicts are not in evidence in modern Israel or in the administered areas. There are political problems but not religious ones. The conflict between the Muslims and the Christians is painfully evident in Lebanon, but not in Israel. Such a conflict could yet become a problem inside Israel, of course, but we hope that a reign of peace may come speedily.

All minorities have their own attitudinal problems, of course, a special kind of complex, something usually of their own creation and not a product of the majority's disposition towards them. There are no religious problems in Israel created by the Jewish majority against the minorities. In fact, quite the opposite is true as evidenced by Israel's support of her many religious minorities in a number of well-known ways. Since 1948 both the Druse and the Arab Evangelical Anglican Church have been designated as *millets* (given community status) by Israel, thus gaining the personal status privileges that are involved in becoming a *millet*. These are now fully recognized religious communities in the legal sense.

If problems do exist for the Druse and Israeli Arabs, they are not religious in nature, but are rather related to the question of representation in the higher echelons of the Israeli government. I find the attitude of the Israeli government towards the other groups (e.g., Christian) to be equally exemplary. There is a section of the Israel Ministry of Religious Affairs that is devoted entirely to the Christian community, assisting the churches with their unique problems—buildings, customs, taxes, and relations one with the other in the holy places. In our own case, the Institute of Holy Land Studies has received assistance on a number of occasions as have all the Christian bodies in Israel. When, for example, a very serious problem was created for us by a small, rather extreme Jewish minority group, mostly from the United States, we received the kind of support one would expect in a democratic society. This help was from both the religious and the secular arms of the Israeli community. I refer especially to the support of the Israeli press, the mayor of Jerusalem, the Minister of Justice, and the police department as well as to the expressions of sympathy from every quarter. The Orthodox Jews of the Me'ah She'arim quarter of Jerusalem refused to become involved in the unfortunate incident that was created by the group on Mount Zion, an incident which has fortunately been settled by Israeli legal processes in our favor. I refer also to my appointment to the board of directors of an Orthodox Jewish hospital, Sha'are Zedek, though my theological stance was fully known, and to my appointment as one of the first two Christians ever named to a municipal commission. I enjoy this work with my Jewish neighbors and colleagues on the commission that names our new Jerusalem streets and suburbs. All of this indicates an attitude of sensitive concern by the majority population toward the minority. One does not usually find such a healthy attitude in the United States. This is not to say that Jews do not serve on municipal commissions in pluralist America. However, we do not yet see in American evangelical circles the level of co-operation between the majority and a religious minority such as is found in Israel. I am happy to say that our Canadian Advisory Committee for the Institute (on which I serve as chairman) consists of three Jews and three conservative Christians. I would like to see more of this kind of co-operation in the United States.

A survey of the Christian sector shows a real pluralism in Israel. There are Greek and Russian (red and white) Orthodox, many orders of the Latin (Catholic) Church, Greek Catholic, Maronite, Chaldean (Iraqi origin), Armenian Orthodox and Catholic, Gregorian Catholic, Syrian Catholic and Orthodox, Coptic, Ethiopian, and Abyssinian.

The Anglicans began their missionary work in the nineteenth century. They were restricted by the Turkish ruling power at many levels, particularly in the matter of church building. Since proselytizing was virtually impossible among Muslims, and similar work among Jews was not "productive," the Anglicans turned their efforts towards the Eastern and Latin Christians and met considerable success, although at many levels serious altercations between the various Christian groups resulted. From these efforts there emerged a strong Arab-Anglican Church which has received *millet* or community status from Israel.

Also in the nineteenth century the German Lutherans began schools, hospices, a hospital, the Church of the Redeemer (1898) and the Augusta Victoria complex on Mount Scopus. This work was taken over by American Lutherans after World War II and now serves some eighteen groups of Lutherans under the banner of the Lutheran World Federation. The vast majority of their work is among Arabs in East Jerusalem and on the West Bank. The work is more social than missionary in the usual sense of that word.

The work of the Church of Scotland (Presbyterian), also chiefly among Arabs, began in the mid-nineteenth century with a school and a hospital. Their churches in Jaffa and Jerusalem were built at that time.

With the British Mandate which began at the end of the second decade of this century, many Protestant missionary groups—some small, some large—entered the area. These groups eventually formed themselves into an organization known as the United Christian Council of Israel, numbering some nineteen or twenty individual groups in all. This organization includes Baptists, Nazarenes, the Finnish Missionary Society, Child Evangelism, the Bible Society, Christian and Missionary Alliance, Mennonites, and others. Outside the Council there exist a considerable number of entirely independent groups such as the Church of Christ, Seventh Day Adventists, Brethren, Pentecostal and National Church groups from European countries—Norway, Sweden, Denmark, Germany, and others. There are also some Christian converts from Judaism, who represent mission agencies from the United States.

In addition there are a great many individuals, some representing foreign mission societies, some representing individual foreign churches, and some who proselytize on their own (including a few who have appeared to convert to Judaism in order to do proselytizing work from within the Jewish community). There are, of course, also a significant number of religious organizations and religious individuals who are *not* involved in proselytizing.

A tabulation of the situation in 1975 might indicate more clearly the nature of the activities of the various Christian groups in Israel.

Kind of Christian Institution	In Jerusalem	In the rest of Israel and the administered areas
Educational Institutions	20	19

e.g., Tantur, Armenian Seminary, Swedish Institute, American Institute, Ecole Biblique

Social Action	10	15

e.g., Helen Keller House, Mennonite Central Committee, Y.M.C.A., Christian Information Center, Lutheran World Federation

Hospices	18	15
Bookshops	6	8
Places where regular worship services are held	75	63

In Jerusalem, twenty-six of these places are Protestant (including Anglican).

All of this serves a population of 120,000 or 3.5 percent of the total population of the country!

Within these Christian bodies (whether Arab or non-Arab) at least two serious problems exist. First, there are the problems among the Christian groups themselves, and second, there are the problems caused by the attitude of these groups towards Jews and the state of Israel.

The first problem relates to the concept of the religious *status quo* and the second problem is simple anti-Israelism. Both exist almost exclusively among the Christians in that part of Jerusalem and the West Bank which used to be in the Jordanian part of "Palestine." Let us take as an example of the first problem, the Church of the Holy Sepulchre. There is virtually no ecumenicity among the Christian groups who worship there. The Greek Orthodox Church, the Latins (Roman Catholic), and the Armenian Orthodox all have possessory rights. The Copts have one small chapel. The Syrian Orthodox, while they have no residence rights, have the right to officiate on holy days. The Ethiopians have the right to use the roof of "Queen Helena's Chapel." History is replete with illustrations of sharp differences of opinion, even of fisticuffs, among these groups over rights within the building. The Turkish *firman* which codified the *status quo* among the groups in 1852 actually led to the Crimean War of 1853-1856! The same problem of religious jurisdiction affects the Church of the Nativity in Bethlehem.

Some Christians have never forgotten the erroneous theological conclusion the church in its earliest days drew from the Jewish loss of sovereignty in A.D. 135—that the Jewish expulsion from the land of Israel meant the Jewish people have been replaced by the church as the "Israel of God." Others simply refuse to adjust to the existence of the modern state of Israel. This segment of Christendom, almost exclusively in East Jerusalem, the West Bank and the Gaza Strip, reflects the typical Arab position—the Jews evicted the Arabs and took over their land; they created the Palestinian refugees by making them homeless; Israel is an expansionist, aggressive Zionist (and currently racist) state, and so on. In part, this is a carry-over from the old colonialist imperialistic outlook, but it also stems from pique at the loss of social and diplomatic prestige, and from such mundane things as rising taxes, the much higher cost of domestic labor, and the problems of security. Nowhere is this negative attitude more evident, and consistently so, than in the pronouncements of the World Council of Churches, the National Council of Churches (U.S.,) the World Conference of Christians for Palestine, and the consultation of the Joint Middle East Churches and the World Council of Churches on the Palestine refugee problem held in Nicosia, Cyprus. We are all only too familiar with these pronouncements. These anti-Israel views are held, often in a *sub rosa* manner, by the church groups in East Jerusalem and the administered areas, and all too frequently they are held firmly by outsiders who are foreign to Israel and know little of the indigenous scene. A friend of mine referred to such views as "the Great White Father Syndrome": Western Christians regard themselves as protectors of those for whom they really have very little personal concern. Those who hold these anti-Israel views fail to see the absence of conflict between Jews and Christians or Muslims in Israel, and they surely fail to see how much they have all benefited under Israel's pluralistic umbrella. The benefits are many and varied: running water around the clock; municipal cleanliness; freedom to visit all holy places in safety at any time they are open; more certified teachers and classrooms; child allowances paid by the government; governmental payments for the restoration of damage to religious property; a department of the government that relates directly to the churches regarding tax problems, customs, and visas; laws that protect holy places from desecration and worshipers from harassment and abuse; and a long list of other benefits including the administration of one million persons (Muslims for the most part) on the West Bank and in Gaza by fewer than five hundred Jews (most of the administration is handled by local Arab leaders). Instead of these benefits those with anti-Israel views see taxes, or union wages that must be paid, social benefits to employees and other social welfare costs. I noted earlier an almost total absence of conflict. Those conflicts of which the foreign public does hear most often relate to the problem of Christian proselytizing. This is not, however, an area of conflict between Israel and the established churches, that is, those Christian bodies that have *millet* status and a constituency of their own.

It should be noted that the problem of proselytizing is treated very differently in Israel than it is in Spain and Italy, both Roman Catholic countries. We all have our own ways of dealing with proselytizers who come to our doors, be they Jehovah's Witnesses or other groups. One basic difference in Israel is that children under the age of fourteen are legally protected by the government.

The problems arise when "free lancers," sometimes well-meaning older ladies or tourists, come to Israel to "do their own thing" in the area of proselytism. It should be noted that there is no complaint against the government or people of Israel by those Christian groups which were in Israel when the state was founded in 1948, or by those who understand and who are concerned about the centuries-old tradition of religious co-existence. Modern Israel is a free and open society where exchanges of viewpoints are unhindered. Some Christians acting in an unethical manner, however, endanger both the principles and the practice of religious pluralism by offending large segments of the Israeli society, thus creating negative reactions both locally and abroad.

In closing, I quote from an article in *Faith Walks the Land* (1961), written by a ranking member of the Israeli Ministry of Justice:

> The situation has remained unchanged since the setting up of the State of Israel. Unless a law was passed by the new State in the very first days of its life, all the laws previously in force in Palestine continue to be in force in the State of Israel, provided that they have not been changed by a legislative Act of the State, and are not incompatible with the fact that a Jewish State has been set up. Since no new laws bearing upon these matters have so far been enacted, and since there appears to be no incompatibility between the existence of the State and the former organization of the Christian communities, it is to be inferred that all matters pertaining to the organization of the Religious Communities and to the jurisdiction of their courts must still be settled by reference to the legislative dispositions in force under the Mandate, which in their turn derive from the legal situation which existed at the time of the Ottoman Empire.[1]

NOTE

1. E. Vitta, "Legal Status of the Christian Communities in Israel," *Faith Walks the Land,* ed. Israel I. Taslitt (Jerusalem: The Jerusalem Post Press, 1961), p. 7.

16

ALBERT VORSPAN

Concepts of Religious Pluralism and Areas of Conflict in the United States

What do we mean by "pluralism"? Whatever else we mean, we mean a rejection of the "melting pot" theory of American group life—the idea that into the pot went people from all national, ethnic, racial, linguistic, and religious backgrounds. Magically, out came *homo Americanus,* presumably in a gray flannel suit. This well advertised new species never materialized, and now the very concept has been abandoned. America has become and will continue to be a pluralistic society in which various races, creeds, and national, ethnic, and cultural groups must co-exist, all the while trying to encourage their own adherents to retain their characteristic values generation after generation. In a land of religious liberty and separation of church and state, in a land of religious and cultural diversity, pluralism is both desirable and inevitable.

Co-existence among faiths within the framework of democratic pluralism has vital corollaries. It implies that each faith is obligated to conduct itself with self-restraint according to the disciplines of freedom and equality, without seeking to impose its will by coercion for its own sectarian purposes. It implies that every religious group is equally free to cultivate its own resources without interference or assistance from the agencies of government.

Leo Pfeffer, in his *Creeds of Competition,* indicated that America has passed through three main periods of inter-religious relations. The first, embracing roughly the colonial period, was dominated by conflicts over dogma and theology. The second, reaching into the early decades of this century, was marked by pronounced religious bigotry and prejudice against individuals. The third period is the present, marked by a decline of religious prejudice but a lively "creative competition" among Protestantism, Catholicism, and Judaism on basic public issues, with the beginning of a more mature, searching conversation about universal theological concerns.

Whether we accept Pfeffer's precise categories or not, I think we can all agree that we are now heading into a new and different era. The intense religious bigotry of past periods seems to have waned. The election of a Roman Catholic President in 1960 and the appointment of a Jewish refugee as Secretary of State in 1973 seem to signal the decline of the old kind of bigotry. The faiths are now relatively benign toward each other. Who is now afraid that the pope will run the White House, or that Protestants will restore prohibition? Why go hysterical about a "Catholic bloc" when one sees that Catholics fight each other even on such issues as abortion, that Catholics—like Jews and Protestants—do not elect "one-issue" candidates to public office? Protestantism is in considerable dogmatic disorder, and who today is fearful of the great power of the National Council of Churches?

And still another era is over—the era of massive and effective interfaith social action which animated the 60s in the fields of civil rights, social welfare, and putting an end to the nightmare of the Vietnam War. Religious coalitions *did* have muscle, *did* speak to the conscience of the American public, *did* mobilize political power in Washington, *did* achieve results. But we also strained the consensus back home, often became generals without armies, causing division and backlash in the ranks, stirring resentment at our moral certitude which sometimes seemed to confuse our particular tactic with a divine commandment. I believe that religious groups made a vast contribution to decency in the 60s, helping to break the back of racial segregation, helping to reveal the war as the moral obscenity it was. But we also brought on the backlash which has denuded so many social action programs, cut budgets to the bone, replaced prophetic audacity with a timidity in which the bland lead the bland, thus introducing the present dark age in the history of religious social action in America.

It is not only religion that has brought on this dark age. The American people have turned inward upon themselves. In the name of a burgeoning ethnicity and in the name of religious inwardness, we have become a nation of independent groupings turned in upon ourselves, separating ourselves from what was once a common agenda for social justice in America. As Martin Marty has pointed out, the cultural systems moving in America today do not follow denominational lines.

They rely more on nation, blood, race, ethnicity, shared experience, class—whether real or imagined. Recently black Lutherans in America, members of one of the most clearly defined "faiths" or dogma systems, announced that they had more in common with black Christians of other denominations than with most whites in their own. . . . One can almost forget about denominations as demarcating influences on the new scene. We might almost say that no one wears denominational jerseys now, nor is it "shirts versus skins." More properly, it is skins versus skins—black, brown, yellow, red, white and the like.

At a time when Americans have lost faith in their leaders and institutions of all kinds, when more and more Americans have surrendered to individual "head trips" in search of individual salvation of a million varieties, religious institutions are also losing their credibility. One reason interfaith conflicts may seem less intense is that many Americans *care less* about society, politics, the moral order, and faith itself. Fifteen years ago the issue of federal aid to education was a critical issue of interreligious tension and conflict. Then it was widely assumed that the Roman Catholic Church had a veto on this issue. No more. The issue itself was finessed by Lyndon Johnson, papered over by the Supreme Court, and largely defused in most parts of the country. Today most Americans couldn't care less about this issue as compared with, say, busing, or even the question of the quality of our public schools.

This is *not* to suggest that there are no issues of conflict in the interreligious sphere. One which continues intense is the struggle over abortion. While I personally support the Supreme Court decision on abortion and strongly disapprove of a constitutional amendment to nullify that decision, I believe the public controversy over abortion rights is a good example of pluralism in practice. The fact that the Supreme Court has spoken is not the final word. Courts have reversed themselves. Courts have been wrong. A Supreme Court decision *is* the law of the land and must be respected, but I believe that pluralism not only permits—but obliges—any religious group whose conscience is violated by that decision to use every legitimate means to sway public opinion and to secure a reversal. If I believed in conscience that abortion is a murder in the eyes of God, I would have every right—and duty—to oppose that practice as a desecration of reverence for human life, just as many of us opposed the Vietnam War in conscience even when it had the acquiescent sanction of a craven Congress and the silent approval of the courts of the land. Are there no lines to be drawn of what is permissible and what is not in a pluralist society? I do not believe that any religious group has a right to impose its theological beliefs by coercion; but in a democratic society no church has coercive power anyway, and so I do not think that lobbying, even threatening politicians, using the pulpit and the church, even using demagogic language like "murder" and "genocide" can be regarded as outside the pale of a robust and dynamic pluralism. The answer to those who are outraged by Roman Catholic campaigns against abortion is equally aggressive and effective efforts on the other side.

I have no doubt that issues concerning the Middle East—and now involving the United Nations as well—will continue to operate in the interreligious community at a white heat. This is the only international issue that divides Americans on religious grounds. American Protestants and Catholics do not seem to have lined up on the Ulster issues; American Christians seem to maintain a strange silence even on the civil war in Lebanon; and the sympathies of blacks are not divided over tribal religious wars in Africa, which are much less vital and relevant to most of them than the economic holocaust in their own communities. But Arab Muslims do feel solidarity with Arab countries, and American Jews are profoundly tied to Israel and see themselves as fighting for survival. Few Christians really seem to understand that Israel is central to the religious vision and sense of peoplehood of the Jews. Few Christians understand what it means to Jews that a Yasir Arafat, who has pledged himself to the extinction of the Jewish state, has been sanctified by the United Nations, and invited to participate in peace talks with the very state whose existence he denies and against which he has waged a mindless and bloody terrorism. Few Christians can understand the sense of loneliness and isolation and indignation which Jews feel when the United Nations, by overwhelming vote, chooses to equate Zionism with racism. To us, Zionism is nothing less than the national liberation movement of the Jewish people—and the only liberation movement in this century which has succeeded in democratic spirit. To us, the debate in the United Nations has deep resonances of the 30s when similar anti-Jewish canards were visited upon the world by another tyrant, and we were told it was only rhetoric. Jews are oversensitive, but we come by our paranoia naturally, for the distance between anti-Jewish rhetoric and Auschwitz in our memory is not so vast.

Let me make myself clear. I believe that Israel is no more exempt from criticism than is the United States or any other nation. While I believe that the biblical covenant involves the Jewish people, faith, and land in an irrevocable unity, I do *not* believe that every Israeli policy was ordained by God or dictated at Sinai. Israel is fallible; indeed, I disagree with many of its policies. But there is a

big difference between disagreeing with a state's policy
and denying its right to exist. What the United Nations has
done is to try to delegitimize Israel, undermine its
sovereignty, make it a pariah state, and make the Jewish
people the only people in the world to be a nonpeople—a
prelude to genocide. I must acknowledge here and now
that not every country that voted against Israel did so out
of anti-Semitic motivation; some were bought, some were
blackmailed, some were registering an anti-American vote;
some were bidding for votes on other issues; some were
sweating under the impact of Arab oil and the power of
petro-dollars. Of course. But for American Jews—and
Jews throughout the world—there is a profound sense of
déja vu, a bitter sense of isolation. Christian voices have
been raised; administration voices have been raised; black
voices have been raised. Yet some Jews are so hysterical
that they do not even hear these voices and choose to
belabor Christian silence. I myself do not remember a time
since World War II when the Jewish psyche was as vulnerable as it is at this moment, when we yearned so desper-
ately for moral voices rising above politics and national
expediencies to shatter the hypocrisies which have been
spread by tinhorn tyrants and military dictatorships that
have turned their own countries into torture chambers,
where Jews have been systematically persecuted and
harassed, where racism is a stench in the nostrils. I think
the Israeli Ambassador was right when he said:

> You dare talk of [Israeli] racism when I can point
> with pride to the Arab ministers who have served
> in my Government, to the Arab Deputy Speaker
> of my Parliament, to the Arab officers and men
> serving of their own volition on our defense
> border, and in our police forces, frequently
> commanding Jewish troops, to the hundreds of
> thousands of Arabs from all over the Middle
> East crowding the cities of Israel every year, to
> the thousands of Arabs from all over the Middle
> East coming to Israel for medical treatment. To
> the peaceful co-existence which has developed.
> To the fact that Arabic is an official language in

Israel on par with Hebrew. To the fact that it is as
natural for an Arab to serve in public office in
Israel as it is incongruous to think of a Jew serving in any public office in an Arab country, indeed being admitted to many of them.[1]

And there is one more area where I wish I saw religious
tension but instead see apathy, separation, and even a kind
of religious narcissism and catatonic despair—the struggle
for the soul of America, the shared struggle we all should
be involved in to bring God's justice to an America which
today stands at a point like that at which Israel stood when
God said: "I have placed before you life and death, the
blessing and the curse, therefore choose life and live"
(Deut. 30:19).

Our beloved America is not only a troubled, heartsick
society, it has lost its ethical moorings; it is wrenched adrift
in the world with no clear sense of national purpose, rud-
derless in a storm-tossed sea, with no sure hand on the till.

America lost its way in Vietnam, deceived by presidents
of both parties and abandoned by a craven and quiescent
Congress, a great-hearted nation reduced to a bloody obsession with body counts. This trauma was followed by the
sordid chapter of Watergate, which was not only a nearly
successful *coup d'état* against the American Constitution,
but also a chilling symbol of the decline of moral standards
in the entire fabric of society. And now we are hammered
daily by new revelations of the Central Intelligence Agency
and the Federal Bureau of Investigation grossly invading
our liberties. These so-called intelligence agencies lack
both intelligence and the remotest sense of accountability
to democratic institutions. We at the Union of American
Hebrew Congregations have always known that the sanctity of the Constitution and the glory of an open society are
not just shining ideals; they are central to our own security
as Americans. When official lawlessness pervades the land,
nobody is safe. We now learn that in 1971 the Federal
Bureau of Investigation used bribery to steal our mailing
lists at the Religious Action Center in Washington, presumably because we dared to express our views on the

Vietnam War. The struggle for an open society goes forward today, but the voice of religion is not heard, or, if it is heard, it is not regarded as pressworthy!

The American people are preoccupied with the economic plight. We have before us an economic disaster in which our present leaders seek to exorcise inflation by neglecting the needs of the unemployed, the poor, the old, the sick and the weak. America has hit its moral depths when it seeks to tighten its belt by slashing hot lunch programs for school children, food stamps for the poor, senior citizens programs, and day-care centers. This is a crisis for us, a holocaust for black youth in the cities. Many of our cities have become warehouses of decay and crime, but the federal government is willing to see even the greatest of them—New York City—gurgle down the drain for the capital crime of "financial imprudence," which is an ugly and hypocritical pretext to punish the city which has virtually bankrupted itself to welcome the poor from Puerto Rico, the hopeless minorities from the South, the weak and despised from everywhere, just as it once welcomed our immigrant parents and grandparents!

Our free enterprise system often serves as a masquerade for private selfishness, and behind our pieties we practice a welfare state for the rich and contempt for the poor. We bail out Lockheed and Penn Central, but we neglect our cities and our poor. America lives above its material means and below its moral means, and the great overarching sense of common national purpose has splintered into a thousand tribal, racial, and ethnic groups looking out for "Number One." And is there a moral protest from religious groups?

In the absence of moral leadership, the American people have nearly lost their faith in their leaders and in their institutions, in their ability to effect change, to make a difference. It is no accident that only 38 percent of the eligible voters bothered to vote in 1972. Our politics have become a charade of plastic images. We Americans have lost our innocence and, even worse, our faith. It is idle to pretend any longer that religious values and American ideals are intersecting. They are diverging, and perhaps that has been true from the very beginning. This free land has become a violent, gun-crazy, materialistic, weight-watching, star-crazed culture which exalts its own heroes, such as Evel Knievel, Muhammed Ali, the Rolling Stones, and Archie Bunker.

America is becoming a moral desert and we all wander about waiting for the voices of moral leadership which will speak, once more, to the best—not the worst—that is in us. We wait for voices which will speak for a heart of flesh and not a heart of stone. We wait for challenges that will make us proud once again to be Americans.

It is no doubt unparalleled *chutzpah* to say so, but I think we have to help fill that moral vacuum. We have to disen-thrall ourselves as religious men and women, to cry aloud and spare not, for why should we choose death and not life? I am not talking about narrow partisan politics nor conservative versus liberal. Both of our political parties have covered themselves with dishonor. I'm talking about caring versus not caring, giving a damn about my neighbor and feeling his pain versus the new American motto of "I'm number one; I've got mine; get off my back." I'm talking about the religious mission to keep man human in an age of dehumanization.

What should we do? We should organize our religious staffs in Washington, who *do* work together, to mobilize our churches and temples all over the country. We should ask religious leaders to come together in every city to speak for a coalition of concern. We should set up a task force of interfaith leaders to speak truth to power, to explode the myths and deceptive half-truths which flow from Washington and pollute the atmosphere of our political discourse. Let us bite the bullet on the Central Intelligence Agency and Federal Bureau of Investigation and their assaults on our liberties, for any threat to the First Amendment is religious business, too. Let us sit with those minority leaders who want to work together on the practical problems of the real world. Let us meet with those in Congress who want to achieve a national health program worthy of America, a tax system that is fair, and a budget that reflects genuine human, moral and social priorities. And let us declare war on the greatest sin of all— despair—and get on with God's business of building a world and an America fit for human beings.

NOTE

1. Chaim Herzog in a speech to the General Assembly of the United Nations, November 10, 1975 (A/PV 2400).

PART 7

The Future

17

A Letter to Richard

Dear Richard,[1]

Thanks for taking time to have lunch with me. If the upcoming conference of Jewish scholars and evangelical Christians does nothing else, at least it got a Jewish rabbi and a Christian evangelist together over Chinese vegetables!

I am honored to be taking part in the dialogue, especially since, as I understand, some of the Jewish members of the invitation committee were among those who suggested I be asked to speak. It's rather striking that an evangelist has been asked to take on this assignment, and as you may imagine I have been musing a great deal as to the significance of my role!

Your suggestion that I try to be quite personal at the session in New York really helped me. The scholars will, I know, provide lots of stimulating ideas. But I really do hope we will meet as people. To quote that learned theologian Charlie Brown: "I love humanity; it's people I can't stand." Let's pray we don't end in that kind of abstraction!

So here goes as first I try to share with you something of my pilgrimage.

I am a Christian. I am an evangelist. The roots of my faith and my calling go back to my early childhood. As a small boy in Canada I came to believe in Jesus. But it wasn't until my mid-teens that my faith really gripped me. Our family was being torn apart and so was I. Mother and Dad fought constantly. When I was fourteen she left home and lived in Western Canada under an assumed name. She was emotionally ill but I didn't realize it then. About that time I met a group of young people whose relationship to Jesus was intensely personal and very radiant. I longed to understand what I saw in them, and this led to a deep experience of self-surrender to God.

I remember going alone into the woods in Canada to pray and read the Bible. Often I'd take one of David's Psalms for meditation and turn it into my own prayer. I became, so I felt, aware that the living God was communicating with me and I with him.

This experience had to overflow from my life to others, so we began a series of youth rallies in my home town. Billy Graham came to speak at one of them, and we developed a friendship which later led to my joining his team. The point I'm making is that from the first I was an evangelist not because I was paid or trained or ordained for it, but because I couldn't help it!

You might ask, how do I *know* I experienced *God?* That's a fair question, but one I don't have time to answer fully now. Perhaps some time we can share further on the concept of an I-thou calling from God. Suffice it to say that my belief that I had encountered God had later to be tested and matured and intellectually undergirded. I came to the conviction there were solid historical and intellectual grounds for my faith in Jesus. But initially, being an evangelist was the overflow of an encounter that had to be shared.

What does this have to do with our dialogue?

Just that I think it's better to state honestly my calling as a Christian to be an evangelist. There's no point in weaseling about this if we're going to have honest encounter.

One of my friends has suggested to me that this dialogue is not the occasion for polemics, apologetics, or evangelism. On the whole I'm inclined to agree. But I do have a problem with his advice. Since I believe the Scriptures are the Word of God, I have to take seriously the teaching given (in what Christians call the New Testament) to go into all the world and preach the gospel to every person. My faith compels me to take this teaching seriously. I think one of your own scholars has remarked that the great commission is as Christian as a prayer shawl is Jewish! For me to disclaim a desire to evangelize all peoples would be dishonest. And yet it is not my intent to turn this dialogue into a platform for proselytism. That would be grossly arrogant.

You may see that, as an evangelist, my taking part in this dialogue is delicate. Some of our Jewish friends will no doubt suspect the worst: that I am there to try to evangelize them. And I'm sure some Christians will probably also suspect the worst: that I am *not* going to try to evangelize!

By the way, I wonder if you and I understand the word *evangelize* in the same way. Quite possibly not! I know that to many people it implies proselytism by trickery, force, or manipulation. But to me it means to witness to the good news of God's liberating love and to invite men to respond freely. I understand this love as revealed according to Scripture in the person of Jesus as the unique Son of God and in his death and resurrection. To trust and follow him involves turning from self-centeredness and serving God and man in the community of God's people.

All in all, I think it's best to get this out on the table, even at the risk of misunderstanding. A greater risk is that fear and dishonesty would make true encounter impossible. And I'm glad that you yourself affirmed to me that you think the risk is worth taking! If I make blunders as I go along, please try to excuse me. They will, I hope, be mistakes of the head and not the heart, for I am seeking to speak from the witness stand and not the judgment seat!

"So," you may respond, "you have set the stage and tried to justify your Christian evangelizing. Are you now going to preach at me? If so, our dialogue comes to a screeching halt."

My response is: No, I am not going to "preach" at you, and I do not think affirming my calling as an evangelist need end our encounter. The experience of getting to know you and of praying for this dialogue has been a great learning experience for me. I've been stretched and humbled and moved and exalted! And I'd like to share with you some of the things I've learned about myself, and, I think, about you.

The first thing I've learned more deeply is how close we really are, though at the same time we seem so far apart. I would reaffirm what I already knew—that when I, a Christian, approach you, a Jew, I do not approach you as a devotee of some religion without biblical foundations. I am not telling *you* this—you know it. I am reminding myself because sometimes we Christians have forgotten.

Last year as I told you we went to Israel. The beauty of the land, the vitality of the people, the sense of history were intoxicating. More than ever before I felt this mysterious sense of kinship. I felt that your book is also mine, that my Lord is of your people, that your land is filled with a sense of destiny for me as well. I was so moved that when we got to Jerusalem I asked for permission to stand by the Western Wall (for the first time wearing a yarmulka!) and to pray alongside the pious folk there for the peace of Jerusalem and for the freedom of Israel.

Some time ago Billy Graham received the Torch of Freedom Award from the Anti-Defamation League. It was a fascinating scene to watch a Catholic priest present this award to a Baptist evangelist in a Jewish temple! I remember vividly how Billy spoke that evening of his strong relation to the Jewish people—his daughter had lived in Israel; his associates conduct tours there; we owe to Israel our Bible and our Lord Jesus; the first apostles were Jewish. In fact he spoke so convincingly that afterwards one of the leading members of the synagogue told me he probably would have responded if Billy had asked members of the audience to come forward as he does in his mass rallies!

In light of this, I confess to a sense of puzzlement and loss that we do not appreciate fully the Jewish roots of our faith. Christians have sometimes, it seems, reduced the Bible to our New Testament. In our worship we do not remember often enough the mighty acts of God through

Moses. We haven't given enough place in our hymnbooks to the rich treasury of the Psalms.

But this is changing! Many of our young people today are singing the Psalms to beautiful contemporary tunes. They are hungry for the Old Testament—perhaps because of the widespread search for roots and identity. My seventeen-year-old daughter is really excited right now about a class which is studying Genesis. Evangelical theology and life are drawing new vitality from the Old Testament. For example, a new sense of community growing from the Old Testament concept of the people of God is emerging to balance the individualism which has been so characteristic of our style.

There's also a new interest in the theme of creation. I suppose that for many evangelicals the expression of faith has been rather limited to phrases such as "Jesus died for our sins." So the emphasis falls on man as a sinner and on Jesus as the Savior. This can result in the idea that God has a very low estimate of man. (I think I mentioned to you the little girl who was thumbing through her Bible and muttering to herself, "Jesus say no, no, no, no, no, no!") I would say that many evangelicals today affirm that the first part of our message is not "Man is a sinner," but "God is really there." The God who has created all things. We see persons as very beautiful and precious in God's sight because they have been created, male and female, in the image of God.

It is precisely because humanity is significant that sin is so tragic. That is why "Jesus died for our sins" is a profoundly meaningful truth to us. Salvation is more than an escape from the consequences of sin. It is also wholeness, the restoring of full and complete personhood. We see embodied in Jesus both the word of the living God and the model of a genuinely human existence.

The theme of creation is also playing a large part in another area—the new surfacing of social concern among evangelicals. Evangelical Christians have had a significant heritage of social involvement. But for a generation or more this aspect of our commitment was somewhat soft-pedaled. Recently we have been rediscovering the mandate of social justice. I'm thinking, for example, of Billy Graham's early repudiation of racial segregation in his public rallies, of World Vision's world-wide programs of feeding and development, of job therapy and rehabilitation work with prisoners, of John Perkins' remarkable black community developments in Mississippi. Evangelical Christians are emerging more and more in an activist role of concern for the peoples of the world.

Two characteristics of this evangelical movement are striking. First, that evangelicals tend to stress personal involvement, and not just institutional and legislative strategies. Here I think is a parallel to many Jewish concerns. And, second, the evangelical social movement has deep theological roots—it is more than a response to secular moods, it is profoundly biblical. And here again I stress an identity with the Jewish community. It's the doctrine of creation that makes us take man and his world seriously, that will not let us look on salvation as mere pie-in-the-sky. Without losing the urgent dimension of eternal life, we also believe salvation involves a new life in this world. We are called by God's grace to obey both the *great commandment* of love to God and neighbor, *and* the *great commission* of mission in the world. When as a Christian evangelist I call for repentance, both personal and social, I am likely to turn to the words of Isaiah and Amos, as well as to Jesus' call for radical discipleship. Increasingly we value the tie between the "old" and the "new" covenants.

This leads to the question: How wide *is* the gap between the "old" and the "new"? I'm sure there are some real issues at stake, but I also wonder if we as Christians and Jews haven't distorted each other's ideas about "faith and works"? In Jewish eyes, the Christian emphasis on faith may look like a kind of buck-passing irresponsibility. In Christian eyes, the Jewish emphasis on the Torah may look like legalism. But is the gap distorted by the spectacles we wear?

I am moved by the statement of a Jewish scholar (one of the speakers at this dialogue) that "the Jew is fully aware that no man can pass muster before God if he rests his case on law . . . rather than the unmerited mercy of God." And I also fully affirm the Christian scholar who writes that Judaism's "deepest Torah-vocation is at the heart of New Testament religion." King David's experience of pardoning grace as he records it in Psalm 32 is cast in words that find an echo in my own spirit. May I ask if you do not also respond to Jesus' words that he came not to destroy but to fulfill the law? When he said that he came that we might have life abundantly, was he not affirming the life of the Torah to the full? I might also mention the ethical imperatives of Paul in the latter parts of most of his letters.

These are a few of the points, Richard, that lead me to say that I've rediscovered how in some ways we really are close. This means that for me as a Gentile Christian to be anti-Semitic is utterly unthinkable! St. Paul (who sometimes, I am told, bothers some Jews!) is the one who teaches me this! He tells me that I am a wild branch grafted contrary to nature into the good olive tree! "Boast not against the branches," he tells me, "you do not bear the root but the root bears you" (Rom. 11:18). No room for arrogance here! And the same Paul teaches me that the Jews have a great future. "Has God cast away His people?" he asks. "God forbid . . . as touching the election they are beloved for the fathers' sake" (vv. 1, 28).

You may respond: Well, if *this* is what Christians are *committed* to, why have so-called Christians treated Jews as they have?

A sobering question indeed.

I've learned in a deeper way that what is very precious to us may be offensive to you. I'm wondering how many of my Christian brothers and sisters realize that while Good Friday is a holy day to us, it is a day on which for many years in many places a Jew was slapped on both cheeks? How many of us know that there were times when Jews were forced by law to go to churches and listen to sermons aimed at converting them? How many of us realize that almost every law passed against Jews during Hitler's Third Reich can be paralleled by a similar church law passed in previous centuries? True, many of these things happened in a darker age. But there were those in our lifetime who professed Christ, yet averted their eyes from the gas ovens of the holocaust. There is a mystery of iniquity here. I find it gross blasphemy that the words of Jesus on the cross, "Father, forgive them," could ever be twisted into, "Father, hold it against them." And we could go on and on with the list of shame, if that would help.

Where we have failed, we must forthrightly admit our failures in order to deserve forgiveness. This is not breast-beating. It is the change of heart which leads to a change of behavior.

Now I suppose it can rightly be said that anti-Semitism in America should not be seen only in the context of religion. It has an economic base not totally related to the Christian community. All anti-Semitism cannot be traced to Christians. I think of clubs and fraternities whose discrimination is beyond the control of Christians.

Also, many people who call themselves Christians are reflecting cultural patterns, not biblical principles. As evangelical Christians we don't believe one is a Christian simply because he or she has been born in a Christian home, or been baptized. A Christian is one who has internalized his faith, who in biblical terms has received from God "a new heart." The evidence for this new birth is in the fruits of righteousness, love, and peace. Don't imagine that everyone calling himself a Christian is one. There are multitudes of people who are only "cultural Christians," not biblical ones.

I wish I could go on to say that every genuine Christian is immune to prejudice. But in honesty, I can't claim that. Even some of our most respected Protestant reformers wrote tirades against the Jews. But there's another side to the story! I'm thinking of Corrie ten Boom, the Dutch lady who with her family hid Jews from the Nazis during World War II. For this "crime" she went to prison, and her father and sister to death. World Wide Pictures has just released the film *The Hiding Place* to tell the story of this brave woman. One of the reasons we produced this film at this time was so that we as Christians might say to Jews: "We stand with you. To be anti-Semitic is to be anti-Christ. Where we have failed you we have failed our own Lord. So as the popular little button reads: BPGNFWMY . . . be patient, God's not finished with me yet!"

Perhaps part of our current problem, Richard, is that we haven't really known each other as people. When we lunched together, it was noted that you were the first rabbi with whom I had ever discussed these things in some depth—and that I was the first evangelical Christian you had ever really gotten to know. Having lived first in a small Canadian town and then in the South, I haven't had opportunity to rub shoulders with Jewish people as I might have in some of the major urban areas.

Also, I was struck by your comment that many Jews tend to avoid evangelical Christians because they think the only thing Christians are interested in is evangelizing. If you have met insensitive Christians who see Jews only as trophies to be bagged in an evangelistic safari, please don't take them as completely representative. And if sometimes it seems to you that evangelical Christians look on Israel chiefly as a key piece in their prophetic jigsaw puzzle, let me affirm that our caring isn't that shallow.

When Israel became a state, many of us felt our hearts leap, not just because this supported an interpretation of biblical prophecies, but because real, suffering people had a place to call home! We try to remember that when Jesus foresaw the destruction of Jerusalem he wept! He didn't exult that what was happening was a fulfillment of prophecy! We were terribly grieved recently when many nations supported a resolution—a resolution we deplore and condemn—which seemed to say that Israel's very existence is racist. We do not suppose for a moment that you who believe in one living God seek to idolize a nation or to make Israel immune from God's justice. Rather, it's because we believe in the righteous, steadfast love of the God of the Bible that we stand for the integrity of Israel, and for justice for all the peoples of the Middle East.

Getting back to what I wrote before, we don't hide the fact that we long for you to believe Jesus is the Messiah. We really do. We can't deny our convictions that he is the fulfillment of the great plan of the God of Abraham, the appearance in history of God himself, our Savior and the Lord of all. This we regard as good news we have no right to withhold from anyone. But we do reject the neurotic approach which would select out Jews alone as some uniquely needy objects for proselytism. We deplore distorted evangelistic methods that involve force or manipulation or deception. We are open to a diversity of responses to the lordship of Jesus Christ, recognizing there are Jews who accept him yet wish to remain within Jewish culture and tradition. And whether or not you believe Jesus is Messiah we want to know you as persons, and to learn much from your experience and traditions. If this happens then a lot of the shallow talk and concerns of the past can be done away with.

I recently came across a statement of Martin Buber which continues to haunt me. As I recall, he suggested that the Christian looks on the Jew as the stubborn man who will not see what has happened; while to the Jew, the Christian is the reckless man who affirms redemption in a world that is yet unredeemed. And this, he said, is a gulf which no human can bridge.

I suppose Buber has put the issue as clearly as it can be posed. We Christians do see Jesus as Redeemer, the one who fulfills the Suffering Servant prophecies of Scripture, and who by his sacrifice of himself and victory over death sets his people free. This does not mean the whole world has been redeemed, but that a crucial event in redemption has taken place. D-Day, the invasion of Normandy, led inexorably to V-Day over Hitler's demonic regime. But many days of struggle lay between D-Day and V-Day. So God calls us to work and pray for the day the prophets foresaw, when the knowledge of God will fill the earth as the waters cover the sea. In this struggle we receive hope from the promises that the Messiah would come not only as Suffering Servant, but also as mighty King. This gives us staying power!

I well realize we differ as to whether Messiah has already come, and I agree with Buber that here is a gulf *no human* can bridge. But must there always be such a gap? Is permanent tension all we can hope for? Can God himself not bridge this gulf? I look for the day, foretold in Scripture, when at the end of the ages he will do just that.

Meanwhile, can we not build some bridges ourselves?

When one of our associates, Grady Wilson, was in Southeast Asia, a whole row of Catholic nuns attended one of his services. Afterwards they said, "Mr. Wilson, you're a Protestant, we are Catholics. But out here we Christians are such a minority that we cannot afford the luxury of divisions we might permit back home in America." In a similar vein, Richard, I would suggest that in a world increasingly godless and amoral and materialistic, all who believe in the God of Abraham may find we have more and more that unites us. When we premiered *The Hiding Place* a few weeks ago in Beverly Hills, a tear gas bomb with a swastika on it was thrown into the theater to disrupt the showing. Jews and Christians together ran out gasping and choking. Was it a warning of what may come? Could the present vacuum of moral leadership open the way for the proverbial strong man on the white horse who with his fantastic powers of technology and mind-control will demand that all men bow down and worship as was demanded of Daniel and his friends? If someday we may meet in some fiery furnace, then we'd better get to know each other now.

Just as I hope our friendship will continue and grow now that you and I have met, I also hope the New York meeting will lead to an expanding circle of personal contacts.

I'd like to see rabbis and evangelical Christian pastors be encouraged to meet, perhaps first on a one-to-one basis in communities across America. And there should be similar exchanges between students and faculties at our colleges and theological schools.

The Hiding Place, the film to which I referred, will be shown across the country for the next year. Couldn't we encourage Christian and Jewish couples and families to attend together, and then to share their feelings and reactions very honestly?

Moving beyond personal contacts, I'd like to think that Jews and evangelical Christians could explore together how we might express mutual concern for some of the urgent human problems which confront us. Perhaps Jewish and Christian young people, for example, could start by working together on the need for food in this hungry world of ours. I even wonder (dare I breathe such a hope?) if the time might come when some of the fine young evangelical Arab Christians might join hands with some of your Jewish young persons in a project of outreach to human need in the Middle East.

You and I both believe in the God of Abraham, of Moses, of Isaiah. So we both realize that we live in a society that is facing a moral crisis, and the judgment of God. We know that no nation which disregards his laws can survive. Are you anguished, as I am, at the breakup of our families, the awful growth of crime, the destructive power of alcoholism, the vicious cycle of poverty, and the devaluation of human life? Do you agree with me that a solely materialistic answer is no answer, that there are moral and spiritual issues at stake, and that as a people we have lost our moral compass? Must we believe that Richard Nixon is right when he suggests that war is the only way to counteract the growing cynicism around us? Can we not, Jews and Christians together, initiate a debate across this land as to what kind of society we want, and what kind of people are needed to create this society? Can we not work together to reintroduce into the bloodstream of our society a consciousness that God is God forever, that his commandments are not outdated cultural oddities, but are his eternally relevant word to man?

It may be significant that this New York dialogue takes place as we move into America's bicentennial year. I believe that the bicentennial needs to be a year both of celebration and of confession, of reaffirmation and of repentance to God.

In that spirit, a summit conference of Christian leaders recently called believers to devote one Friday a month during 1976 to fasting and prayer for the soul of the nation. The theme of this movement is borrowed from God's promise to Solomon: "If My people, who are called by My name, will humble themselves, and pray, and seek My face, and turn from their wicked ways, then will I hear from Heaven, and will forgive their sin and will heal their land" (II Chron. 7:14).

If Jewish leaders who are equally concerned for spiritual and moral renewal could stimulate a companion movement in their own community, who knows what might happen to bring a new beginning to America?

And who knows what God might do to bridge that gulf between us which no human can bridge? I do not suggest we abridge our deep convictions. I do dare to believe that the day will come when in God's timing, and by his action, the natural and wild branches will be joined in the olive tree. Then, and then alone, will the universal mission of the people of God be carried out, and then only will Isaiah's prophecy come fully true: "Arise, shine, for your light has come, and the glory of the Lord has risen upon you. For behold, darkness shall cover the earth, and thick darkness the people: but the Lord will arise upon you, and His glory will be seen upon you. And nations shall come to your light, and kings to the brightness of your rising" (Isa. 60:1-3).

Sincerely, your friend,
Leighton Ford

NOTE

1. Rabbi Richard Rocklin, Temple Israel (conservative), Charlotte, North Carolina.

18

A. JAMES RUDIN

Prospectus for the Future

This was the first national conference that brought together evangelical scholars and leaders with their counterparts from the Jewish community. The group reached a general consensus in several main areas:

1. *Israel.* Evangelical Christians and Jews must resist all attempts at the United Nations and elsewhere to judge Israel by an unfair and dishonest "double standard." The grotesque United Nations resolution of 1975 that linked Zionism with racism is but the latest and worst example of this outrageous "double standard" at work. Since evangelical Christians and Jews are rooted by faith to both the Hebrew Bible and the land of the Bible, both communities must continue to express positive support for and solidarity with the people and the state of Israel to insure her survival and security. Professor Carl Edwin Armerding of Regent College (Vancouver, B.C.) strongly urged his fellow Christians to condemn all one-sided and unbalanced attempts to undermine Israel's right to survive as a free and secure state.

2. *Anti-Semitism.* Much more systematic and serious work by both evangelical and Jewish scholars is needed to eliminate all forms of anti-Semitism in Christian teaching, preaching, and liturgy. Jews and Judaism cannot be seen only as ancient biblical categories; rather, Christians must experience the contemporary Jewish community today *in situ.* Intensive work and study need to be undertaken by Christian scholars to eradicate all traces of the infamous

and murderous "Christ killer" (deicide) charge that has historically been used against the Jewish people. Evangelical seminaries especially need to interpret the Easter story, the Gospel of John, and the Jewish roots of Christianity in positive and theologically authentic terms to their students. Rev. Pamela Cole (New Bedford, Mass.) has warned that "mere neutrality" by evangelical Christians in the face of Christian anti-Semitism is an inadequate response. A fuller understanding of the rabbinic background of the New Testament and the life of Jesus is needed by evangelical Christians.

At the same time, Jews need to see the evangelical Christian community as it truly is, free from stereotypes and caricatures. The accidents of demography and geography in the United States have often prevented Jews and evangelicals from interacting with one another in a meaningful way. Both groups need to view one another with mutual trust and a sense of loving respect. For Jews this means an understanding of the central factors that have decisively shaped the evangelical ethos—the authenticity of Scripture, the importance of the personal as well as the corporate religious experience, the historic commitment to a separation of church and state, a free and independent congregational life and an extraordinarily rich inner spiritual life.

3. *Human rights and social justice.* Both religious groups have an obligation to support the cause of human rights around the world, especially in the Soviet Union and Eastern Europe where Jewish and Christian believers are currently being persecuted.

Evangelical Christians were urged by Leighton Ford to "reject the neurotic approach which would select out Jews alone as some uniquely needy objects for proselytism." Christians need to disassociate themselves from all forms of evangelistic methods "that involve force or manipulation or deception."

Jews and evangelicals can join together in a host of critical concerns: gun control, world hunger, energy, pollution, racism, ethics in government and business, quality education, fair housing, and full employment.

In addition, specific recommendations were made to organize a series of regional evangelical-Jewish conferences that would focus on the various themes and issues that were articulated at the New York meeting. Such conferences would bring evangelical and Jewish leaders together in a co-operative effort to develop new resources for positive teaching and preaching that would lead to improved understanding and mutual respect, interreligious study tours to Israel, and intensive dialogue in the area of theology, Scripture, and history.

Even as dramatic and significant strides have been made in Catholic-Jewish and mainline Protestant-Jewish relations in recent years, the present moment offers a great opportunity to deepen and enhance evangelical-Jewish relationships. The moment must not be lost because of inherited ignorance of each other. The evangelical-Jewish encounter, at its best, promises to break exciting new ground for both our "Peoples of God."

Bibliography

I. Evangelical Works

Barker, Glenn W., William L. Lane, and J. Ramsey Michaels, eds. *The New Testament Speaks*. New York: Harper & Row, 1969.

Bloesch, Donald G. *The Evangelical Renaissance*. Grand Rapids: Eerdmans, 1973.

Bright, John. *The Kingdom of God*. New York: Abingdon Press, 1953.

Bruce, F. F. *Are the New Testament Documents Reliable?* Second edition. Chicago: Inter-Varsity, 1946.

Grounds, Vernon C. *Revolution and the Christian Faith*. New York: Lippincott, 1971.

Harrison, R. K. *Introduction to the Old Testament*. Grand Rapids: Eerdmans, 1969.

Henry, Carl F. H. *A Plea for Evangelical Demonstration*. Grand Rapids: Baker, 1971.

Ladd, George E. *A Theology of the New Testament*. Grand Rapids: Eerdmans, 1974.

LaSor, William S. *Israel*. Grand Rapids: Eerdmans, 1976.

Packer, James. *Fundamentalism and the Word of God*. Grand Rapids: Eerdmans, 1958.

————. *Knowing God*. Chicago: Inter-Varsity, 1973.

Pfeiffer, Charles F. *Old Testament History*. Grand Rapids: Baker, 1973.

Quebedeaux, Richard. *The Young Evangelicals*. New York: Harper & Row, 1974.

Ramm, Bernard L. *The Evangelical Heritage*. Waco, TX: Word Books, 1973.

Schaeffer, Francis. *The God Who Is There*. Chicago: Inter-Varsity Press, 1968.

Stott, John R. *Basic Christianity*. Grand Rapids: Eerdmans, 1958.

Tenney, Merrill C., ed. *The Zondervan Pictorial Encyclopedia of the Bible*. Five volumes. Grand Rapids: Zondervan, 1975.

Wells, David F. and John D. Woodbridge, eds. *The Evangelicals*. Nashville: Abingdon Press, 1975.

II. Jewish Works

Baeck, Leo. *The Essence of Judaism*. New York: Schocken Books, 1948.

Bamberger, Bernard J. *The Story of Judaism.* New York: Schocken Books, 1970.

Baron, Salo. *A Social and Religious History of the Jews.* Sixteen volumes. Philadelphia and New York: Jewish Publication Society and Columbia University Press, 1952.

Buber, Martin. *I and Thou.* Translated by Walter Kaufmann. New York: Scribners, 1970.

Donin, Hayim Halevy. *To Be a Jew.* New York: Basic Books, 1972.

Encyclopedia Judaica. Sixteen volumes. New York: The Macmillan Co., 1972.

Heschel, Abraham Joshua. *God in Search of Man.* New York: Harper & Row, 1955.

_____. *The Insecurity of Freedom.* New York: Schocken Books, 1972.

_____. *Israel: An Echo of Eternity.* New York: Farrar, Straus and Giroux, 1971.

Kertzer, Morris N. *What Is a Jew?* New York: Macmillan, 1968.

Lacqueur, Walter. *A History of Zionism.* New York: Holt, Rinehart & Winston, 1972.

Neusner, Jacob. *The Way of Torah: An Introduction to Judaism.* Second edition. Encino, CA: Dickenson, 1974.

Siegel, Richard, Michael Strassfeld, and Sharon Strassfeld. *The Jewish Catalog.* Philadelphia: The Jewish Publication Society of America, 1973.

Silver, Abba Hillel. *Where Judaism Differed.* New York: The Macmillan Co., 1956.

Silver, Daniel J., and Bernard Martin. *History of Judaism.* New York: Basic Books, 1976.

Steinberg, Milton. *Basic Judaism.* New York: Harcourt, Brace & World, Inc., 1947.

Wiesel, Elie. *Night.* New York: Avon Books, 1958.

III. Books Dealing With Both Communities

Ahlstrom, Sydney E. *A Religious History of the American People.* New Haven, CT: Yale University Press, 1972.

Baeck, Leo. *Judaism and Christianity.* New York: Atheneum, 1958.

Buber, Martin. *Two Types of Faith: The Interpenetration of Judaism and Christianity.* New York: Harper & Row, 1961.

Carlson, Paul R. *O Christian! O Jew!* Elgin, IL: David C. Cook Publishing Co., 1974.

Eckardt, Roy. *Elder and Younger Brothers.* New York: Schocken Books, 1973.

Isaac, Jules. *Jesus and Israel.* New York: Holt, Rinehart and Winston, 1971.

————. *The Teaching of Contempt: Christian Roots of Anti-Semitism.* New York: Holt, Rinehart and Winston, 1964.

Jacob, Walter. *Christianity Through Jewish Eyes.* Cincinnati: Hebrew Union College Press, 1974.

Littell, Franklin H. *The Crucifixion of the Jews.* New York: Harper & Row, 1975.

Oesterreicher, John M. *The Rediscovery of Judaism.* South Orange, NJ: The Institute of Judeo-Christian Studies, Seton Hall University, 1971.

Olson, Bernhard E. *Faith and Prejudice.* New Haven, CT: Yale University Press, 1963.

Opsahl, Paul D., and Marc H. Tanenbaum, eds. *Speaking of God Today.* Philadelphia: Fortress Press, 1974.

Parkes, James. *Conflict of the Church and Synagogue.* London: Temple Books, 1969.

Sandmel, Samuel. *We Jews and Jesus.* New York: Oxford University Press, 1973.

————. *We Jews and You Christians.* Philadelphia: J. B. Lippincott, 1967.

Strober, Gerald S. *Portrait of the Elder Brother.* New York: The American Jewish Committee and the National Conference of Christians and Jews, 1972.

Index of Subjects

Aaronides, 58-60, 71
Acts of Pilate, 170
Akiba, Rabbi, 48
Allegory, allegorization, 40, 143, 207
America
  democratic pluralism in, 230, 279, 286, 289
  Judeo-Christian heritage of, 11, 12
  moral crisis in, 11, 215, 250-52, 255-57, 258, 260, 271-73, 288-89, 292-94, 309
Amin, Idi. *See* Dada, Idi Amin
Amnesty International, 214, 220
Anti-Israelism, 282-83, 290
Anti-Semitism, 99, 109, 113, 155-56, 210, 225-27, 290, 291, 305
  Christianity and, 10, 11, 100, 109, 110, 113, 114, 156-57, 158, 167, 180-83, 304-5, 311, 313
  in New Testament. *See* New Testament, and anti-Semitism
  in Protestant Church S.S. materials, 183-84
Anti-Zionism and United Nations resolution, 74, 137, 267-68, 290-91, 306, 311
Apocalypse, apocalyptic, 87-88, 242
Apostolic Fathers. *See* Church Fathers and anti-Semitism
Arabs. *See* Israel (State), Arabs in; Middle East
Arms race, 223-24, 231

Baal Shem Tov, 68
Bar Kochba revolt, 65, 109, 114, 127, 166, 169
Ben Pandera stories, 164. *See also* *Toledoth Jeshu*
Ben Sira, 58
Berith. *See* Covenant
Bible, 5, 6, 7, 11, 13, 16, 18, 116, 206, 211, 212
  centrality of, in Christianity and Judaism, 13, 34-35, 39, 117, 154, 197, 204, 301, 311
  evangelical view of. *See* Evan-

gelicalism, and Biblical authority & interpretation
  interpretation & criticism, 35, 38, 92, 142, 144-45, 146, 206-10
  Jewish view. *See* Hebrew Bible, Jewish interpretation of
  Word of God, 39-40, 93, 252, 299
"Black Panthers" (Israel), 277
Britain, and Israel (State), 131-35. *See also* Christian Zionism; Evangelical Awakening
British Mandate, 280, 284

Canon, 17, 36-37, 40, 197
Chosen People, 18-19, 56, 72, 99, 102, 107
"Chosenness." *See* Election
Christ. *See* Jesus
Christian Zionism, 119, 123, 132-34
Christianity, 2, 15, 17, 18, 19, 49, 109, 116, 126, 137, 163, 252, 312
  and anti-Semitism. *See* Anti-Semitism, and Christianity
  and Israel (People), continuity with, 119, 121, 128, 302
  and Israel (State). *See* Evangelicals, and Israel (State)
  and the Law, 42, 45, 109-10
  as Judaism of the Gentiles, 51, 117
  evangelical. *See* Evangelicalism
  fundamental. *See* Fundamentalism
Christianity and Judaism, 2, 9, 10, 11, 15, 34, 109, 111, 116, 129-30, 161, 230, 301, 304, 307
  antagonism, 110, 112, 115-16, 126
  common heritage and destiny, 11-13, 17, 24, 117, 122
  dialogue. *See* Jewish-Christian dialogue
Christology
  and Hebrew Bible, 9, 37, 39, 77-79, 84-86, 90-92, 93
  in early Church, 88-89, 91, 124-25, 179

317

Index of Authors

Index of Scripture
and Other Ancient Writings

Hebrew Bible

New Testament

Ancient Jewish Writings